STEEP HILLS & LEARNING CURVES:

Cycling Land's End to John O' Groats

DAWN RHODES

STEEP HILLS & LEARNING CURVES

Cycling Lands' End to John O' Groats

Some of the information in this book – for example, location of campsites, volume of traffic
on specified roads, facts I knew about people at the time, facts and statistics about political and
social landscapes – was all relevant at the time of my ride in 1997 but may not be relevant or
accurate now. But it has been left in so I can describe my journey just as it happened back then

Matador
Unit E2 Airfield Business Park,
Harrison Road, Market Harborough,
Leicestershire. LE16 7UL
Tel: 0116 2792299
Email: books@troubador.co.uk
Web: www.troubador.co.uk/matador
Twitter: @matadorbooks

ISBN 978 1803130 156

British Library Cataloguing in Publication Data.
A catalogue record for this book is available from the British Library.

Printed and bound in Great Britain by 4edge Limited
Typeset in 11pt Adobe Caslon Pro by Troubador Publishing Ltd, Leicester, UK

Matador is an imprint of Troubador Publishing Ltd

In loving memory of my parents

RULES OF CYCLE TOURING

1. Break yourself in gently.
2. Until you have arrived at the place you intend to sleep, then the ride isn't over.
3. It always costs more than you think.
4. The camping routine can be just as tiring as the cycling.
5. Seek advice from the locals.
6. Sadly, busy roads can't always be easily avoided.
7. Purpose-made cycle clothing isn't just a gimmick to make you feel ridiculous. It really has been designed to be the most comfortable, practical option.
8. Knowledge of basic bicycle mechanics will spare you pain.
9. Concerning alcohol: have a guess!
10. Never underestimate how many calories you will need to consume.
11. Beware of fellow travellers bearing gifts.
12. Don't invite strangers to sleep in your tent.
13. If cycling uphill gets too arduous, stop for a rest.

14. Cycle tourists will always look out for each other.
15. Eight miles at the end of a long hard day may as well be eighty.
16. Be certain how far away your next source of food is and never risk running out.
17. Beware of getting directions from car drivers.
18. When you see a sign that says *Scenic Area Ahead*, it means the area you are about to ride through is very, very hilly.
19. As a rule of thumb: main roads tend to be built *around* the hills or mountains, whereas back lanes traverse up and down each and every one.
20. Gradients can be deceptive.
21. The further you travel, the further away your destination feels.
22. No matter how capable the body is, if the mind isn't willing, then you're screwed.
23. Looking for the perfect saddle is like looking for the perfect partner: There are no set rules which, if followed, lead to success. You simply have to endure the trial-and-error method.
24. Make absolutely sure your saddle will be comfortable over longer distances.
25. Taking care of your mental health must be a top priority.
26. It takes time to adjust back to normal life after a tour.
27. There are no rules.

PROLOGUE

'*T*hat must have been easy. I know a man who ran it.' The woman's words were a sucker punch to the midriff and as I hurried outside, they rang around my head. *That must have been easy... I know a man who ran it... that must have been easy.* Those callous words threatened to take the most challenging, most exciting feat of my life thus far and turn it into something so ordinary, it shouldn't even be *called* an achievement. I slumped against the wall, blinking back the tears I knew were coming and stared vacantly for a long, long time. Had I been deluding myself, believing I was doing something worthwhile with my life whilst other people disparaged me?

ALLOW ME TO INTRODUCE MYSELF

*C*laiming my cycling adventures were inspired by a dream (and by dream, I mean *thoughts and images occurring in the mind during sleep*) will likely sound rather banal. But before I come to that, I would first like to talk about the other kinds of dreams: *our cherished aspirations, ambitions, or ideals,* because I believe these are at the cornerstone of everyone's existence. They keep us alive, move us out of our stupor, and they can be swayed by the most unexpected event or person we encounter.

As far back as I can remember, my head had always been full of rather wild, ambitious dreams. At the age of ten, I began planning a walk from my home in Sussex to Bangor in Wales. (What can I say? It felt at the time like a far-off mystical place.) My intention was to rescue all the neglected or abandoned horses I might encounter along the way and then live in the Welsh hills, surviving on berries and other wild foods whilst my horses roamed free. I already had my route marked out in my parents' road atlas, but by the time I was fifteen, my dreams had morphed. I began saving my wages from my Saturday job so that as soon as I was old enough, I could buy a van. My plan was to convert it into a campervan and join a convoy of New Age travellers. The dream I held on to involved cooking over open fires, living in a like-minded community (lots of people with dreadlocks and guitars) and sleeping out under the stars. But when I had to give up my job in order to concentrate on exams, life continued more conventionally. I went to college to study for A-levels, but there was always a part of me that was lured away by other wayward souls, who chose to consume cheap lager in the park rather than attend lectures. Somehow, I still passed my exams and then found a job working for a railway company, and I began to save my wages again. Only this time, my dream was to buy a field so I could live in a caravan and run a small holding.

Then I met a man called Jason and the pendulum of my life began swinging once again when he introduced me to the concept of long-distance cycling. On weekends, we would load our bicycles with camping gear and head for a beauty spot, but whilst I struggled up even the shallowest of ascents on my old, heavy bicycle, Jason would be miles ahead on his sleek new tourer. It was not the most promising of starts, to an activity that would become a life-long passion. But I persisted and gradually my fitness improved, and I started to enjoy cycling for the first time since childhood. I parted company with Jason just then and became entwined in another relationship. It was around this time that I had my dream.

I'm stood atop a mountain road in the Scottish Highlands. I close my eyes so I can sense the world in all its splendour: the warm breeze on my skin, the sun on my face, the smell of bracken in my nostrils and the distant "peee-uu" call of a buzzard. I open my eyes and reach out my fingertips, longing to touch the rugged mountains in the distance. Then I pick up my bicycle and begin the long descent down this twisty mountain road. Everything feels so tranquil, and I feel so happy. More serene than at any other time I can recall.

Up until this point, I'd never believed that dreams have hidden meanings. I thought they were just a person's thoughts, memories and emotions all jumbled together at night, which result in some pretty wacky images. But to believe in the sensible scientific explanation all of the time, to always hear horses not zebras, is to be in danger of becoming closed-minded. And so, not long after, when I read an interesting proposal that: *dreams are answers to questions we haven't yet realised we need to ask ourselves*, I froze. I reread this paragraph several times, thinking, *yes, I like this. I like it very much*. Then I recalled not just my dream but also the holiday a few years ago, when I'd first clapped eyes on the Scottish Highlands. I remembered how it had felt akin to falling in love (an affinity that clearly had not gone away), and the concept whirled around my mind that maybe the two definitions of *dream* were more similar than I'd realised. But one thing was crystal clear: I was going to explore the Highlands by bicycle.

Without mentioning this to anyone, I began to scour cycle shops and research the different types of bicycles available, and a few months later, I'd bought myself an expedition bicycle: a mountain bike-touring bike hybrid. It was beautiful. This red bicycle, which had been handmade in Sheffield, was marketed as suitable for any terrain… *from Iceland to Indonesia* was the boast. Even though my plans didn't extend much beyond the Scottish Highlands at the time, it was hard to resist. Almost immediately I took my new bike (which I named Loopy Loo) to Scotland for a trial run, and the cycling was every bit as enjoyable as it had been in my dream (although maybe not as warm).

The next year, my sister, who was working in Thailand at the time, invited me to go and stay. As I'd browsed the airport's bookshops, I'd stumbled across a book written by the late Anne Mustoe called *A Bike Ride*. For anyone who doesn't know, Mrs Mustoe decided at the age of fifty-four to take early retirement and set out on a solo cycle tour around the world, despite being totally unfit and incapable of even mending a puncture. Her story was captivating. Coupled with the fact that my Thailand trip turned into a three-week holiday of a lifetime, I returned home reoriented in my thinking. I know that many people feel renewed and ready for change after a holiday, but as I struggled to pour myself back into the mould of my conventional life, I became convinced that *something* would be along soon to stir up the waters. And there was. But it didn't happen in a way I would have chosen.

A few months later, I was physically assaulted by the person I had believed I was in a genuinely loving relationship with, and after, events just spiralled further and further out of my control. In the wake of all this, I'd felt slain. My legs had been metaphorically kicked so far from beneath me that I wondered if I'd ever get over it. I felt heartbroken, grief-stricken, as well as guilty that I'd brought it all on myself. One blustery weekend, I spent the day on the beach, staring out to sea and hoping to find answers in the immutable power of the waves. Events from the last few horrific weeks played over and over in my mind like a videotape stuck on a loop. And I worried: *was this all life had to offer in terms of happiness?* But from the ashes of this mess rose a realisation that the waters had probably been stirred up some time ago. Life, maybe not in the subtlest of ways, had been trying to tell me for a while now to get moving. I didn't need a caravan or a field in five years' time. I needed to save my life… *right now.*

Once the decision was made to walk away and start afresh, the rest followed easily. Four weeks later, I'd said farewell to all my work colleagues at a leaving party and packed up the contents of my rented bedsit. I can still remember how it felt to leave that life behind; to close the door firmly behind me knowing I had made the right decision. I cycled back to my parents' house with all of my possessions filling just two pannier bags, and feeling relief and freedom like never before. Finally, I had the chance to do what I wanted; to find out who I really was in this world. Shouldn't everyone be given this opportunity at least once in their lives?

The first half of that summer of 1997 was spent Interrailing around Europe. Rather than Paris or Rome, I headed for a little-visited area of Germany, Steinfurt, where I lodged with a pal of mine who tried to teach me German in return for cooking her family traditional English fish and chips three nights a week. Then I went to see Ziggy Marley perform live at a concert in Amsterdam, complete with a spliff in my hand. I met Russian soldiers in Poland, visited

Bran Castle in Transylvania, sat in steaming natural spas in Hungary and had lunch with Italian railway workers at their staff canteen in Venice. I made dozens of new friends and surprised myself with my newfound confidence, shaking off the shackles of timidity and fear of the unknown. Once my rail tickets had expired, a lump in my throat accompanied me home, but I comforted myself with the thought it was only June; summer wasn't gone yet and neither were my savings.

I began to think about how I could spend the rest of my precious gap year. I knew I wanted to explore my own country. The seed had been sown one balmy night, drinking with fellow backpackers in Budapest. I had been in full flow: ribbing an American guy because I couldn't believe he'd lived all his life in the States and had never seen the Grand Canyon. He was hastily defending himself, describing the huge distances in the States (always in hours' drive, never in miles), when he suddenly stopped and said, 'Hang on a minute, Dawn, you've never even been to the Lake District and your country is *tiny*. So, what's your excuse?' He made a good point. As a keen environmentalist, the notion that our green and pleasant land would eventually disappear under a bulldozer seemed a bona fide worry and, with my newfound passion for cycling, I couldn't think of a more appropriate way to travel. The idea swelled in my mind for weeks. I had a romantic notion of myself as a cycling nomad: travelling wherever my heart desired, sleeping in the great outdoors, visiting beautiful and historic places and searching for a place to call home.

Without really understanding the logistics and effort involved in such an expedition, I naively pored over maps and began circling all those places I wished to visit (including, of course, the Lake District). And by the time I'd finished, I had a wibbly-wobbly line from Cornwall to Caithness that nowhere near resembled the shortest distance favoured by most Land's End to John O'Groats cyclists. As the days ticked down to departure, I had some doubts. Considering the furthest I'd ridden in one day was 30 miles (and that was a one-off), I did wonder how the hell I'd manage those sorts of distances *every* single day. But, I figured, what the hell; I'd just build up my fitness as I went. I was actually more concerned about my mental health, because whilst I'd coped well in Europe when travelling alone, that was only occasional. On my upcoming cycle tour, I would be alone almost all of the time. What would I think about to fill in the long hours and make sure my old foe, depression, didn't raise its ugly mug? A few days before departure, I was given some clues.

By chance, I heard a young monk being interviewed on the radio. He'd gone off to the hills to live alone for a few months and meditate. He lived off rice and water and never saw or spoke to another soul in all that time. On his return, he found he'd become a bit of a celebrity and was subsequently interviewed by the local radio station. He was asked the predictable question, 'So, what did you do all that time alone?' to which the monk replied quite honestly, 'Well, one day, I spent the entire day thinking about roast chicken.'

And later in the interview he was asked the equally predictable question, 'So, what will you do now?' Again, he replied honestly, 'I'll probably go and eat some roast chicken.' I decided my journey would be nothing if not interesting.

PART 1

THE WEST COUNTRY

As fresh as a daisy at Land's End

DAY 1

38 MILES

*H*ow many people cycle from Land's End to John O'Groats each year? Whilst no official records are kept, my guess would be hundreds, maybe even thousands. They arrive at the most south-westerly point of the British Isles mainland with the sole purpose of traversing to its most north-easterly extreme, and the nickname for these extraordinary people is *End-to-Enders*. And they don't just come by bicycle. Oh no. People walk it, run it, hitchhike, ride their horses, or go by public transport. (Imagine waiting for that many buses which half the time never show up.) Even more remarkably, people have skateboarded the distance, travelled by wheelchair, walked whilst hitting golf balls, and a few heroic types have even swum around the coastline. The youngest person to have

3

completed the End-to-End was a lad called Henry Cole, who in 2006, at the age of just four, cycled it in thirty-one days, whilst Reg Sevill, aged seventy-four, is the oldest man to have walked the distance. The record for the fastest cycle is forty-one hours, four minutes and twenty-two seconds. Being that the shortest possible route is 874 miles, the rider must have kept up an average speed of… well, I will let you do the maths, but it blows my mind.

So, what is the big attraction? At first glimpse, it is hard to fathom, since Land's End itself is a rather unspectacular, bleak and windy headland. And if that wasn't off-putting enough, in 1987, a millionaire purchased the headland after outbidding the National Trust and turned it into a kitsch mini theme park. So, here you will arrive, filled with all that anticipation for the coming days, weeks or months of your challenge ahead. And what of this grand destination after all your efforts? Another bleak headland, as windy and grey as this one.

Back in 1997, it was my turn. It was 10am on 30th July and I had just turned twenty-one. The previous day, I'd made the long journey down from Sussex, and I must confess I'd felt ridiculously excited. But by the time the train pulled into Penzance at dusk and I found I still had ten very hilly miles to ride before dark, that bravado began to slide. Once at the campsite at Land's End, I'd fumbled with my new tent, glad I was well practised in the art of its erection, and then I'd crawled inside, feeling hungry and a long way from home. With the darkness came the fretting, particularly concerning my bicycle. Who would even want to steal my red paint-chipped bicycle, I don't know, but I could visualise the humiliation:

End-to-End cyclist has bicycle stolen before she's even cycled anywhere. The bike's silhouette was cast upon the tent canvas and I watched it carefully, and by the time daylight rolled around again, I'd hardly slept. I sipped black coffee, counted seagulls and watched the grey clouds also on their way to Scotland. They would no doubt be there long before I would.

Packed and ready to roll by 09.30, I wheeled my way through the handful of tourist attractions: *Smugglers Cove, Shipwreck Supreme, Fond Fumbling at the Bottom of the Sea* (I made that one up) and other nauseating names, before I found the official Land's End signpost that so many people have posed beneath. Although you can pay to have your own name inserted onto the sign, I decided to save myself the money and asked another tourist to take my photograph. And there I posed beneath the names *Kane and Fay from Rochester*.

As all my friends and family were 300 miles away (and at least eighty per cent knew nothing of my whereabouts, for the simple reason I hadn't told anyone), I had to give myself a pep talk. I pulled on my homemade tabard, on which I'd painted the words *Land's End to John O' Groats* on the back and *In Aid of Landmines Clearance International* on the front. And for good measure, I hung a collection tin on my handlebars. There are thousands of good causes out there, any one of which I'd have been happy to raise money for. But after reading a newspaper article recently, explaining how there were enough unexploded landmines to kill every man, woman and child in the countries in which they are still prolific (Cambodia, Rwanda and Angola to name just a few), I decided I would like to give this largely unknown and little-reported-on cause a boost. (Imagine my surprise when just a few days later, I turned on the television and saw Princess Diana also bringing the world's attention to the landmines problem.)

I was ready, and at 10.01 my epic voyage began… halting again at 10.04 when I noticed my bicycle's odometer (which I'd fitted that morning) remained stubbornly on zero. Now, I am sure I'm not alone in my belief that instruction manuals are too boring to read, and substitute them for my preferred method, which is to fiddle with the object until I eventually work it out for myself (because it surely can't be *that* complicated). As methods go, it rarely lets me down, but, on the odd occasion I can't work it out for myself, then some sort of divine intervention usually shows up to help me. I am not entirely certain the tall man on a racing bicycle could be described as divine. But he did intervene. He appeared at my shoulder and after thirty seconds of watching my novice repair attempts, he practically snatched the odometer from my hands and within a minute, he had fixed it, spinning my front wheel to demonstrate the repair. I thanked him profusely. I was grateful for his help but a teeny bit annoyed I'd relinquished my independence at the very first hiccup.

Finally on my way, I picked up speed down the first exhilarating descent and a car driver, who'd slowed to overtake me, shouted good luck through the open passenger side window. And he wasn't alone. As car after car overtook, this same show of moral support was repeated again and again. I was so touched that I felt tears welling up in my eyes. It was one hell of a start to my journey.

The road back to Penzance was easier in this direction, with more descents than ascents and the bonus of a tail wind. I was amazed by how quickly I got back into town and I decided I would skirt the centre to avoid traffic. I followed the road out east and here I encountered my first fellow End-to-Ender. A man was walking towards me. He held a *John O'Groats to Land's End* banner above his head and his fast pace hinted at his seriousness. As I got closer, I read the anti-abortion message that was screaming out across his placard and I shuddered involuntarily. It seemed a little audacious to go trudging the length of the British Isles condemning people for difficult decisions they've made, or spouting emotionally loaded arguments, all of which conclude that bringing unwanted children into this world is always the best option. As I passed this man, our eyes met briefly and I saw his tiredness. He looked glad his long trek was over and I wondered what lessons the road had taught him. Had he learnt to be less condemnatory of those whose situations he couldn't possibly know anything about? I wondered what lessons my journey might teach me. I certainly hadn't missed the coincidence of that first meeting.

Two miles east of Penzance lay the small town of Marazion and, if it were a person, it would surely have been a supermodel. Pristine sandy beaches, blue sea and an island in the bay with its own castle; it must have lured many a tourist to stop in the expensive beachfront car parks. But not me. Buoyed by the miles disappearing so easily behind me, the last thing I wanted to do was stop so soon. Even the local pub tried to catch me in its tentacles with a sign promising *delicious pub grub and real ales*. During the run-up to this trip,

I had often daydreamed about what it would be like, and one of the things I'd imagined doing was enjoying leisurely lunches in pub gardens up and down the country. But after only 15 miles I could see the absurdity of the idea. A heavy lunch and a pint of beer would be most unconducive to an afternoon of further pedalling. Crossing the main road again, I began winding my way inland. It was a shame to be leaving the coast so soon, as it is one of Cornwall's chief attractions, but what little I saw of the azure waters left me spellbound.

I eventually settled for a more modest lunch: a pre-packed sandwich bought from a village shop. As I ate, I peeked at my bike computer and felt immensely proud. I had already clocked up 27 miles and even better, I didn't feel tired. I had visions of catching those clouds up after all. Oh boy, was I about to learn the hard way what cycle touring was really about. Rule number one of cycle touring: break yourself in gently, because only half an hour later I was *exhausted*. In the distance of just 5 miles, the zippy, energetic thoroughbred had been reduced to a bedraggled donkey. It was time to call it a day and look for somewhere to spend the night.

Fortunately, this seemed a good place to run out of energy because, scanning my map, I saw there was not one but four campsites close by. Result. Rule number two of cycle touring: until you have arrived at the place you intend to sleep, then the ride isn't over. So, this was how my next hour went. A small wooden arrow (with a tent symbol and "2 miles" carved onto it) pointed me down the correct road. Even in my knackered state, I was confident I would soon be there. But after 2 miles, instead of a campsite, I found another arrow, again with a tent symbol carved into it, only this time it said

"1.5 miles". Again, I followed compliantly, and let me just explain something: being that this was Cornwall, the road was going sharply uphill and down dale and I was growing more and more exhausted by the second. So, at the end of the next road, what do you think I found? Well, here's a clue: it *wasn't* a campsite. Just another small wooden arrow that now said 2.5 miles. If only I'd had a hacksaw, I would have gleefully put that arrow firmly in its place. Whether it was one campsite badly signposted or the directions for all four campsites intermingled, I have no idea. (And at this stage, no one had explained to me the phenomenon of the Cornish Mile.) But eventually, someone must have decided to take pity on me and stop moving campsites around, because I finally found one.

The campsite was nice enough, but my heart sank when the proprietor asked me for five pounds. Because I was financing this trip myself, I hadn't budgeted on spending more than five or six pounds each day: two to three on food and the same again for a campsite. Even back in 1997, this would be considered a tight budget. But listen, in those days, I was the master of frugality (or more commonly known as tight-fisted). I am the woman who, every day for two years, went to the shop at lunchtime and spent forty-five pence on two bread rolls and two tomatoes. I am also the woman who lived in a bedsit for an *entire year* and only put four fifty-pence pieces into the electricity meter. (My landlord accused me of breaking into it and stealing back the money.) But my extreme frugality had allowed me to save most of my wages and was why I could now afford this gap year. Anyway, back to Cornwall, and last night, when I was charged five pounds to camp, I assumed it was an overpriced campsite; Land's End being a popular tourist destination. Now I was realising, five pounds is a pretty standard charge and at some point, I would have to sit down and recalculate my budget. Rule number three of cycle touring: it always costs more than you think.

Right now, though, I had a desperate longing for a hot shower and afterwards, my first Cornish pub. The campsite proprietor kindly drew me a map and said it was a little over 1 mile's walk across the fields. Who was I trying to kid? By the time I'd pitched up my tent, showered and fixed something to eat, I didn't even have the strength to walk 20 yards to the phone box. Rule number four of cycle touring: if you are camping as well, then the daily chores of pitching the tent, cooking and washing up afterwards can be just as tiring as the cycling. Day one had proved itself to be a steep learning curve, and there would no doubt be more lessons coming my way over the coming days. I manoeuvred my aching legs into my sleeping bag before it was even dark, but once again found it difficult to fall asleep on the hard ground.

DAY 2

40 MILES

*J*ust keep breathing, I told myself as I approached the top of a particularly gruelling hill which, for Cornwall, is really saying something, because *all* Cornish hills are gruelling. My eyes were locked onto my bike computer and in a beautiful coincidence, the clock flicked over to 50 miles at the exact moment I reached the brow of the hill. This was momentous. Fifty whole miles. Fifty damn wonderful miles. I felt as though I'd just won the lottery. But I wasn't the only one monitoring my progress that morning. As I rested in the lay-by, a family of four got out of their car and to my delight they came over to donate money into my collection tin. The Morgan family were lovely people and most generous with their time. Whilst hundreds of people must have driven past me that morning and read *Land's End to John O'Groats* on my back, these guys actually stopped because they wanted to be involved, and I was touched by their attention. We ended up talking for over an hour. Sue was from Scotland and after a few seconds' thought, she concluded I'd be arriving in the Highlands just in time for midge season. Chuckling away, she described the gruesome details of aerial attacks suffered by campers who dared to camp in the Highlands during this period. Words such as *plagued*, *crazy* and *agony* were mentioned on more than one occasion, whilst I listened with what I hoped was good humour and optimism that they were *surely* exaggerating. Rule number five of cycle touring: seek advice from helpful locals.

Midway through our natter, another car pulled over and a smartly dressed man got out to stretch his legs. Before he even had time to appreciate the views, my new friends were upon him.

'Come and meet this brave lass. She's cycling all the way on her own and she's doing it for a good cause.' After their impressive gambit, he had little choice but to donate to my collection tin which, to his credit, he did with grace and a smile. I was inspired. I wished I could employ this family as my personal fundraisers, for they were far bolder than I when it came to asking for money. But all they wanted was to take my photograph against a backdrop of wind turbines (in case I was ever famous, they joked), before bidding me a fond farewell. The three coins now rattling around my charity tin felt like a good luck charm.

The road wound its way through a valley, which was enclosed on either side by dozens of looming, rather stark-looking wind turbines. I learnt from reading the back of a postcard (it was the days before the internet) that Cornwall was where the first UK wind-powered farms were built. One can't help noticing how contentious the issue of wind farms has become in Britain, whereas on the continent, they've been embraced. As I'd travelled around Germany, Switzerland and the Netherlands this summer, I saw how they'd popped up all over the place. I'm not saying every proposed wind farm should get the thumbs-up, but I wonder why other schemes, which are arguably more damaging, go largely unchallenged. Permission is given to dump nuclear waste in national parks, roads are built through areas of outstanding natural beauty and open mines are dug on sites of special scientific interest. For me personally, whenever I see the forces of nature being utilised in such a simple yet clever way, it brings a lump to my throat. It stirs inside me a mixture of emotions: of sadness because the change needed is coming too slowly but also of hope, that there are those who understand and might yet save our planet from climatic catastrophe.

*

On reflection, I was starting to think that 38 miles on only my first day might have been a teeny bit over-ambitious, because this morning, my body felt like it had been in a car crash. Now might be a good time to warn other potential End-to-Enders that if, due to lack of time, you decide not to train beforehand and instead think, *I'll just build up my fitness as I go*, just as I had done, then please, *don't*. Because there is *nowhere* in Cornwall where you can break yourself in gently. The county has a network of quiet back roads that should be heaven for cyclists, but (and this is a big but) they are steep. Really steep. Many come with warning signs of gradients of between 10-20%. (The steepest being a place called Millook at 33%.) There is nothing about the Cornish topography that is in any way forgiving. Aside from the obvious strain of going up, I soon found out that coming down wasn't any fun either. There may be riders out there who are happy to let go of the brakes and enjoy the ride. But for me, there was no pleasure to be had in reaching speeds of 40mph, not when there was every chance a car would appear around the blind bend at the bottom and end my tour, with bicycle and body twisted and bloody wrecks. And finally, you should know that these hills are relentless. It isn't just certain parts of Cornwall that are hilly; it's the whole of the damn county, over 100 miles in length, that will have you going up and coming down like a bleedin' yo-yo. That said, I persisted with the back roads because I believed the alternative (cycling on the A30) was probably worse.

But it was not just the gradients that caused me grief. Navigation was also infuriating. The back lanes were like a maze and as the morning wore on, I found myself becoming angry with the road signs. Anyone who has been to Cornwall is probably now smirking and thinking, *aha, the Cornish Mile*, but for those who have not had the pleasure, then please allow me to explain. I would arrive at a T-junction and examine the signpost. To reach destination A, it would clearly say turn left and for destination B turn right. Heading for destination B, and most definitely away from destination A, right I would turn. Only to find a signpost half a mile up the road saying that destination A (the place I should now be headed away from) was suddenly the place I was headed for. And as for the mileage stated on these road signs, please… *how* can somewhere you have been cycling towards for the last ten minutes suddenly be two miles further away than stated on the previous signpost?

So that you don't think I'm going to spend the rest of this book complaining about how tough the cycling was (although once you've ridden around Cornwall, you may sympathise), I would like to reassure you that even on a day like today, when muscles, miles and maps all seemed hideously against me, there was still plenty of interesting things to see. Through a tiny hamlet, I stopped to look at a garden full of old Land Rovers and military tanks, a formidable sight and a far cry from the usual gnome collection. I also noticed this area was occupied by folk who were fiercely patriotic towards their corner of the world. Cornwall is called Kernow in local dialect and I noticed the flag of St Piran (black with a white cross) being flown on many houses and farm cottages. I wondered if these were proud families, long-standing occupiers of their county. But I'd also read recently that Cornish citizens liked to fly their flag in defiance against what was described as: *the increasing encroachment on communities by people buying up property for holiday homes*. Up one of these back roads, a man raking his lawn stopped to watch me cycle past and I saw his eyes read my charity tabard with, I noted, great amusement. Leaning on his rake, he called out, 'You won't find John O'Groats up here.' I forced myself to smile back, unsure whether he was trying to patronise me or just have some friendly banter. Either way, it wasn't good for my moral.

What also wasn't good for my moral was finding the morning long gone but I was still no nearer to my destination. Wandering about lost in this maze of lanes meant I'd cycled 10 miles further than I'd meant to and, in light of this, I felt my decision to use the A30 after all was the right thing to do. At least, I consoled myself, it would now be one straight road from here into Bodmin town. I digress here to recall that one afternoon prior to departure, my father had looked over my shoulder whilst I was engrossed in route planning and he voiced a rare opinion.

'Whatever you do, stay off the A30. It's the main speed link through the West Country.'

But typical of a child listening to their parent or, should I say, not listening, I replied, 'Yeah, okay,' whilst my brain thought *whatever*, and I continued route planning, oblivious to those words of wisdom.

I halted where minor road merged with the A30 and I must confess, I did a double take. Three lanes of traffic roared past me in both directions and approaching speeds that looked suspiciously like 90mph. Worse still, the road builders seemed to have forgotten to add any kind of hard shoulder where a cyclist might take refuge. *Shit*. I pulled out my map to double check this wasn't a motorway. But no, it was either this or more of the leg-aching, muscle-wrecking, lung-exploding, soul-destroying Cornish mile. The former just about won. Rule number six of cycle touring: sadly, busy roads can't always be easily avoided. To start with, I tried to stay as close to the edge as was possible, but it didn't take me long to realise that this action simply encouraged traffic to overtake me closer than ever. I was horribly aware of just how fragile the human body is, particularly my head, which I now found compared well to a freshly laid egg, ready to be smashed and smeared across the tarmac. The constant roar of engines drowned out the sounds of the world around me and I thought miserably, this was not how I'd envisaged my trip. My head began to thump and my eyes span in their sockets as I tried to watch the traffic coming at me from all angles. But it wasn't just my vulnerability that bugged me; the speed of the traffic made it seem as if I was travelling extremely slowly in comparison.

My moral was on the floor by the time I'd reached the outskirts of Bodmin town where mercifully, the traffic returned to a much saner speed and I dared to uncross my fingers. My bicycle computer was once again reading 38 miles; so much for taking it easy today. I wobbled into the first pub I came to and collapsed dramatically onto a picnic bench. Then I ordered a large baked potato and ate it in three minutes flat. Out in the beer garden it clouded over and I had to pull on my coat again. All day long I'd been plagued by typical British weather, with hot sun one minute and downpours the next. As a consequence, the day had been one long farcical juggle, as I'd struggled on and off with jumpers and coats, trying to maintain the perfect temperature for a cyclist. I wondered if other riders found it as much of a pain as I did. In those days, racers in shiny Lycra were not such a common site and as a novice, I had no clue as to the benefits of proper cycling attire. Instead, I opted for everyday shorts, t-shirts, leggings and sweaters. Rule number seven of cycle touring: purpose-made cycle clothing is not just a gimmick to make you feel ridiculous; it really has been designed to be the most comfortable, practical option.

I could feel the carbohydrates reviving me slightly and the beer acted as liquid anaesthetic. According to my map, there should have been a campsite next door to the pub but that would have been too much to hope for, and a quick chat with the barmaid revealed it had closed down years ago. But, she assured me, I would find another campsite further into town. As I supped the last of my pint, the benches around me began to fill up with holidaying Lancastrians. They had just returned from a 30-mile cycle ride around the local vicinity and all of them looked remarkably fresh-faced. Even the young children had barely a hair out of place. I was included in their conversations and before long they had wheedled from me the details of my trip. As they patted me on the back, they joked that I looked fit for bed rather than for a 1,000-mile bike ride, and I felt embarrassed because I knew how true that was right now.

'So,' asked one, 'which charity are you supporting?'

'Landmines Clearance International,' I smiled back, hoping another donation was heading my way, but their faces looked blank.

'Princess Di's thing?' I added as an afterthought, which brought nods of understanding from them and raised eyebrows from me.

*

The over-enthusiastic campsite manager came rushing out of his office when I arrived, promising me a favourable spot by the ladies' wash block and then spent ten minutes trying to recruit me into the Caravan and Camping Club. Nearly insensible with fatigue, I finally persuaded him that I would consider this later and then he offered to wheel my bicycle over to my pitch. I was continually forgetting that people don't realise how heavy a fully loaded touring bicycle is... and before I could warn him, he'd bent down to pick up my bike off the floor where I'd left it. In slow motion, I watched the look of surprise and then panic cross his face as he was pulled off balance by its sheer weight, and he fell with a painful crunch on top of it. I did my best to hide a smirk.

Because I was so tired it took me ages to set up my tent... so I won't repeat the language I wanted to use when that same over-enthusiastic manager reappeared and *gleefully* informed me that I had pitched up closer than the recommended six paces from the neighbouring tent. He ordered me to take it down and repitch it further away. Had this guy been *watching me*? Had he waited until I was finished scrabbling around before he decided to tell me this? Was this retribution because I'd smirked at his fall? I tried a series of faces: the reasonable face, the pleading *I promise I won't set fire to my neighbour's tent* face and eventually the *I don't give a shit about your stupid fire recommendations* face. But all to no avail. Later on, when I was finally settled inside, the lady from said neighbouring tent brought me out a cup of tea. I thought this very kind and wondered whether she had witnessed the whole tent-pitching debacle and was bringing me a cup of tea in solidarity.

DAY 3

15 MILES

*T*he question of what to pack for this trip had been a difficult one, since I had no prior experience of cycle touring, and in the end, if there was even the slightest chance I thought I might need something, then into my bags it went. The result (*quelle surprise*) was four over-stuffed panniers and one *very* heavy bicycle. Fortunately, it soon became obvious which items were going to be worth keeping (the camping stove) and which should be binned off at the first available opportunity (the cagoule). But the one thing I hadn't even considered bringing was something to keep me entertained each evening. With weeks of solitude stretching ahead, I began to realise my well-thumbed copy of *A Bike Ride* would not be enough, and so I decided to purchase a portable radio.

The shopkeeper didn't even look up from what he was doing when I entered his shop, only nodding in a barely interested fashion towards the radios after I'd stood right in front of him for ten minutes. And when two days of my budget disappeared into his till, he still couldn't raise a smile. Okay, so maybe he was just having a bad day, but I found this indifferent attitude pretty consistent amongst the locals; there were residents in this town who were not going to hide their aversion to tourists.

So today I was heading for the wilds of Bodmin Moor and it occurred to me that whilst I had a puncture repair kit (and knew how to use it), it might still be a good idea to carry a spare inner tube. My imagination had already played out scenarios of what might become of me across the moors…

The puncture occurred late in the day and by the time I concluded it irreparable, darkness had fallen. It was 20 miles to the nearest town; it would take me until midnight to walk there. And so, I set out along the empty road in the pouring rain, resigned to my fate and tripping into potholes without bike lights to guide me. After hours of painful trudging, I rounded a corner and my heart leapt with hope. There, with all the windows illuminated like a beacon of light, was a lone farmhouse… was someone home? I banged on the door and eventually a wizened man answered. I said good evening and hurriedly explained my plight, asking if there was anywhere nearby to stay. The man thought for a moment before answering that yes, there was an inn, 3 miles away. My spirits rose and then instantly fell as he added, 'on the far side of those hills'. In his thick West Country burr, he told me to follow a track that would lead me right there, pointing in a vague direction, before shutting the door in my face.

I found this track easily enough, and followed it as it wound its way into the hills. I was quietly confident I would soon be sipping a warming brandy by the inn fireside, but after a mile or so, the track just petered out. Nervously, I decided to keep going. Across fields and through woodlands I traipsed, struggling to push my bicycle through ankle-deep mud. I kept hoping the track would reappear, but as I stumbled blindly in the dark, the panic began to rise. I cut my arms on brambles as I went and heard unseen wild animals snarling as I passed, whilst all the time I desperately tried to remember the old man's final directions. 'And you'll come to a tree…'

Okay, let's not get carried away. It's not as if I had to cross the swamps of the Amazon or anything, but having said that, even the comparatively small 80 square miles of Bodmin Moor should be treated with reverence. I'd heard it said many times that misadventure in the wilderness can usually be traced back to one simple mistake from which everything else escalates. And in light of this, I decided a spare inner tube and some bike lights would be no bad thing to have (as well as a healthy scepticism of directions from elderly men).

Inside the only cycle shop in town, I found myself staring cluelessly at a shelf full of inner tubes of varying types and sizes. Thankfully, the man who ran this shop was kind and helpful and pointed to the inner tube I'd need for my bicycle with its 26-inch wheels. *Hang on. Did he say twenty-six?* And at that moment I realised I had done something really, really stupid. I recalled the debacle with the odometer a few days earlier, and that I'd set up my bike computer for… (I'm blushing now just thinking about this) … a bicycle with 16-inch wheels. You know, like on a child's bike. Oh, the shame. Outside, and I went through the whole set-up procedure again, only this time *with* the instruction manual, and here's what I found. I had *accidently* set the odometer for 26-inch wheels after all. Who says two wrongs don't make a right? Rule number eight of cycle touring: knowledge of basic bicycle mechanics will spare you pain. (And just so you know, I did consider calling this book *An Idiot on a Bicycle*.)

Back on the A30, Bodmin Moor was invisible below a damp, thick fog. It lay heavy on the land and felt claustrophobic against my chest, which heaved in and out in protest of the hills. It was too warm to wear my cagoule and soon I was as wet as the moors. A stray mat of damp hair dangled in front of my eyes and I was faced with the irritating task of sweeping it aside every 30 seconds. Alas, the night had brought no relief to my aching leg muscles and every push on the pedals was a grim reminder of the one hundred miles so far covered… and the almost nine hundred left to go. A familiar red-hot flair of temper began to well up inside. I was angry at myself. *Why, oh why hadn't I done the sensible thing and taken a day to rest? Why was I even trying to cycle another 30 miles in this state of exhaustion?* I also realised that it wasn't just an illusion created by high-speeding cars, I really was moving at a snail's pace. And I was even more worried for my safety in the poor visibility, which did nothing to curb traffic speeds. In vain hope, I wore my fluorescent tabard and kept my new back light on flash mode.

Exhaustion… bad weather… busy roads. These unappetising statistics swam around my brain until I could think of little else; self-pity had set in and it was here to stay.

Stopping for a breather in a lay-by, I pulled out the map and traced my finger along the A30, expecting to see, I don't know, maybe a sign from the Gods for inspiration. And after a few moments, I found one. There, nestled in the soggy folds of my map, was a smudged symbol of a tent and caravan. *This* is where I would head. Measured in thumbnails, the campsite was only 8 miles further. I folded the map away. Astonishingly, as soon as I had a more achievable target in mind, the cycling seemed easier. I liked my new plan. *That's it*, I encouraged myself, *cycle at least as far as the next campsite and then give up and go home.*

The rest of the journey passed in a blur. My mind was lost to the sweet pleasure of daydreaming. *I was Dawn, the brave eco-warrior princess. Dashing into the road, halting all the traffic and coaxing drivers out from their air-polluting cars.* But even this was too exhausting, and instead, I thought about what it would be like to peel off my sodden clothes, slip into a hot bath and sip a glass of Chardonnay. Yes, now that was more like it, although not very likely on my five-pounds-a-day budget. But, as always, daydreaming succeeded in making the time pass quicker and when I looked up again, the sign for the campsite was just ahead. I felt no elation at seeing it. Just a saddened sense of relief.

When the woman on reception at the Red Woods Campsite (described by the leaflet as an 'Oasis' on Bodmin Moor) heard I was cycling for charity, she immediately waived the camping fee. (I later placed the cost of the pitch into my charity tin myself, something I made a habit of doing.) As she wrote down my details, I imagined she must have been thinking: *This girl... Land's End to John O' Groats?*

Pah, no chance. I must have looked like the most sorry-arsed cyclist the world had ever seen, and the one least likely to reach John O' Groats. Luckily, this woman was perceptive enough to notice my depressed state and did not make any quips at my expense, for which I was grateful for.

I spent further precious minutes out in the rain assessing the half-empty campsite for the perfect location to pitch my tent, and picked a spot sheltered by some ornamental pines. Half an hour later, I was curled up inside asleep, thankful that today's ordeal was finally over. As I dozed, I dreamt peculiar dreams about legs that flailed round and around on a bicycle that went nowhere… until I was startled awake by a voice from outside.

'Hello.' Poking my nose through the tent flap, I was rather surprised to see the receptionist standing in the rain clutching a brolly and looking rather peeved, whilst behind her stood a monstrous motorhome.

'Look, I'm sorry,' she said, 'but you weren't supposed to pitch here. This spot is reserved for caravans who pay for electrical hook up. I'm afraid you'll have to move.' How can the same shit happen to the same girl twice? Under the eyes of the sneering motorhome occupants in whose spot I was pitched, I made it policy to move my tent and all my gear as slowly as possible so I could be as much of an annoyance to them as I felt they were being to me. I was then forced to repitch my tent on the windy, rain-lashed side of the trees. Considering the wind has a far more detrimental effect on a tent than it does a motorhome, this seemed grossly unfair.

I may not have been able to afford the swanky hotel with large bath and complimentary vino, but we work with what we've got, and this campsite had a bar. A large, cosy, heated onsite bar; and this was where I was headed. But it wasn't only the prospect of warmth that lured me in. Not once since starting out had I managed anything that even resembled a good night's sleep, and I blamed it squarely on my inability to adjust to sleeping on the ground. (Note, I did have a sleeping mat, but it was one of those old foam mattresses which were basically no different from sleeping on the ground.) Now, I don't like sleep deprivation. I know that no one does, but I *really* can't handle it. It upsets every molecule in my body, including my mental health, and that was what worried me most. Because unless I could rustle up some positivity from somewhere, I might just find myself catching a train home from the nearest station and Landmines Clearance International wouldn't be receiving very much money. So, here was my big idea… I was going to get drunk. Absolutely sozzled. If my body couldn't get used to camping, then I figured if I drank enough, it wouldn't even notice the lack of a bed or soft pillows, and my mind might finally get the restoration it needed.

I made myself comfortable in a corner of the pub, pint glass in one hand and pen in the other. I wrote my daily diary whilst intermittently pausing to sip beer, but every time I looked up it was to find a different pair of eyes staring in my direction. At first, I thought it was just my imagination, but after it'd happened half a dozen times, it really started to bother me and I decided to say something.

'Hi,' I called out to one staring couple. 'My name is Dawn. I'm from Planet Zog and I've come here to vaporise your dog.' Okay, I didn't really say that, but God, I *wanted* to. I get that I wasn't a run-of-the-mill client in this place. I'd have had to be blind not to notice that everyone else was in groups of family and friends. But would a little friendliness have killed them? For their looks of curiosity to be accompanied by a smile instead of their standoffish, unresponsive expressions? I know I should have ignored them but I was only twenty-one and had yet to develop the necessary thick skin. Eventually, I left my pint unfinished and fled back to the sanctuary of my tent, but once again spent the night tossing and turning. Looking back now, I can see that this rather distressing day was the nadir of my trip, both mentally and physically. Hopefully from now on, things would look up.

DAY 4

(30 MILES)

O n any trip, there will usually be some niggling little issues which, on their own, seem trivial. But only once you're free of them do you realise how they were collectively grinding you down. This was the position I found myself in this morning. The rain, for now, had finally beat it, but something else had gone, and it took a few seconds to figure out what: all those aches in my legs, back and posterior had vanished. I wondered if pushing myself those 15 miles yesterday had been a good idea after all. It had been far enough to feel like I was still making progress, but short enough to be almost as good as a rest. I crawled out of the tent, blinking in the morning light and happy to see colour in the sky again.

Now in a more optimistic frame of mind, I felt I could rest today if I wanted, without feeling like an abject failure, but it wasn't only the break in rain that made me want to push on. The truth was, I did not want to stay in this campsite a second longer than I had to. Maybe I was a bit oversensitive after the pub last night, but as I passed back and forth between tent and shower block, I felt I was being watched. But just like in the horror movies, when I turned around to look, there was no one there. But I could take a good guess at the kind of comments being made behind twitching caravan awnings.

'That poor girl, all on her own, doesn't she have any friends or family?'

'Perhaps she is hoping to pick up a man'

'Hanging around all alone in the bar last night, it's not becoming of a young lady.'

'There she goes, the scarlet woman.'

Whether real or imagined, I'd had it with Red Woods. But as I prepared for my departure, I was surprised to find I was actually dying to get back in the saddle; it seemed that sometime in the night, I had crossed an invisible divide. As I cycled away from the "Oasis", I began to notice a pattern in my days. The first few miles were always a struggle. My legs felt like lead weights and I would be convinced someone had smuggled rocks into my panniers during the night. During this time, it was not uncommon to hear myself inwardly whining, *I can't do this*. But after a time, usually within that first hour, the wheels seemed to turn more easily and I began to relax into my own rhythm and at a pace I was comfortable with. Once I'd settled into this zone, I could stop seeing the trip as an endurance test and believe I was actually doing this because I wanted to. Even the uphill bits.

The final wisps of mist cleared and Bodmin Moor was transformed from the dank, depressing place of yesterday and into a green and picturesque landscape. I wished hard for the sun to emerge to complete the tranquillity. I stopped to observe Bodmin Moor's adorable native ponies from a distance. None of Britain's native equines are truly wild but feral, i.e., domestic animals turned loose. Like a lot of horses, they seemed most perplexed by my bicycle, and I watched them watching me until finally the handsome stallion turned tail and protectively herded his mares away.

So, another day, another maze of Cornish back lanes. Twice I took a wrong turn and ended back on the A30, which I'd sworn off after yesterday. I altogether missed the miners' memorial I wanted to see (another wrong turn) and unfortunately the caves I planned to explore after lunch were, to my surprise, closed on a Saturday. But any frustrations were quashed by an inner glow of satisfaction that was growing within me. Not only had day four brought respite from muscle pain, it also marked a momentous hike in my fitness levels. That morning, I lost count of the number of hills I made it up and, unlike the previous few days, I found I could now reach the top with my heart, legs and lungs in a reasonable functioning order.

Along the A390, heading for Tavistock, I finally met the sunshine.

'Delighted to make your acquaintance,' I called out to the sky, and basked in the unexpected warmth. The road, having risen sharply for 2 miles, now rewarded me with easier riding along the crest of the hills. It was a great opportunity to study the finer points of the West Country landscape which

I would describe later in my diary as: *soft on the eyes with green rolling hills, covered in a patchwork of smaller fields and still separated by traditional hedgerows.* It made me want to reminisce about a bygone era, where man not machine still toiled the earth. The disappearance of traditional hedgerows (and the wildlife within them) began in the late 1500s, as they were torn out to make way for much larger agricultural fields. Naturally, there was an outcry from various quarters, including the Church and writers of the time (Shakespeare), who were most concerned with what they called the "ripping up of England". By the mid-1700s, England had the most productive agriculture in Europe and by 1850, only twenty percent of the population were now required to work the land (rather than the traditional eighty). It marked a significant shift in population; from country to city and from field into factory.

After a gloriously long freewheel down the other side, I spied a fully loaded touring bicycle, albeit a riderless one, propped up against a bench. I felt a pang of excitement as I stopped to make myself comfortable and wait for John to emerge from taking a leak in the bushes. We introduced ourselves and I listened intently as he told me in his thick Leeds accent that he too was cycling the End-to-End, also alone and unsupported and with a tent. I cannot describe how happy I was to meet another cyclist attempting the same challenge, and I listened keenly whilst he told me of his charity fundraising attempts. He was raising money for his local school for children who are hard of hearing, whilst his wife, who was a presenter for their local radio station, interviewed him daily to boost donations. He had tried writing to companies both large and small but found, as I had, they were only interested in funding large or famous events. We shared a grumble about the tiresome Cornish roads, and it was comforting to know I wasn't the only one struggling. Unfortunately, John had to rush on. He needed to be at the top of the hill for his next interview with his wife, and that's when I realised, not only was he cycling with all his clothes and camping equipment, he was lugging a heavy transmitter around in his panniers too. Total respect to this man. At least it was proving to be worth the effort; he had already raised £1,300. I tried not to think of the measly few pounds rattling around the bottom of my collection tin.

As I watched John ride away, I stayed to eat an apple. Now I had met an ally, I sensed a shift in my perspective. Instead of envying the ease at which passing cars could cover distances, I now eyed them almost with sympathy. The occupants had no idea how serendipitous this meeting had been, and nor would they ever get to feel their self-respect building like the determination of two cyclists, defeating their own limitations. As I idly flicked apple pips into the hedge, I mulled over the odds. In four days, I'd encountered just one other touring cyclist and goodness knows how many cars; hundreds, maybe thousands must pass me each day. How different the world would be if those figures could be turned on their head. Suddenly brimming with optimism and overwhelming happiness, I hit the road again. This long road that snaked into the distance would always lead to John O'Groats. I felt I could travel the whole world on my bicycle

It wasn't long before I spied a speck in the distance which, as I got nearer, morphed into a cyclist, which in turn morphed into John. Together we struggled onwards towards the town of Tavistock and I must admit, I was secretly pleased I could cycle easily up hills John struggled on, but he said this was because I had a much lower gear ratio on my bike. (I have mountain bike gears that are designed with a small third cog on the front chain ring, which enables the rider to cycle up steeper hills, even if it isn't much faster than walking pace.) And I should add, John was twenty years my senior. But when he explained he had given himself *only sixteen days* to complete the whole ride, I suddenly had a happy mental picture of myself really doing this. If he could finish it in sixteen days, then I should have no worries in my allotted time of four weeks.

Freewheeling down the final road into Tavistock, it felt as though we were already a team. And now that I was no longer alone, I thought I could sense a marked difference in people's attitudes. The locals, who sat in the afternoon sun, still watched us keenly as we arrived on our loaded touring bikes, but it felt no more than mild interest. It was hard to decipher whether those intense stares I often received were even real or whether, on this occasion, John's presence simply provided a shield for my acute self-consciousness.

We tracked down the tourist office but were disappointed to learn that the youth hostel (marked clearly on both our maps) had never actually existed. We were redirected to a campsite out east of town on the edge of Dartmoor National Park and arrived some time later, both complaining bitterly about the hilly West Country, no easier despite having passed out of Cornwall and into Devon. I pitched my tent in a sunny corner between John's tent and one belonging to Annie and

Steve, a friendly pair who frequented this particular campsite on a regular basis. Finally, the weather was clement enough for me to sit outside and write my diary, but I soon gave up writing in favour of being sociable. Annie and Steve invited John and I to join them in the campsite's bar, and we justified the move by saying we needed to celebrate the completion of our first county. The bar was dingy but comfortable, with a small restaurant next door, and was full of other holiday regulars like Annie and Steve. I perched myself on a bar stool with a beer and was soon immersed in barroom banter. It had to be one of the most enjoyable camping experiences of my entire trip, and it restored my faith in people after the chilly atmosphere of the night before. Quite naturally, this meant one or two pints became a sociable four or five; probably not the best move for someone who has to tackle Dartmoor by bicycle in the morning.

It was good to talk about cycling with John and as the beer loosened my tongue, I shared some of my ideas I'd been dreaming up, of cycle tours through Scandinavia and Eastern Europe. When he told me he'd seen many a good cyclist walk up hills I'd ridden today, the beer as well as the compliment made me blush. I teased John, saying it was because I hadn't smoked a single cigarette since setting out, whilst he was sat there filling up the ashtray. As the evening drew on, I watched him puff through nearly a whole packet of cigarettes whilst occasionally waving them temptingly under my nose. I think it was somewhere between pints three and four that I succumbed to my addiction.

DAY 5

(8 MILES)

*I*t's not as though I am totally naive to the consequences of too much alcohol, but like most of us at some time in our lives, I allowed myself to get caught up in the moment, as I transformed into a social butterfly for the evening. And even if someone had taken me aside and laid out in no uncertain terms how awful I would feel next morning, I would no doubt have waved away their kindly concerns with the dismissiveness of a glassy-eyed drunk who firmly believes they have everything under control.

As I lay on my back staring up at the tent roof, I performed a quick mental rundown of the world around me. Mouth? Dry and tasting as though I'd licked out the ashtray. Head? Danced on by pregnant hippos. Legs? Well, having braved 30 very hilly miles yesterday, those painful, dispiriting aches had, alas, returned. Wallet? No doubt emptied. And finally, the weather? I pushed an experimental finger into the sagging canvas above and realised copious amounts of rainwater were sat just over my head. Every now and again, the tent walls flapped violently, like a ship's topsail out at sea. And as my fuzzy, alcohol- blocked senses began to clear, I heard the rain beating down outside. Rule number nine of cycle touring… have a guess! Half of me didn't want to move, whilst the other half was all too aware of the beer still sloshing around my otherwise empty belly. I needed to get food into it quickly before I vomited. Somehow, I got myself together and ventured outside and with my only protection my useless cagoule, I crouched in the rain. I rustled up a couple of boiled eggs with my last remaining bit of bread, but it was a far cry from the full English I craved. I cursed the rain and I cursed my own stupidity.

After eating, I was slightly revived and I began the laborious process of taking down a tent in the rain. I was aggrieved to realise that saturated as it was, it was now twice its normal weight. I suspected John must be suffering too, but if he was, he wasn't about to show it. The last I saw of him was an impressive show of bravado as he swung into his saddle, muttering he would make it to Bristol today even if it killed him; anything to leave these hills behind. And then he was gone. It was my turn. Steve and Annie were there to wave me off. They brushed off the weather as a typical day on Dartmoor, but I wondered whether they would be tempted to head for a hotel and hot bath once I was gone. I know I would have, given the chance. Annie put some money into my collection tin, whilst Steve handed me a ready-to-eat army ration: rice pudding in a bag that you heat up in boiling water. I guess he wasn't confident of my survival in the storm either.

The problem with this campsite (aside from selling copious amounts of alcohol) was its location. Out of the main entrance, turn right, and immediately you are looking up at one of those hills so steep, it is marked on ordnance survey maps with small black arrows that might as well say, "only four-wheel drives need bother". Standing at the bottom in a puddle, I had to crane my neck right back to see the top. I slipped into that small front cog I told you about, gritted my teeth and ever so slowly began toiling upwards. I had no clear idea where I was heading and I don't mean which direction (there was only one road), but I had no idea where I would end up. Two youth hostels were perfectly located on my route but disappointingly, an answerphone message last night informed me they were both fully booked out for the next month. In a demonstration of youthful optimism, I went anyway.

I managed the climb in alternate stretches, slowly pushing down hard on the pedals and then pausing to regain my breath. But just as I made it over the brow of the hill, I was greeted by a gust of wind and rain that slammed into my face and made me gasp. At that moment, I knew; far from having got the difficult bit out of the way first (had I *really* thought that was what I was doing?), the hell had only just begun. The wilderness of Dartmoor National Park lay at my feet. It was my first-ever glimpse and my heart sank. It was far higher and more exposed than I'd realised, but worse than that was, of course, the hills. From what I could see of the road as it snaked away into the murky distance, the gradients were longer and steeper than anything I'd encountered up to now, even by West Country standards. The wind, a strong breeze when I'd left the campsite, now reached near gale force on top of the moor. And I need not explain to regular cyclists what cruel fate awaited. But for those still newbies to cycling, it can be explained in just one word… *headwind.* Now, I *know* what you're thinking. You're thinking, why didn't I just head back down to the campsite and wait for the wind and hangover to subside? It's a fair question, and one I cannot answer easily. Only to say that there seemed to be some invisible force pulling me on. Whether it was a love of cycling or some egotistical motive that wouldn't allow me to stop, I don't know. But whatever it was, I was glad of it, because without it, I sure as hell wouldn't have made it to Somerset, let alone Scotland.

So here follows a brief description of how I survived that difficult ride. I now see the last few days as some kind of warm-up, with Dartmoor as the grand finale to my *Tour-de-West-Country.* I found the best posture to adopt was to keep my head down, thus protecting my face from the wind and my gaze from the gradients. *Head down, mind blank, legs on autopilot* became my mantra. Water fell in torrents on my head and ran down my face, off the end of my nose and into my mouth. It leaked through my cagoule, saturating every article of clothing I wore. It filled my boots too. It ran in rivers down the road and as I passed drainage ditches, it roared in an ever-constant waterfall off the moors. For a while, I tried singing to raise my spirits but instead, a line from one of my favourite poems, *The Rhyme of the Ancient*

Mariner, kept repeating itself in my head: "Water, water, everywhere, nor any drop to drink". Aside from the usual panting up every hill, the cold weather made my nose run like a tap (have you ever tried using a tissue in the rain?) so that I felt I was in danger of drowning in a deluge of rainwater and mucus. The headwind was so strong I had to get off at regular intervals and turn my back on it just so I could catch my breath. And I didn't make much progress on the downhill stretches either. The wind slowed me down so much that I had zero momentum left to get me even a teensy bit of the way up the next climb. Halfway up one hill, when I'd stopped for a breather, a flying twig smacked me in the face and I screamed angrily into the wind, 'Oh, for crying out loud, just ease up, will you?' And then I begged, almost in a whisper, 'Please, just for a few minutes?'

After nearly two hours, I glanced at my bike computer and saw I'd only managed a soul-destroying 8 miles. I could have *walked* that distance in the same time. Just as I was wondering where this day might end, being that I didn't have anywhere to stay, I rounded a corner and my heart leapt with hope, for there, with all the windows illuminated like a beacon of light, was a lone farmhouse. Was someone home? I banged on the door for a few minutes until a wizened man answered. Okay, just kidding. What was *actually* around the next corner was a sign for the village of Princetown and, joy of joys, a campsite. Now that really was a welcoming beacon. And I needed no persuading to abandon my ride. My progress was so incredibly slow that it was futile to continue. But unlike that day on Bodmin, I knew this did not mean I had failed. This time, I knew I would be back in the morning, fresh-faced, fully rested and ready to hit the road once more.

Turning right, I rolled on down the road, and Dartmoor prison appeared eerily through the swirling mists. The prison was first built in 1809 to hold French and American prisoners of war before it became a criminal prison in 1850. It was said to be the hardest, most severe prison in Victorian England and until recently, it housed some of the most dangerous and notorious inmates in British history. I wondered if it was always this grey and depressing here.

Princetown (actually a village) was a curious place. Originally the idea of Sir Thomas Tyrwhitt, secretary to the Prince of Wales in 1785, his original idea had been for a farming settlement and only later decided it would be the perfect place to build a prison. I was astonished to learn that up until 1956, the village had benefitted from its own railway service, astonishing because the place is 1,400 feet above sea level and seemed extraordinarily remote. As I cycled into "town", I realised it was one of those places that had more facilities for tourists than for locals, and as I so often do with remote communities, I wondered if the residents moved here specifically because they love the National Park and the great outdoors. Or, were they here because this was where they were born, but barely gave their surroundings a second glance anymore?

Stepping inside the bar at the Plume of Feathers pub was like stepping into another world. A warm, dry world where people were drinking beer, eating lunch with friends and watching the football match on the television. You know, *normal* Sunday things. Maybe I should have felt a little foolish, standing there all pink-faced in a puddle forming around me. Perhaps the people in the bar knew better than to be out cycling on Dartmoor in this weather. But I certainly didn't feel foolish; more like inwardly satisfied at having got here at all. I thought the landlady might have been annoyed by the mess I was making of her carpet but she didn't seem to notice. In fact, she very kindly told me to go and get myself settled in and pay later. I was delighted to learn the pub offered another cheap option besides camping: a bed in a bunkhouse for just seven pounds. Did I want a night in the dry? In a proper bed? You bet I did. And it got better because I had the entire room to myself. I hung up every last sodden item of clothing and equipment to dry, including the tent, before having a hot shower. Then I towel-dried my hair and went down to the bar to treat myself to a bit of TLC.

Can there be anything more inviting than the site of a roaring fire after a morning spent out in the rain? I bagged the table in front of the hearth and then ordered a starter, main and dessert from the extensive menu and devoured them greedily, with barely a thought for my budget. But I figured, what the hell, I deserved it, right? And for good measure, I tried a half pint of each locally brewed ale on tap. And all the while, my boots were sat drying by the fire whilst my feet were tucked under my bum for warmth. The afternoon was far from a solitary affair and several fellow travellers, keen to share the warmth of those logs, joined me. A Danish couple sat morosely with their pints, clutching a soggy copy of *The Lonely Planet Guide to Walking in Britain*. They'd hoped to sit out the rain in the pub but they couldn't hide their disappointment at the Dartmoor weather. Later, a couple from Scotland joined us. They too were walking but were remarkably nonchalant about the weather, and they seemed to be facing the prospect of an afternoon in the pub with considerably more cheer than their cousins from across the North Sea. That afternoon, my collection tin, which I'd got into the habit of taking everywhere, swelled by several more pounds. Landmines Clearance International would be glad of the rain that day.

That night, I was sharing my bunkhouse with a group of youngsters who, in the morning, were attempting part of their Duke of Edinburgh gold award. This particular part of the challenge involved walking for eight hours a day across Dartmoor over three days, living under self-built shelters and putting their map and compass skills into practise. It all sounded terrific fun. I chatted to their team leaders, who were most impressed, not that I was cycling the End-to-End but that I was doing it alone and without any back-up support. They were all banging around till late that night, preparing their equipment for the next day, and were all up again at the crack of dawn. Because they'd felt guilty for disturbing me, as a (literal) peace offering, they'd left me some of their supplies for my breakfast and I dined on tea, toast, cereal and eggs. But really there was no need for them to feel bad; an earthquake couldn't have kept me awake that night. After five nights of uncomfortable, disturbed sleep in the tent and five days of physically pushing myself further than I ever have in my life, I was *exhausted*. I turned in at seven o'clock and lay on the softest, warmest bed in days. At five minutes past seven, a shouting match started up in the street outside; a couple were having a jealous row over another man. I got as far as wondering *how long will this go on for?* and then I fell asleep for twelve straight hours.

DAY 6

(34 MILES)

*D*artmoor: a wild, windswept landscape, beautiful and rugged with miles of breathtaking vistas. Or at least, that was how I imagined it might look. With only 15 yards of visibility, I had to guess at the rest. But having everything hidden in mist did have one advantage: not being able to see the next steep hill before I'd even made it up this one. Shortly after leaving Princetown, it became apparent that today would not be as bad as yesterday, since the road now headed in a north-easterly direction, and the wind was still coming from the east. Being battered from the side might be off-balancing but it's nowhere near as bad as riding into a full frontal.

An hour went by before I saw another living soul, and the cocooning effect of the mist gave me some unsettling thoughts: that perhaps the rest of the human race had vanished out of existence. The only sound was the relentless wind buffeting at my ears, but every now and again I would glimpse tiny signs of life. Crows and sparrows flapped their wings, fighting their own battles with the elements. I watched intently as they struggled to fly a few yards before the mighty wind deposited them back whence they'd come. I could certainly sympathise as I struggled on with them for another 15 miles.

Just as I suspected, the world became instantly brighter once I'd descended off the highest plateau of Dartmoor and I left the mist behind. The wind dropped, the rain ceased, but sadly the hills continued. I took a rest in the village of Moretonhampstead, a pretty market town with a good array of shops, and I wasted no time buying and devouring six large bananas and a family-sized malt loaf. Rule number ten of cycle touring: never underestimate how many calories you will need. Although malt loaf was a food beloved by my mother, it had never really appealed to me, but now I couldn't get enough of it. It came neatly wrapped and was full of calories and carbohydrates, and it became my ideal pannier filler.

After six days in the West Country, I now considered myself something of an expert at differentiating between tourists and locals. The tourists were easy to spot, especially the ones who eyed my bicycle and my unorthodox luggage distastefully. The locals, however, seemed happiest just ignoring anyone who wasn't from their local community, and I quickly got used to their blank expressions, even when I bought food from their shops or sat mere feet away from them in the park. I guessed they must get pretty sick of us tourists. I'd heard that Devon and Cornwall suffer a double whammy: high unemployment rates whilst being an extremely popular holiday destination. So, whilst many areas are, to some extent, reliant on tourists' money, it also meant constant disruption to daily life. It isn't too hard to imagine that if your only source of employment is seasonal work serving other people on holiday, one might begrudge the fact that these same hoards keeping you in brass are the same ones making day to day life difficult. Imagine a constant traffic jam from June to September. Or knowing there is no chance of quickly popping to the shops because it invariably means tripping over holidaymakers on every corner. And you can forget any chance of a quiet afternoon at the beach in the summer.

After leaving Moretonhampstead, I made a number of frustrating wrong turns and so when I bumped into Dave, a friendly grey-bearded cycle tourist going the opposite way, I was more than happy to ask for his help. Studying both my map and his more detailed Ordnance Survey, he set me straight on my whereabouts and then offered a gem of advice.

'Head for the Exeter Youth Hostel. They'll let you camp in their garden and you can order a cooked breakfast for the morning.' Now that sounded like a good plan. Dave praised me for cycling my route independently and he added several more coins to my collection tin. As he was headed the way I'd just come from and vice versa, it was the perfect opportunity to enquire about any upcoming topographical difficulties, e.g., how many hills? and his answer made me laugh out loud.

'I've definitely come up way more hills than I've come down today, so you should have quite an easy time of it into Exeter.' It was funny because I would have said *exactly* the same about my morning. I'm not sure if we both said this to encourage one another, or it just felt that way. But one of us must have been wrong, or else it meant we were standing on the highest point on Dartmoor.

It was turning out to be a good day for meeting fellow cycle tourists. After only encountering one (John) in five days, I met four more this day. I guessed Exeter must be a bottleneck for cyclists heading west. I rolled into the city centre (definitely more downhill than up for me. Oops, sorry, Dave) and headed straight to the tourist information centre. Here I met Peter, a cycle tourist from South Africa. He'd lived and worked in London for the past few years and was now on his way to Plymouth to catch the boat to Spain to enjoy a two-wheeled adventure in the sun. As we were heading for the same hostel, I followed in his wake through the city but struggled to keep up with his far speedier pace.

The youth hostel was lovely. A modern, purpose-built affair where just as Dave had suggested, I did pitch my tent in their garden and I did order the full English veggie breakfast for the morning. I also met my third and fourth cycle tourists of the day, a father and his ten-year-old daughter who were cycling around England on a custom-made tandem; little and large to the rear and helm respectively. To say I was in awe of this duo would be an understatement, but when I asked the girl how she was finding her trip, she shrugged it off like it was nothing more than a trip to the shops. I found myself willing her never to grow out of cycling. I hoped she would never become a sullen teenager, who found her dad an embarrassment and took to riding around in the back of boys' cars instead.

Meeting these two brought to mind the number of holidaymakers I'd met who'd complained bitterly about traffic congestion.

'We love Cornwall but the traffic has been terrible,' they'd all said. Although a passionate cyclist, I am also a car user, so I feel I have a clear grasp on the futility of grumbling about traffic congestion... as if it is all somebody else's making. I know that when I use my car, I'm a part of the problem. I'm not simply sitting *in* traffic. I *am* the traffic. And if I really want to do something about it, then the only thing for it is to try and use my car less. And I'm not talking about long-distance cycling now. I'm talking about the shorter everyday journeys that are only a mile or two, the ones to the shops or to the train station. Since I'd became a regular cyclist, I've tried to have this conversation with perfectly healthy able-bodied people. They'd nod their heads and *sound* interested, but when I *dared* suggest that maybe they could sometimes walk or use a bicycle, to help combat traffic congestion and air pollution, more often than not my suggestion would be met by a barrage of excuses as to why this would be completely impossible for them. After meeting this amazing ten-year-old girl who thought nothing of cycling right around England, I would have these conversations in the future and raise my eyebrows sceptically.

That evening, I struck lucky with Peter. What I mean is, it turned out he was a chef by trade, and chefs are some of my favourite people. After my shower, I made my way into the kitchen where I found him pulling a tray out of the oven, full of awesome-smelling pasta bake. And before I had time to say, 'That smells good,' he had thrust a plateful my way. Afterwards, I offered to buy him a drink to say thank you and we went next door to the pub. Sadly, it was a bleak, sombre affair that held none of the Devonshire charm I would have liked a first-time visitor to experience.

I was dying to ask Peter about life in South Africa. When I was a teenager and just beginning to take an interest in the world at large, South Africa, with the whiff of apartheid still lingering in the air, was always in the news. A million miles from my English rural life, it seemed in equal measures beautiful and ugly, alluring and terrifying. I had been in Brixton hoping to see Nelson Mandela the day he came to visit in 1996. And afterwards, my friends and I had sat in the pub whilst Bob Marley's *Redemption Song* played over and over on the jukebox, whilst a number of elderly Black Men sat misty-eyed in corners. So, meeting a person from South Africa for the first time intrigued me and I was dying to hear a first-hand account of life in that country. But Peter was having none of it. Maybe he was sick of the same old questions about his infamous home country, or maybe he felt I would pigeonhole him into a stereotype. Neither was my intention, of course, but about the only thing he was willing to say was that, in the last five years living in Britain, he'd witnessed far more racism in London than he ever had back home, and then he clammed up. I can't deny that I struggled to believe what he'd just said, but the walk back to the hostel was a little frosty after this.

I bade Peter good night and was about to retire to my tent when I spotted some figures lurking in the courtyard.

I sidled up to them causally, asking for a cigarette, and I introduced myself. I met Anna, Stephan and Ivan, who were backpackers from Germany, and their buddy Roy from London. As international relations had not gone too smoothly with South Africa, I thought maybe I should try for a more convivial time with Germany. The four of them were very friendly, and clutching three bottles of cheap Russian vodka, they insisted I join them for a tipple. My sensible head thought, *just the one won't hurt.*

Two hours later, I vaguely recall my rusty German improving with each finished glass. But when a member of staff yelled at us to keep the noise down, instead of going to bed we moved into the kitchen annex and carried on drinking. Around one in the morning, a young Frenchman about my age showed up looking rather forlorn. He had arrived at Plymouth dock only two hours before and become separated from his friends. He barely spoke English and the hostel's reception was closed for the night. The five of us drunkenly debated how best to help him. The others thought they should let him into the hostel with their key so he could help himself to a spare bed. Yours truly thought this might not be wise, and high on all the kindness strangers had shown me lately (as well as vodka), I was dying to repay some of this goodwill back into the world: I told the guy he could sleep in my tent for the night. Heaven knows what time later, I walked a little unsteadily back to my tent and found *Monsieur arrivée tardive* had not only helped himself to most of my tent, he had also blocked the entrance with his enormous rucksack. It took me quite a few minutes and several attempts before I could coordinate myself, giggling and swaying over the obstacle and into my sleeping bag. I realise now that when I'd shown this guy to my tent, he probably hadn't realised I intended to sleep there too and now he was wide awake, but desperately pretending not to be. I still chuckle to this day, thinking of that poor man. Hiding in the depths of his sleeping bag, scared of what the mad drunken woman might do next. But he need not have worried, because the only thing I was interested in was sleep, and within seconds, I was unconscious.

DAY 7

(28 MILES)

I awoke to find myself alone. The French guy had quietly slipped away and for this I shall remain eternally grateful. It turned out he was neither thief nor madman, who could have done any manner of unspeakable things whilst I was unconscious. In fact, the only sign he was ever there was a small plastic baggie containing a tiny square of cannabis. Whether he had dropped it in his haste to get away or it was left as a thank you wasn't entirely clear. What with the sharing of vodka and now this? I'm not sure if rule number eleven of cycle touring should be: beware of fellow travellers bearing gifts, or the more accurate rule number twelve: don't invite strangers to sleep in your tent.

I lay still for a while listening to the deluge falling outside. My watch read five minutes to eight and, never one to let a hangover stand in the way of a good breakfast, I went in search of the canteen. As always, I believed fried food could work miracles. But on this occasion my taste buds had given up in disgust of the vodka excess and my breakfast tasted of nothing more than cardboard. I went back to my tent hoping to sleep it off. I squeezed my eyes tightly shut and tried to ignore the rain falling hard on the canvas, but dehydration prevented even this respite. Up again and to the kitchen, I found my fellow partygoers also nursing hangovers, and suitable banter was bandied around. I was touched when they asked if I wanted to join them for the day; they were off across Dartmoor in their hire car. In some ways, I was sorely tempted, what with the awful weather (again), my hangover (again), and the chance to actually enjoy breakfast tomorrow. But when I learnt they intended to drive the exact way I'd already ridden, I changed my mind.

As if on autopilot, I began packing up my belongings and folding up the tent in a torrential downpour that clearly wasn't going to go away. I'm not sure who was more surprised at my eagerness to get going, myself or my friends? They watched incredulously as I packed up and swung my leg keenly over my saddle. But as we said goodbye, I knew something they did not: I was *really* beginning to love this trip. Somewhere across Dartmoor, something within me had changed. I was no longer cycling just to cover the mileage and to get from A to B. I now cycled for the absolute love of it. I had found my passion and every hill I topped was accompanied by a big smile. And always, I couldn't wait to see what was around the next bend.

It was to be a peculiar day with many interesting encounters, and one where all manner of people stopped to question my rationality for making my trip alone. A German motorbike rider clad in all his shiny leathers was the first. As I pedalled away from Exeter Youth Hostel, he pulled over to chat. Don't you get bored, lonely or frightened? he asked, to which I replied no to all of the above. He recounted that whilst travelling in Southeast Asia last year, he'd noticed nearly all the women travelling alone turned out to be British. I found his observations interesting but not surprising. Speaking personally, I became a young woman in the 1990s. And aware that female equality and independence had been hard-fought for by previous generations, I thought using this independence was not just my right; it was my *obligation*.

Trying to negotiate my way out of Exeter with a hangover was a formidable task, since the whole city was one long traffic jam. When vehicles weren't queuing at the traffic lights, it was for a roundabout or a level crossing. I was happily doing that thing cyclists do the world over: filtering through the traffic, overtaking car after stationary car on the inside and, contrary to popular belief, it is perfectly legal under UK law. But when a small blue metro pulled left, deliberately blocking my path and prompting me to brake hard, I took the move as an act of aggression and issued forth a tirade of abuse at the driver. If I'd wanted to be a good ambassador for cyclists, I should have kept my mouth shut. The old woman in the passenger seat wound down her window, gingerly holding out money for my collection tin and only enquiring which charity it was for as an afterthought. Humbled and embarrassed, I thanked her profusely.

Today, I was back with my old friend (though more often my enemy), the good old A30. At least now it was reduced to a less intimidating one lane in either direction and with a speed limit of 60mph. Yesterday, I had felt duty-bound to warn Peter that if he intended to make it from Exeter to Plymouth in one day to catch his ferry, then the one thing he should do was to absolutely *not go via Dartmoor National Park under any circumstances*. But he'd waved away my advice like an annoying fly, saying it would be no problem because the previous day, he'd cycled along the exceptionally hilly A30 into Exeter and was well prepared.

'Watch out,' he had even warned me, 'it's a killer of a road.' I'm not sure *which* A30 he had been referring to exactly. Because *this* A30 was what I'd have called pretty flat in comparison to Dartmoor. If Peter had thought this hilly, he was in for one hell of a shock across Dartmoor, and my heart went out to him. I would still love to know if he made it.

I nicknamed the A30 *the vagabond's road*. Trucks, trailers and caravans loaded up with people's worldly possessions passed by me frequently and many of them, who I presume had read the back of my tabard, beeped their horns in a show of support. At one petrol station, a guy watched me fill up my water bottles, before daring to come over to say hello and make a donation. All of these people did not know it, but they helped me keep my spirits raised on that dreadful day. To begin with, I still felt slightly tipsy, and it put me into a trance-like state that allowed me to ride without feeling anything. But the deluge didn't let up for a second. I had water pouring off every inch of my saturated body and eventually the continuous damp ruined my trance and the tiredness and headache took a hold.

I seemed to be living in a very wet and watery world that first week, something I would later refer to as my *aqua-cycle* experience. The skin on my hands and feet was permanently wrinkled and I mused on how I wouldn't be surprised to wake in the morning and find I had sprouted gills. I thought ahead to the forthcoming rigmarole at the next campsite:

1. Struggle to put up an already saturated tent in the wind and rain.
2. Head for campsite shower block and peel off sodden clothes, stuck to my body like superglue.
3. Stand in shower with temperature up as hot as I could bear for at least half an hour, the requisite time it took to warm my body right through.
4. Return to tent and invent ingenious ways to dry out clothes in the limited space of my home.
5. And finally: wake next morning to find it was still raining and my clothes were still damp.

And don't even get me started on wet tents; they're a headache all of their own. Not only are they heavier to carry, but they are impossible to fold/unfold without getting soaked yourself. I would recommend some research before purchasing a tent, because aside from the more obvious considerations of cost and weight, it turns out there are variations in the way you erect them. With some tents you put the inner skin up first and then the outer shell. Some, like the one I have, the outer shell goes up first and comes down last, which I liked because it meant the inner skin was easier to keep dry. And some, you can just leave them attached together and put them both up at once, thus saving time. It will all come down to personal preference in the end. But ultimately, I chose mine for three reasons: I could afford it, it only weighed 2.5 kilos, and because it was deemed a 1.5/2-person tent. This meant it was big enough for me and my multitude of panniers, or it could accommodate a second person when needed, like my friend Sarah who would be joining me in Scotland. Or, for example, a French drug dealer.

Another ten miles passed where I was aware of nothing but the rain and the occasional whiff of vodka fumes seeping through my pores. Where the road crossed the flooded River Otter, I leant over the bridge to watch the swirling torrents of muddy water passing just below my feet and that's when I decided my original target of Glastonbury could wait. A truckers' roadside café provided some much-needed sustenance and I sat devouring veggie burger and chips, surrounded by an audience of big burly truckers and their exclamations of *Ooh, aren't you brave* ringing in my ears. With my last kilojoule of energy, I made it to a campsite just outside of Honiton.

I hadn't even finished struggling with my voluminous, flapping tent when right on cue, a man appeared from a neighbouring caravan and invited me in for a cup of tea. I had a slice of carrot cake with his wife, Amy (who'd sent her husband to fetch me in out of the rain). They were a friendly couple, about my parents' age, but during our chat Amy kept telling me how brave and courageous I was to ride alone and I started to feel embarrassed. All day I'd heard enough compliments to make anyone's head swell but, in all honesty, I felt a bit of a fraud. Being courageous suggests you had fear in the first place, whereas for me, embarking on a cycling holiday in my native country, which is relatively safe and stable, where I can converse freely in the native language and where I have lived all my life did not produce fear. Caution maybe, but certainly not fear. However, I didn't want to hurt anybody's feelings or appear rude, so when they asked if I was afraid of attack or rape or whatever other gruesome images were shadowing their minds, I simply replied that, as they were kind and meant me no harm, I wasn't expecting the next people I met to be any different. Now don't get me wrong; *obviously,* there are always going to be a number of malevolent humans in the world (and later I would experience some first-hand), but I am still firm in my belief that ninety-nine per cent of people don't mean you any harm. Moreover, quite a number of them would be happy to help you out if you got into a real pickle.

I sometimes wonder if this unhealthy fear of strangers is partly because, instead of going out to experience the world first-hand, people's opinions are too easily influenced by the media? And one look at any newspaper will confirm they generally report the bad stuff: the rapes, murders, swindling, poor state of the hospitals or the pensioner robbed by drug addicts. Whilst I'm not denying this all goes on, I feel the media could do with being a little more *balanced* and report more on the positive stuff as well: the man who donated a kidney to save a stranger's life, the nurse who went the extra mile to make her patient smile, the woman who drove the children to the soccer match because their mothers didn't have cars, or the homeless man in Delhi teaching street kids to read. Really, when you start looking into it, the world is dripping with the milk of human kindness, and yet most news is doom and gloom with a token fluffy story thrown in at the end. If this trend could be reversed, then couldn't the world become a very different place?

You have to wonder (or at least I do) why the media does it. Is it simply because bad news is sensationalistic and it sells? Or is there another reason, with more insidious consequences? Because, actually, people's fear is good for business and good for the politicians. *Don't talk to strangers, stay home where it's safe and watch your television. Buy more stuff to bring you comfort in this terrifying world, and don't question us when we make laws and legislations, because we are doing it for your protection. Remember, the world isn't safe anymore.* And in the meantime, the government and the multinational corporations carry on with their slippery dealings, filling their already swollen bank accounts by whatever means necessary. Rainforests are burnt, indigenous populations are displaced, seas are polluted, thousands are laid off whilst CEOs are paid bonuses, children are targeted by junk food marketing and blind eyes are turned to genocide. And meanwhile when *our* lives are going wrong (rising living costs, job losses, hospital waiting lists), instead of turning on those who are really responsible, we (with plenty of encouragement from the media) turn on each other, squabbling for the crumbs that are left.

Will we ever band together and work out just how far we've been conned? Realise we live in a world where a small handful of people rules it for their own financial benefit and at the expense of everyone and everything else. That we live in a system that encourages us to feed our stomachs junk and ditto our minds. A system that tells us the whole point of our existence is to earn and spend, earn and spend. But suppose we do fulfil all our consumer obligations like the good citizens they want us to be, then what exactly will be left of us? Empty shells? Walking clichés? Flabby, unhealthy beings, imprisoned by our belongings and our debts, with no time left for creativity or love in our lives. I don't know about you, but I think people are capable of and *deserve* so much better than this.

DAY 8

(58 MILES)

I was immersed in a nightmare, of deluge and cloud. Of inescapable chill and wet, tangled hair suffocating against my face. But it wasn't just a dream, this was my reality, and now that I was fully awake, I felt as cold and wet as before I'd gone to sleep. Miraculously though, I had actually slept. And not just my usual, itty bitty intermittent doze, but an all-out nine-hour coma of a sleep. Was my body finally ready to accept a summer of sleeping on hard surfaces? Had I toughened up at last? I stacked this latest victory alongside my hard-fought for fitness and with a wave of confidence I sprang from the tent... only narrowly dodging the small lake that had gathered outside. Ho-hum.

But there was something else I needed to get a handle on before I could declare myself the Zen Master of Cycle

Touring, and that was packing. Each morning, I endured the same frustrating rigmarole where, no matter how hard I tried to stay organised, my pannier bags, saucepans, clothes and tools would get scattered about whilst I muttered and crawled around, swearing because I couldn't find this or couldn't locate that. But I have to say that, once it was all packed up, I would stand back and admire the end results. I loved travelling in such a minimalistic way and knowing that all I ever needed in life could be fitted into four small bags and be carried on the humble bicycle. This morning, though, it took me an incredible two and a half *hours* to get going. (Perhaps staying for two more cups of tea with Amy and her husband didn't help matters.)

Somerset: I had only been here for one day and it was already winning me over. The main features of Cornwall and Devon had been their quaintness. The gorgeous chocolate box houses, pretty villages and surrounding countryside with its patchwork of fields. But due to its hilly terrain, my mind had been a little over occupied by my discomfort; but things were about to change. Somerset's chief features, I noted for my diary later: *lots of flat bits*. Like leaving behind a tumultuous relationship, I felt liberated. Without those muscle-destroying hills, I was now free to soak up the rural idyll before me. My plan for today was to head for the town of Langport and then, for the very first time, I would head directly north towards Glastonbury. According to my map, this would take me through an area known as the Somerset Levels. North *and* level? Excitedly, I felt I would finally be making some real progress in the direction of John O'Groats... Oh, how the Road Gods must have laughed.

Not 500 yards further down the road, I almost ploughed into a police notice which read: *Road Closed Due to Flooding*. Rolling my eyes, I realised that flat regions of the country came with their own unique sets of problems.

Two teenage boys on mountain bikes were coming along this road and judging by the state of their attire, I think they'd been playing *in* the flood. I asked them how bad it was and they muttered something about it not being too bad, though in some places it was bad. So, nothing concrete. They headed off but I remained stubbornly by the police sign. My map said Langport was 4 miles this way, or I had to take a 12-mile detour. I watched for the next ten minutes as each car stopped in front of the sign and then turned around, but I didn't want to. Surely, I couldn't get any wetter than I already was, and I didn't have an engine to ruin. Before I could change my mind, I began stripping off my panniers and balancing them on the handlebars. Cautiously, I waded into the murky water that was once a road, proud that bicycle and rider could go where cars could not. But only a quarter of a mile on, as the brown water began swirling around my thighs, I started regretting the decision, for I could no longer tell if I was still on the road, or if I'd wandered off into the adjoining field. I couldn't see me keeping this up for another 4 miles, so mainly out of respect for my bicycle, I aborted my mission and about-turned. Setting off on the 12-mile detour, my cycling song for the day became the one about Noah's Ark: *The animals went in two by two, hurrah, hurrah.* Fortunately, I was still bursting with energy after all that sleep, and what I expected would be a lengthy detour was over very quickly.

I'd never heard of Langport until today but that was no surprise, since it didn't appear a particularly touristy place. Perhaps that was why it was so friendly. Maybe, once out of tourist-clogged Devon and Cornwall, people actually said good morning to you whether you knew them or not, and, if you caught someone's eye, they smiled and nodded. You could be forgiven for thinking I'm a wee bit oversensitive about this issue, but it was a very real pattern I'd observed across the West Country. Many tourists had gawped at me in a manner usually reserved for bizarre zoo animals. (Come back, anteaters and armadillos; all is forgiven.) But in areas unused to large influxes of visitors, like Langport, I was made to feel welcomed. As if to prove my point, a group of locals out on an afternoon stroll stopped to chat, and each donated to my collection tin before they bid me farewell. It's funny, but if you had asked me what I thought would be the hardest part of cycle touring, I'd probably have said the rain or hills. Never would I have guessed it would be the cold, hard stares from fellow holidaymakers.

The hot topic on everybody's lips right now was, of course, the weather. It had gotten to the stage when you didn't have to utter a single word about it with those you exchanged pleasantries with; you simply cast your eyes up at the sky and that was enough to get people tutting and shaking their heads. It turned out that I'd crossed the West Country during the wettest summer recorded for fifty years. Whilst on the subject of weather, I'd recently heard a radio report claiming that, at any given time, at least one third of the British population is, has, or is about to talk about the weather. Yes, we Brits are *obsessed* by it. In reality, it was just

63

one of those spurious reports where you think, *how the hell can they possibly know that?* but still, I thought it was pretty funny, mainly because I fit this stereotype. But what, I ask, could be more important than the observance of nature and the one element in life that links us all? Of course, these days, there is a much-diminished link with our environment because we have air-conditioning and central heating. But for those people who still work the land or make their homes from natural materials, or for people whose lives have been profoundly affected by a natural disaster, it is not so easy to forget we are just as susceptible to nature's intense power.

Twice now, I've been scared out of my wits by Mother Nature. The first time was on an organised jungle hike in Northern Thailand. Crossing a waist-high river, everyone else in my group made it to the other side without problem, whereas I, totally unprepared for the current's strength, was swept off my feet. I remember how terrifying it felt to be carried off against my will by a force so incredibly strong, I was utterly powerless to beat it. Luckily for me, some Thai villagers fished me out further downstream. But it was a lesson I would never forget.

My second experience came some years later, cycling across the Isle of Skye in Scotland. The weather forecast had been pretty decent for mid-March: cold but clear, but how wrong it was. I was riding a single-track road through the mountains when the weather turned bad, but I carried on, believing that my destination was nearer than my starting point. Within an hour, the wind had become so incredibly strong that at one stage, it blew me into a roadside ditch and then, it picked up my bicycle, panniers and all, and hurled it straight over the top of me too. Miles from anywhere, face red raw from hailstones slamming into me, I was powerless. I was in a nightmare, trapped in by these mountains which went on forever, and I felt I would be stuck on that lonely mountain road until hypothermia and then death took me. The sheep carcasses lining the road and recently dead from exposure mocked me as I went. I was but a tiny speck of insignificance lost to the almighty Mother Nature. Luckily, just as I was on the brink of giving up, a woman whom I'd met the previous night passed me in her campervan and stopped. Both rider and bicycle were rescued in the nick of time. But later, when I was safely tucked up in bed, as I closed my eyes the whole experience came flooding back. The vastness of that wilderness and the fear of being so powerless against it. I remembered the tears of frustration at the wind and it finally hit home, just how close I had come to perishing.

Back in Somerset, the weather was a complete contrast to my memories. The sun came out and I felt surprisingly at home as I crossed King's Sedgemoor. To one side lay farmer's fields and on the other, the hills were reminiscent of the South Downs in Sussex where I grew up. An abundance of birdlife appeared in the skies above. I spotted sparrowhawks and jays and listened whilst skylarks sang their songs in the skies above, intent on drawing my attention away from their nests, which they make on the ground. Hoverflies chased my fluorescent yellow cycling tabard down the road in the sunshine. Unfortunately, the common fly was also in abundance and I suspect this is due to an abundance of dairy farms in this area and the millions of cowpats available for flies to lay eggs in.

Yesterday, my left knee started to ache but had healed overnight after a liberal application of Deep Heat gel. Now, though, as I approached my sixtieth (... *sixtieth*...) mile, the combination of sore knees and accumulated insect bites that itched with maddening vigour meant I had reached that time of day where, no matter how well it was going, I flipped from thinking: *I love this,* to: *I can't wait for this to be over.* With much elation, I finally homed in on the campsite just outside of Glastonbury town. I wanted to crawl into my tent and escape all the ailments that were making my life uncomfortable right now: damp, hunger and flies. I went to pay my levy at the reception desk, only to be told that most of the camping field was under 2 feet of water. I knew I shouldn't have packed that snorkel away just yet.

DAY 9

(14 MILES)

*W*hen I switched on the radio and discovered it was ten o'clock, I couldn't believe my ears: I had been asleep for almost fourteen hours. Sleeping this well, and without the aid of medication or alcohol, is not something I'd experienced before, but considering our culture is built around the sedentary lifestyle, I don't suppose many of us have. With doctors and health departments begging us to eat healthily and take more exercise, I wonder why we find it so hard to comply with this advice, especially as we all know the consequences if we don't. I'm going to stick my neck out now and say that I think, by our very nature, we humans have a tendency to take the easiest way when it's offered, and having identified this human weakness, the manufacturing companies have exploited it fully. Just think what big business human indolence has become, with the manufacture of ever new labour-saving devices for an insatiable market.

Make your life easier, the companies whisper in their advertising campaigns. *You work hard so you deserve it.* Trouble is, I believe that by adopting such sedentary lifestyles, people are doing themselves a great disservice. You see, there is something that the corporations who sell you these gadgets won't tell you... something the doctor who advised you to lose weight probably didn't mention either: that ditching the car and getting around under your own steam makes you feel *fantastic*. Picture yourself if you will, cycling (or walking) to work. Zipping past the queues of traffic, arriving all pink-faced and healthy with those exercise endorphins pumping through your body. Imagine how proud you'd feel, knowing you are quite capable of cycling 5, 10, even 20 miles without breaking a sweat, or that your journey to work didn't cost you a penny. Imagine knowing you are not only transforming your health but helping to curb air pollution. I personally *love* this. It's a real feel-good factor and one I believe could be the secret to an altogether happier life. All those lethargic insomniacs take heed: the more energy you use, the more you will have overall, the better you will feel, and the better you will sleep.

*

By half past ten, the day was a scorcher; it seems the West Country knows how to have a summer after all! The only fly in the ointment (if you'll pardon the pun) was the flies.

It seemed their mission in life was to buzz around my face and get on my nerves as I tried to eat breakfast. But even they couldn't spoil that sweet feeling of a hot summer's day, and I set out for Glastonbury Tor. The local council had thoughtfully provided bicycle racks for visiting cyclists, but for reasons known only to themselves, they had positioned these racks on the other side of a high gate which was chained firmly shut. Marvellous. And so began the farce, as I tried to hoist my bicycle up and over that gate, and pretty soon, I was red- faced, covered in chain oil and swearing profusely. Just when I was on the verge of giving up, a local bus stopped. The driver got out and leaving his bemused passengers for a moment, he came to my assistance. He lifted my bicycle and all its panniers right up and over that gate as though it weighed no more than a kitten. I could have kissed him.

As there are already more books devoted to Glastonbury Tor than you can shake a stick at, I will just run through a few highlights to whet your appetite. Glastonbury Tor is the name of the hill itself. (*Tor* is an old English word meaning high hill or rock.) It's rather a bizarre-looking 518ft hump in the middle of the Somerset Plains made of layers of clay, blue limestone and capped by hardy sandstone. It is the sandstone that ensured this tiny piece of Somerset lingered whilst the rest eroded down to the flat plane it is today. We humans have always revered high-up places (is it to be closer to the sun, to God, or the universe in general?) and so the Tor, not surprisingly, has hosted human settlements since Neolithic times. There is also evidence of Christian worship in the form of St Michael's Church. It was built from wood in the 11th century but destroyed by a fire in 1275 and then rebuilt from stone a few hundred years later. It is this tower that remains today. The place is literally awash with legends. Just take your pick: a gateway to the underworld, association with King Arthur, medieval terraces forming a giant 3D maze, or even that the Tor is hollow. And it has seen some pretty dark times too. It was used as a place for hanging, drawing and quartering, with one of its most notable victims being Richard Whiting, the last abbot of Glastonbury, whose abbey was dissolved during the reign of King Henry VIII.

I followed the footpath to the top of the Tor and was greeted by an impressive if slightly hazy view of the surrounding countryside. Just to warn you, if you prefer solitude then unless you visit on a wet weekday in February, you are likely to be disappointed. It's a very popular place. However, I think the real attraction is what it means to people personally, for it has long been a place of spirituality and mysticism. On the day I visited there were some pretty interesting characters: hippies in varying states of nirvana smoking and chanting, people in contorted yoga poses, not to mention a fair few King Arthur wannabes. (At least for once I wasn't the one being stared at.) A little later, I watched a group of friends form a circle at the base of the tower. Holding hands, with their eyes closed, they said they could feel themselves flying upwards towards the top of the tower. Maybe I am just a little too conventional in my thinking because whilst there was no denying the beauty of Glastonbury Tor, I wasn't really sharing their spiritual vibe in quite the same way. I briefly wondered if the Tor really was hollow, and if so, might the top open up and swallow everyone into the dark clutches of the underworld below us?

But it didn't look like it, so I dedicated the rest of my visit to examining flora and fauna, photographing wild flowers and locating the source of a thousand wasps which smattered the hillside in yellow.

I headed into Glastonbury town for lunch. I don't quite know what I was expecting, maybe an ordinary Somerset town which, once a year, gets swamped by hippies and other alternative types during festival time. But as I sat eating four organic bananas and a strawberry soya milkshake, everywhere I looked, I saw dreadlocked heads and sandalled feet toing and froing. It seemed the town has an active, all-year-round alternative vibe, with health food shops outnumbered only by shops selling crystals and rune stones. As I sat on a bench people-watching, I found my attention focusing inwards. I remembered the sixteen-year-old me who couldn't really envisage a future spent chasing high-salaried jobs, big houses or expensive clothes, and I was sure I'd prefer life in a back-to-the-land commune than life with a mortgage. My greatest ambition had been to travel the world, and whatever job I had to do in between to earn the money, I didn't really care. That I'd ended up with a regular job in the city and a rental agreement instead wasn't a bad thing, but being here now, watching the Glastonbury residents contentedly living out their wildest hippie dreams beneath the shadow of the Tor, sparked a hankering for a different path. One more in tune with who I really was. But hey, wasn't that *exactly* what I was doing? For a second, my mind had become so embroiled with the past that I'd forgotten I was in fact free. And searching the British Isles for a place to settle down. I said a little thank you to the universe for my good fortune.

Despite fourteen hours of sleep, I was still pretty worn out after my marathon ride yesterday (two and a quarter marathons to be precise), and I wondered what I should do next. It was very hot and the wind was humid and strong (was there any such thing as perfect cycling weather?) and suddenly I didn't feel much like another long day in the saddle. Studying my map, I saw there were quite a few tourist attractions within the vicinity. There was Wells Cathedral and Wookey Hole Caves just 6 miles away. And then Cheddar village was a further 10 miles after that. Sixteen miles seemed like a good distance in this heat and so I opted for a day spent sightseeing and taking it easy. But things took an unexpected turn when I bumped into Les in Wells. Les was forty years old, part Brit, part New Zealander. He was a mountain bike enthusiast and he too was cycling Land's End to John O'Groats. Only to put a more interesting spin on things, he was pedalling via the forty-two cathedral cities. And as if that wasn't enough, he was also diverting to the three peaks of Snowdon, Scafell Pike and Ben Nevis to put down his bike for the day and scale each one. Phew. But, most interesting of all, he was also raising money for a landmine's clearance charity. Within minutes of this extraordinary meeting, we both agreed to call a day on our cycling schedules and hang out together. Locking our precious bicycles in the market square, we took a tour of Wells Cathedral, followed by one around the city's pubs, and then finished the evening in a very good curry house.

It was an interesting afternoon, exchanging information and swapping stories. But despite a shared love of cycling and a desire to rid the world of landmines, there the similarities ended. Les' long spell in the military had made him so well organised, it put me to shame. He took me on a tour of the expensive equipment he'd purchased for this trip: the clothing that simultaneously warmed you up *and* cooled you down, a tent which was so light it could be carried on the back of a pigeon and erected by pressing a button, the water canteen that kept your water chilled and the miniature robotic cycle mechanic you could carry in your panniers. (Okay, I'm exaggerating… you had to press two buttons to put the tent up.) Whilst this demonstration was going on, I used my foot to quietly slide my bags beneath the pub table out of sight; my panniers I'd converted from old army bags, my draughty sleeping bag, the excruciatingly uncomfortable sleeping mat and the non-waterproof cagoule all felt amateurish by comparison. I enjoyed Les' company, for he was an intelligent and friendly guy. His energy and enthusiasm for life were second to none and were matched only by his confidence. His life story, which he managed to chuck in over a few beers, read like the CV of an Eton graduate: brigadier in the army, CEO of a city finance company, then moving to New Zealand to become a successful independent financial advisor before returning to England to become an MP. After his ride was finished, he was certain he would be meeting Princess Diana, the patron of his charity.

Despite liking him, I would not have chosen Les as a travelling companion. That drive and energy I mentioned could feel a little overbearing at times, and it seemed I wasn't the only one to share this sentiment. As Thursday night got into full swing in the city of Wells, alcohol-fuelled locals were none too impressed by this stranger in their town, with his overly loud BBC English accent and confident male manner. On three separate occasions, complete strangers picked an argument with him, and when a fourth looked set to erupt, I decided I would get on my way… although not before Les had tried to invite me back to his bed and breakfast for the night. I politely declined.

DAY 10

(44 MILES)

Nine o'clock in the morning, and another scorching hot day awaited me, but in the caves of Wookey Hole it was dark, damp and wonderfully cool. I was hesitant to go in at first because of the ten pounds fee (an entire day's budget for me). But I took the plunge and in spite of our tour guide's lame jokes, it was worth every penny. The limestone underground caverns were formed over many millennia, carved out by naturally acidic groundwater slowly dissolving the rock away. The full extent of them is yet to be uncovered, but so far, twenty-five chambers expanding over 13,000ft have been explored. But who knows how much further and deeper they go? The discovery of Palaeolithic tools suggests people were residing in these caves some 45,000 years ago. The caves are also the source of the River

Axe, thus allowing people to use the place for industrial purposes. Examples include a corn grinding mill in the 9th century and a paper mill in the 15th century. These days, aside from tourism, the caves are now used to store and age local cheeses made in nearby Cheddar. Their constant temperature of eleven degrees Celsius provides the perfect conditions for doing this.

One of the most impressive sights are the stalagmites and stalactites. I must confess that before I visited, I had imagined them to be thin icicle-type formations but they were nothing of the sort. They are great irregular-shaped pillars made up of minerals and calcium carbonate deposits that slowly drip through the cave roofs. With their rate of formation at 1 millimetre per year, the oldest are around 120,000 years old. The stalactites grow from the ceiling downwards, as further mineral drops run down them and crystallise at their end. The stalagmites are formed by drops that drip onto the floor below and then crystallise, growing upwards in an ever-increasing pile. (The way I remember it is that stalactites hold *tight* to the roof and stalagmites *might* one day reach the roof.)

Despite the fact the caves have housed residents since the Stone Age, guess who was the main focal point of the tour? …The Witch of Wookey Hole. The legend tells of an old woman who lived alone in the caves with her dog and her goats. She was, unsurprisingly, blamed by superstitious locals for everything that went wrong in their lives, and they long suspected her of boiling cauldrons, casting spells, that sort of thing. The locals turned to the Abbot of Glastonbury for help, who in turn sent a monk, Father Bernard, to exorcise the witch's spirit. (Talk about delegation.) The young monk ventured forth into the caves and there ensued a long chase, followed by "the witch" being turned to stone. I found this story boringly predictable (where there's a cave, there's usually a witch legend), and it was no doubt dreamt up after the archaeological recovery of an almost complete human skeleton in 1912. Found with a dagger and goat bones, the skeleton is thought to be around 1,000 years old. The fact the deceased turned out to be male should have brought a sledgehammer down on the whole witch thing, but I guess the story bulks out the tourist literature. Personally, I'm not fond of "witch" legends, since this title was a fabricated label made up by powerful men in the 15th and 16th centuries, and used as an excuse to legally murder some 60,000 innocent, unmarried and intelligent women across Europe in the most horrendous way.

Included in the entrance fee was a tour of Wookey's Victorian papermaking mill, one of the few places left in this country that still makes paper by hand. These days, the paper is made for demonstration purposes only, but during the 18th century, as much as 35,000 sheets were turned out every week. They were used for banknotes and top quality paper for legal documents, and all were made from cotton rags. These days, the cotton is imported from the United States, but apart from that, the process remains unchanged. Cotton is mixed with caustic soda, lime and water and made into a pulp which is then shaped and flattened out in a mould and left to dry. I was delighted when the opportunity arose to make my very own piece of paper, and I lined up enthusiastically with the rest of the under eights, preparing to get my hands gooey. Proudly, I smoothed out my finished work of art, which was placed between two pieces of hessian cloth to dry. Unfortunately, I was unable to take my masterpiece home, as the paper takes up to five days to dry. But I would like to think that somewhere in the world, maybe in the European Court of Human Rights, some important international agreement has been carefully signed on my very own handcrafted piece of paper.

By the time the tour was over, it was one o'clock and the sun was at its harshest, but after a week of persistent rain I wasn't going to complain. As I pedalled along the A371 towards Cheddar village in temperatures reaching twenty-six degrees Celsius, I marvelled at the lack of traffic on the roads again; back home in Sussex, most B roads were busier than this. And save for the odd passing car, the ride was peaceful and I could hear birds singing their hearts out. It was going to be a good day. As Cheddar was already swarming with tourists, I decided not to stop, and on the hottest day of the year thus far, I set off for the long and arduous climb out of there. Cliff Road, as it is rather unimaginatively called, winds its way up through Cheddar Gorge and into the hills beyond. Cheddar Gorge is a natural phenomenon, carved out by the melting of glacial ice over the last 1.2 million years, with a depth of 449 feet. The whole area is a site of special scientific interest. The calcareous grasslands are home to peregrine falcons and horseshoe bats, whilst grazing Soay sheep are used to keep the scrubland in check.

As I set off up Cliff Road, I found it disconcerting that people driving the other way were not only staring, as was the norm by now, but were actually shaking their heads at me. Twenty years on, I wonder if this was due to the hot weather that day, or because my bicycle was overloaded with pannier bags? Maybe cycling wasn't as popular back then? (I'll wager that same road today is chock-a-block with riders on racing bikes, competing with each other up that climb every weekend.) Anyhow, I flashed those doubting Thomases a confident smile. The thing is, by now, I had stopped dreading the hills. So, it induced a bit of panting and puffing and an awful lot of sweat, but so what? The main thing was that it didn't hurt anymore. To anyone still in the early stages of fitness, let me give you some advice. Rule number thirteen of cycle touring: if cycling uphill gets too arduous, then you can always *stop for a rest*. I know. Radical, isn't it? I don't mean to sound flippant, but you'd be amazed how many cyclists live by the attitude that to stop halfway up a hill to rest for a while somehow equals failure. And sadly, this attitude then gets conveyed to new cyclists, who get very dispirited if they can't manage a hill in one go… and I think that's a crime. But please listen to me… it *really* doesn't matter one jot how many times you have to stop. What matters is that you've tried. And each time you try, it will get easier and easier until one day, you'll surprise yourself and simply fly up those hills, just as I did.

In the end, the climb wasn't so bad. The first half a mile out of Cheddar was the hardest, with the road rising at a rate of 1 in 6. But after this it became a much shallower gradient. As I toiled upwards for another four and a half miles, I tried to look out for the rare bats, birds of prey or Soay sheep that may wander across my path, but the sweat dripping in my eyes meant I was virtually blind for the duration of the ascent. And about an hour later, I reached the summit. I took shade behind a thorn bush, removing most of my sweat-saturated clothing so I could enjoy the cool breeze on my bare chest and back.

Cycling across the Mendips felt like cycling on the top of the world. The road, which was now practically flat, made the cycling effortless; the temperature was cooler than in the heat-hazy valleys below and the 360-degree views were breathtaking. I passed a number of travellers setting up camp in lay-bys with their beautifully painted caravans and signs advertising "Real Romany Fortunes Told Here". By late afternoon, I was seriously considering giving one a go when I realised that, yet again, I had managed to get lost. Well, I say I was lost. What I actually mean is that, when I looked at my map, I wasn't where I should have been, which I suppose is the same thing. Fortunately, a more conventional form of help rolled up: another cycle tourist called Martin. I explained my predicament and together we studied both my map and his, and he identified *why* I kept going wrong. Because I was using black and white photocopies of a map, without the aid of colour, I often thought my intended route was just a bend in the road, when really, I was supposed to be turning onto a different road. (Which would have been easily identifiable if I'd had a coloured map.) I wanted to hug Martin, as I'd never have figured it out myself. Gratefully, I let him pinpoint which way I needed to go now in order to get back on track, and then as a double dose of serendipity, he topped up my diminishing water supply with his own. Rule number fourteen of cycle touring: cycle tourists will always look out for each other.

After I'd bid Martin farewell, the road began its descent off the Mendips. It was the thrill I'd been waiting for. With the wind through my hair and the sun on my back, I swooped down that scenic road without a care in the world and feeling like the luckiest woman alive. Alas, it was all over far too soon, only taking around fifteen minutes in total. Somewhere nearing the end of my slalom run, my attention was drawn away from an impatient Volvo which almost ran me off the road and towards a man who had stepped out of his car and was waving frantically for me to stop.

'Hello' I called out curiously. The man said he'd seen my charity tabard as he'd passed and desperately wanted to make a donation. He told me his son had been in Cambodia for two years and they knew all about the horrors of landmines. I was so touched by his donation and by his praise that I kicked myself afterwards for not asking more about his son's story.

For some reason, I'd expected that once over the Mendips, my final 10 miles into Bath would be easy. Where in the hell had I gotten that idea from? The road went repeatedly up, down, up and down, up and down with a regularity that made me want to weep. Worst of all, it was composed of short, sharp ups and downs. Or in other words, it meant the descents weren't sufficiently long enough for me to get my breath back before starting on the next steep accent. Pretty soon, the sweat was pouring off me again as I struggled to push my post-Mendip legs around. I tried taking comfort from a sign that said Bath was only 8 miles away, but rule number fifteen of cycle touring: eight miles at the end of a long hard day may as well be eighty.

It was no good. I needed to rest *right now*. Halfway down the next descent I came to the perfect place: a lay-by with grassy picnic area and benches shaded by trees. Then I noticed the young man parked there, leaning against his car bonnet, staring out across the fields. It was an innocuous enough scene, but some barely audible niggling sensation told me not to stop. *Hello, what was that?* But it was quickly forgotten again as I struggled on up the next three ascents, before finally, I found a grass verge suitable to collapse onto. I laid motionless for many minutes before dragging myself into the sitting position. I dusted myself off and drank the warm dregs from my plastic water bottle. Then I heard a car pull up and the driver get out. I stood up, half expecting it would be someone requesting directions, which happened often. Then I recognised the driver as the man from the lay-by. He came straight over and asked, 'Excuse me, do you fancy a shag?' I stood there, dumbfounded. I was a sweating, smelly cyclist in a daft sunhat, trying to study a map... did I *look* as though I did?

Momentarily in shock, the only word I could gurgle was 'Pardon?'

The guy repeated his lurid offer, but in those three extra seconds I collected myself enough to reply, 'No, but if you come one step closer, I will knee you in the bollocks. Just fuck off.' I surprised myself by how fierce I sounded, and luckily, this guy *did* fuck off. Back into his car and drove away. I watched him go, trembling slightly. As I packed up my map and my snacks, I remembered the feeling I'd had, telling me not to stop, and I recognised that something important had occurred back there. Was it a sixth sense or intuition? Whatever you want to call it, I made a mental note to listen to it again in the future.

Whilst the whole episode had an air of ridiculousness about it... actually, I'll rephrase that... *he* had an air of ridiculousness about him... I did wonder; if the guy was weird enough to introduce himself to a complete stranger in this manner, then exactly how deep did this weirdness reach? Was he a one-time chancer or was he someone graduating up through the ranks; going from propositioning lone women, through to sexual harassment and far worse? I definitely did *not* want to find out. I picked up my bicycle, and as hot and exhausted as I was, believe me, I did not stop once until I got to Bath.

DAY 11

(FIRST DAY OF REST)

*T*he morning began sooner than expected, thanks to a fellow camper who, in his infinite wisdom, thought, *hey, you know what? It's only six o'clock on this peaceful Saturday morning. Wouldn't it be an awesome idea to start up my 1200cc motorbike?* (The one that just happened to be missing the exhaust silencer.)

I can rev it continuously for a full five minutes before I go so everyone else here can appreciate what a magnificent machine I have.

This particular campsite had an area set aside for campers without cars, but sadly, the management hadn't thought to ban *all* combustion engines. I clearly wasn't the only person who harboured these thoughts because all around me, tents began unzipping furiously and the air turned blue. Everyone was cursing motorbike man for the rude awakening, and many references were made to the guy's masturbation techniques and (assumed) small genitalia.

But I felt far too euphoric to stay annoyed. I'd had another fabulous sleep, again brought on by physical exhaustion. Interestingly enough, when I'd arrived yesterday, a fellow guest (a man in his late fifties) had commented on my weariness and enquired about my ride. When I'd told him I'd just cycled 40 miles across the Mendips in the heat, his reply went along the lines of, 'Is that all? I walked further than that today.' I can't deny it, the remark both impressed *and* annoyed me. The insinuation that someone else's efforts are less worthy than yours is rather unkind, because isn't achievement relative to each individual? Still, I forced a smile and congratulated him. Maybe he hadn't meant to belittle me. Maybe, when you've done something amazing (and walking 45 miles in one day *is* pretty amazing), then it's only natural to crave some praise and recognition for your efforts.

The campsite was located 2 miles outside of Bath and soon after my arrival I'd dubbed it "the gift that keeps on giving". With spacious pitches, cheap rates, fabulous showers and an onsite pub, it was catnip to a tired cyclist. I sat outside in the fading heat and ordered the veggie burger with a large salad and extra chips, washed down with a pint of lager so cold that it numbed the back of my eyeballs. But before I could even empty my glass, I was practically asleep in it. I weaved my way back to my tent, drunk on tiredness rather than alcohol, and fell into a contented coma, listening to tawny owls calling one other across a gurgling stream.

So, today was my first planned break and at exactly the time they had said, my parents arrived with my elder sister in tow. I had expected that, by now, my sister would be in Copenhagen on her latest English teaching assignment, but as her start date had been delayed for a week, she had come along to check out how I was going. It was the icing on the cake. After a quick discussion, we decided against going into Bath because really and truly, all any of us wanted to do in this heat was to eat ice cream on the beach.

Weston-Super-Mare, or Weston-Super-Mud as it is affectionately known by locals, is located on the Bristol Channel and as such, it is shaped by the wide tidal ranges of the estuary. The resulting beach at low tide is *enormous*. My mother, sister and I quite fancied a dip, but ten minutes later we found ourselves still walking. It transpires that the low-tide mark is an entire mile from the shore. However, it would be most unwise for anyone to try and reach it; go that far out and you'll likely find yourself stuck in the mudflats of the Channel. In the end, we made do with a splash-about in the shallows before making our way back to shore, where my father was eyeing the ice cream van covetously. I was surprised to learn the beach itself is used as an overflow car park and stern warnings are posted everywhere, reminding people what will happen if they don't return to their cars by a certain time. No wheel clamps needed here.

It was a day for idling and I revelled in the novelty of not having to move. I lay on my back and stared up at the cloudless blue sky, absorbing sun rays like a lizard. As requested, my parents had brought me some things from home which I thought could be useful: another one of my favourite reading books, a stack of mail and an eagerly awaited jacket. After despairing over my cagoule, I'd remembered that I did in fact own another coat… Cue the "British Rail" coat. Earlier that year, when I'd quit my job with British Railways, it had coincided with rail privatisation and, long story short, I got to keep the now defunct uniform. Most of it went in the bin, of course, but I'd kept a good pair of boots and waterproof jacket, both of which were still like new, and I thought this coat would be worth trying out. Let's face it, it couldn't be any worse than that bloody cagoule. It was strange to see the jacket again here; a little reminder of the life from which I'd fled.

We lunched in a seafront pub, where I piled my plate with nut loaf and roast potatoes, then watched my family raise their eyebrows when I declared, not an hour later, that I was peckish again. (I refer you back to rule number ten.) And then we returned to the campsite. Over a final cup of tea, my sister discovered my still rather empty charity tin. I think it contained about twenty pounds (although I should mention that I had almost seven hundred pounds in sponsorship promised from friends and family back home). My sister suggested I might actively seek out more donations, maybe by standing around in high streets, jingling my tin under people's noses. I didn't tell her the very thought gave me sweaty palms, but I said I would give it a try. All too soon, it was time to say goodbye. They left for their long drive back to Sussex and I was left to my owls and my gurgling stream, silently counting my blessings for a loving and supportive family.

PART 2

THE MIDDLE BIT

Flooded roads in Somerset

DAY 12

(45 MILES)

*T*he campsite that kept on giving proffered me one last gift: its café opened early enough for breakfast. As I made my way through a plate of scrambled eggs, beans, mushrooms and toast, I worked out that by not having to cook or wash up, it would save me nearly an hour, and in that time, I intended to get at least 10 miles under my belt whilst the temperature was still in the low twenties.

Having hovered around the periphery of Bath for two days, I finally got to see the city itself. The stunning architecture is made from Bath Stone: a warm honey-coloured material that gives the city its unique look and is just one of the many reasons why it was declared a World Heritage Site in 1987. I was surprised to find the streets so quiet. Occasionally, I'd pass people busy with those quintessential Sunday activities:

young men washing cars, old ladies pruning flowers in their beautifully kept front gardens, and parents strolling to the park with their children, loaded down with pushchairs, footballs and tricycles. And without exception, those lovely, friendly Somerset folks all bid me a cheery good morning.

Whilst I have never cared much for people harping on about "the good old days", you'll have to forgive me now, because this is precisely what I am about to do. Because the tranquillity of Bath that morning had me reminiscing about how Sundays used to be. (Or, at least how I perceived Sundays were back when I was a kid.) In the 1980s, Sundays still felt different to the rest of the week, and whilst many of my school friends bemoaned how boring they were, I loved them. In many ways, my childhood sounds idyllic now; playing out in the fields all morning and then returning home at two o'clock for a sit-down Sunday lunch. But whatever memories people have of that time, I would say that, up until the Sunday Trading Act of 1994, people's activities were (at least partially) influenced by the fact that shops shut all day and pubs were only open for limited hours. People simply had to find other things to do. And because shops weren't open, a pleasant by-product of this was less traffic on the roads, and life, just for one day a week, was more peaceful and less hectic. I'm not saying the '80s were better times, but I do think it's a shame there isn't at least one day out of seven where people can focus on something *other* than shopping.

Over long periods of time, it can be difficult to notice social change within one's country, but it was highlighted by my month in Germany. Germany still had restrictive Sunday trading laws. (Even as I write this twenty-five years later, these laws have not eroded over time.) And when I was there, I became intrigued by the way young adults conducted themselves of a weekend. With no shops or bars open on Sundays, other means of entertainment were found. My friends visited one another's houses to chat and drink coffee. Sometimes they would head to the park for a game of football or frisbee or, as this particular crowd liked to do, they would sit and play their musical instruments. They explained that they saw Sundays as a time for relaxation; in preparation for the working week ahead. And it didn't even enter their minds that they were being deprived because they couldn't shop. At the time, it struck me as being rather old-fashioned, and I could have easily believed we were in a rural backwater of Catholic Ireland rather than a highly modern borough of Dusseldorf in Germany. But thinking about it now, it did make a refreshing change from our 24/7 consumer culture.

*

Once again, my photocopied maps led me a merry dance around Bath before I finally found my intended route out of the city. I headed up Bannerdown Road, which was a quiet but extremely steep lane. The only way I could manage such a gradient was to cycle for a few minutes, then stop to regain my breath, drink water and carry on for a few more minutes, then stop, rest and repeat, over and over. And in this way, I made it to the top in easier-to-manage baby steps. Every time I stopped, I remembered to look over my shoulder at the view, which grew increasingly spectacular the higher I climbed, and it helped spur me on.

The Cotswolds were similar to the Mendips in that once I'd made it to the top, the road flattened out. For once, I was confident I wouldn't get lost, because today I was following an old Roman road: the Fosse Way, and like a lot of Roman roads, this one was built in a straight line. The Fosse Way runs for 230 miles, linking Exeter to Lincoln, and marks the western frontier of Roman rule in Britain. *Fossa* is actually the Latin word for a ditch, not a road, and the theory goes that the Fosse Way was originally a defence ditch that they later decided would be better used as a road. Can you imagine being on *that* works crew?

'Er, sorry, guys, there's been a change of plan. We've got to go back and fill it all in again.' The name Fosse Way is unique because it's the only Roman road in Britain to retain its original Latin name; the rest were renamed once the Saxons arrived.

The Fosse Way made for a pleasant ride. Once the sprawl of Bath had petered out, the road ran through open farmland but was tree-lined and shady and there were barely any cars. The only people I saw all morning were two armed policemen guarding an MOD airfield, who met my cheery good morning with a stony silence. I also passed from Somerset into Wiltshire, my fourth county. Despite some problems with flooded roads and dubious men, overall, I had really enjoyed Somerset. With its more cycle-friendly topography, it's even friendlier people and charming villages, it was definitely a place I would consider returning to one day, possibly even to live.

I passed through the beautiful market town of Malmesbury where only a part of the old abbey remains. It was from this abbey tower, around 1010 AD, that the flying monk *Eilmer of Malmesbury* became famous, by leaping off the top of the tower in a primitive hand glider, in his attempt to become the first man to fly. Surprisingly, he made it an entire 200 metres before a crash landing broke both of his legs, after which the Abbot refused point-blank to let him try again. Poor Eilmer. I expect he became something of a local character after this, as he spent the rest of his life limping around town, where a few unkind souls no doubt would have sniggered behind his back. I stopped to rest beside a riverside pub where drinkers spilled out of the beer garden and down to the river's edge. A couple of young men asked me to join them for a drink but I declined. Although it *looked* as though all eccentricities in the population had been bred out thirty generations since Eilmer, you can never be too sure.

Further on down the A429, I passed from Wiltshire into Gloucestershire. Three counties in one day; not bad, huh? But by mid-afternoon, I was beginning to melt in the heat and so apparently was the road. Rather alarmingly, I could hear tarmac squelching beneath my wheels and I hoped it wouldn't stick to the tyres. By three o'clock, I was forced to rest in a field. I flopped under the shade of an enormous oak tree and dozed off immediately, and I had one hell of a time trying to coax myself up again.

The next place circled on my map was located just off the A429 near Kemble. I kept a sharp lookout for the sign and spotted it buried in a hedge:

Source of the River Thames – 1 mile. As I was locking up my bike, a man and a woman coming from that direction saw me and came over.

'It's dry,' said the woman.

'What?' I asked.

'It's dry… the River Thames. There's nothing there.'

'Oh, I see. Well, erm, thank you.' More curious than ever now, I set off quickly along the path. Certainly, on the day I had left London, the River Thames had been as swollen and full as ever, gushing its way through our capital city. But the woman was right, because that's just how I found it; the source of the River Thames was as dry as a bone in a desert.

The river originates from a natural underground spring called, rather logically, the Thames Head. After heavy rainfall, the spring bubbles up and water begins to flow on its 215-mile journey to the North Sea, but during dry spells like now, the water is too deep underground to reach the surface. I could see clearly the empty riverbed: a channel cutting across the field where the water should flow, and I walked along it. (Well, it's not everyone who can say they've walked along the bottom of the Thames.) During these drier spells, the shortage of water is boosted by Lyd Well, an old Roman well about a mile east from Kemble, and from there on, it swells with the addition of many tributaries along its route until it becomes that mighty torrent that we see flowing through London each day.

It was past five when I finally reached Cirencester, and the first thing that I had to do was find a cash machine. As I searched for my purse, I heard a group of rowdy teenagers hollering and pointing and coming my way. *Uh-oh*, I thought, and braced myself for trouble but surprisingly, they were genuinely interested in what I was doing and they bombarded me with questions.

'How far is it?' they asked, wide-eyed.

'You're cycling a thousand miles?'

'With only one water bottle?'

'Why not drive a car?'

'Why have you come through Cirencester?'

'Are you a traveller?'

'You shouldn't wear those big boots for cycling.'

I stemmed a giggle and decided to stay a while, happy to have some genial company after a long day. But I remembered I still needed a place to sleep and asked if they knew the whereabouts of the campsite. They did not but to my surprise, they dashed into the road to hail down a passing police patrol car to ask them. I thought the officers would be angry, being stopped for unofficial police business, but here in small-town Gloucestershire they were nothing but helpful (and I think somewhat amused by my sudden appearance in their town). This was an eye-opening situation for me. Maybe I was still comparing everywhere to the last place I'd lived (an undesirable location in South London), where teenagers would menace a stranger rather than welcome them, and police officers would likely arrest hobo-esque strangers wandering their streets. But the PC and WPC in the patrol car began digging out their loose change for my collection tin and asking me what charity it was for. When I told them, once again I heard, 'Oh, so you're one of Princess Di's friends?' (Enough with the quip already.)

I waved goodbye to the teenagers and the police officers and headed off in the direction they'd pointed me in. As I cycled, I hummed contentedly, occasionally wiping spots of rain from my face. There was an almighty storm brewing in the skies above and as the cloud thickened, it became hotter still, if that's possible, and I longed for the relief of rain. I could feel the electricity building in the air as a great tension. Distant rubbles of thunder brought, as always, a deep-rooted longing for something I have never managed to put my finger on. Something primeval and beautiful, reminding me that I am nature and that I often ache to return to its bosom. Alas, despite putting my tent up in record time, the storm clouds passed that campsite by and I was left to a sticky night, thrashing around in a sweat-soaked sleeping bag.

I was happy to see this campsite doing its bit to promote energy conservation and recycling, (the only one I stayed at that did), and it had even left the boundaries of its camping field to grow untamed to attract wildlife. The loss of species diversity in the UK has happened so quickly that even in thirty short years, I can see it with my own eyes. I remember as a child seeing "moth storms" in the car headlights at night: when so many would appear, it would be like driving through a blizzard of moths. But you don't see that anymore, not like you used to, and that's because forty percent of all British moths have been wiped out because of habitat loss. Another thing I've noticed is the shocking diminishment of garden birds. Again, when I was a child, my mother used to feed the birds each morning in winter, and we would watch thrilled as dozens of species flocked to our garden. These days, spotting certain species has become a rare event rather than the norm, and the Royal Society for the Protection of Birds confirms the figures. Since the 1970s, tree sparrow numbers have dropped by ninety-five per cent, corn buntings by eighty-eight per cent, willow tits by seventy-eight per cent, starlings by seventy-one per cent, song thrushes by fifty-six per cent... I could go on and on. And again, it's all down to loss of habitat. Did you know that sparrows have lived amongst humans for 11,000 years, but now, ninety-five per cent of them have been wiped out in just *thirty years*? If that's not something to get angry about, then I don't know what is.

DAY 13

(48 MILES)

"*T*otally and utterly exhausting" is how day thirteen is described in my diary, but it had been exhausting for the most unexpected of reasons. In the morning, when I realised I'd run out of food, I wasn't overly worried. I made do with a cup of coffee and resolved to hunt down the nearest shop. Of course, I could have cycled the 3 miles back into Cirencester but that would mean me doing something too ghastly to contemplate… *Backtracking*. (Dirty word. Filthy concept.) And rather than do that, I headed onwards, thinking it must only be a few miles to the next shop. But I was about to encounter a bizarre trend in the UK which, unbeknownst to me, had been steadily increasing since the 1950s.

The terrain that morning was very hilly and would have been tough even after a big bowl of porridge. I pedalled slowly and dreamt about greasy spoon cafés, with red-chequered tablecloths, serving hash browns on toast with brown sauce. I love a good breakfast. I love it so much, I even love the word: to break the overnight fast. But it didn't take me long to work out I wouldn't find any food stores around here. My route led me through miles of farmland, interspersed with patches of woodland and not a lot else. But a little further on, I began to see signs that the developers had been here also. By now, ravenous to the point of distraction, I was looking out eagerly for the many villages on my route. I say villages because to all intents and purposes, this is what they appeared as on the map, but as I arrived at each one, I was disappointed to find nothing more than a housing estate of new homes. Each time I passed a sign saying *Welcome to blah-blah-blah*, I looked for recognisable signs of civilisation: a shop, post office, tearoom, children's playground with requisite ice cream van. But there was nothing. Just row upon row of identikit new builds.

I rode on through each soulless, sterile settlement, growing evermore morose. Here were estates without centres, villages without a heart, communities without a spirit. Where were the shops? The community hall? Where was the local pub? (A very long drive away, I shouldn't wonder) What were the planners thinking? I wasn't too far from the big cities of the Midlands, where housing was no doubt in high demand. Maybe these developments were to ease a housing shortage in the cities. Was the aim to relocate families here, with the promise of affordable housing? Or were they hoping to entice white-collar workers by promising them a (semi-) rural idyll after a stressful day at the office? It was hard to tell anything actually, since the streets were abandoned, and the only people that I saw were far from friendly; eyeballing me suspiciously from behind the shield of their car's windscreen.

Why build homes without facilities for thousands of people? You would certainly need a car to live here, and you'd have to drive a 20-mile round trip just to reach a town that offered the kind of facilities most of us require on a day-to-day basis. This smacks of the American idea of town development, or should I say *out-of-town* development. To me, they were environmentally unfriendly, community-less places, where the daily interactions that would normally occur whilst shopping or on the school run just wouldn't happen because there was nowhere *to* interact. Everyone would be too busy driving backwards and forwards to the nearest town to have *time* to build community spirit. No wonder the locals weren't smiling. Maybe travellers should be told: beware of villages without shops.

After many more exhausting miles, I finally reached a real town: Stow-on-the-Wold (or Thank-God-I'm-Here Town, as I renamed it). Rule number sixteen of cycle touring: be certain how far away your next source of food is and never risk running out. Stow was an attractive place and displayed a proud sign declaring itself the highest town in Oxfordshire. But I didn't need to know any of this... all I needed to know was... *where was the food?* My eyes were out on stalks and in the first fifteen seconds, I clocked a bakery, mini-mart, delicatessen and a butcher's shop window stacked with pies. And five minutes later, I was sat in the sunshine devouring pies, cake and a pot of yogurt so fast, I gave myself the hiccups. Now I was back in a real town, I discovered the people became real again, and I fell easily into conversation with those around me. First up was a woman visiting from Blackpool who stopped for a chat. Then a man in his fifties, who was originally from Cornwall but now lived locally, also sat with me. On hearing about my expedition, both of them donated some money. I learnt that Princess Diana had been visiting victims of landmines this week and it had all been thoroughly televised. This explained the increase in the, *oh, you must a friend of Princess Di* wisecracks. And then a frail, elderly man approached and told me he'd seen me arrive and had returned home to fetch some money to donate. Very slowly, with hands shaking from the onset of Parkinson's, he proceeded to empty all his loose change from every coat and trouser pocket, around twenty pounds in total, and put it all into my collection tin. I had to fight back a tear as I thanked him.

The afternoon became so hot that I worried I might soon end my days in a sticky mess, stuck to the road like a blob of ice cream dropped by a child. Outside a café where I'd stopped to fill my water bottles, I chatted to a young man on a motorbike. He shared his cigarette with me and we talked of common concerns: the weather, traffic volumes and idiotic drivers who endangered the lives of anyone on two wheels. He popped two pounds into my collection tin before flashing me the most beautiful smile and roaring away on his bike. But when I turned around, I was amused to see that every person in the café had been watching us like hawks.

I entered Warwickshire and rolled into Stratford-upon-Avon; the birthplace of Shakespeare. It'd taken me thirteen days, but I'd finally discovered the best way of finding a campsite was to head straight for the tourist information centre and ask them. Their offices were well signposted and, unlike campsites, were always easy to find. Then once on my way to the campsite, I made sure to stop off somewhere to pick up some food and supplies because once I'd arrived at my campsite, the last thing I ever wanted to do was to go out again... until tonight. As I waited for my kettle to boil, Roger, a fellow cycle tourist from Birmingham, came over and sat down for a chat. He said he had been touring around Kent for two weeks and expected to be home by tomorrow. Now this was music to my ears: Birmingham already? Okay, so it's not even a third of the way through my tour, but for the girl who at one point didn't expect to make it through Cornwall, reaching the Midlands was *massive*. I began to suspect poor old Roger had been a bit lonely on his tour and may have mistaken me for another lonely person, because from the moment he opened his mouth he didn't stop talking. I tried to be as genial as possible but I couldn't get a word in edgeways and, as I was too polite to tell him to go away, I ended up sitting there for two hours whilst he conducted a one-sided conversation. Finally, I could take it no more, and I had to resort to the one thing I really didn't want to do: I had to make my excuses and ride off, leaving him sitting there *still* talking.

It really wasn't my day. Within minutes of leaving the campsite, I felt myself sliding irrevocably into the Bonk; a term regular cyclists will be familiar with. For those who aren't, then let me explain, lest you think I was heading for some kinky bicycle-induced experience. The term, bonk (or hitting the wall as it's also known), is a sudden loss of energy during long-distance exercise, caused by a depletion of the body's glycogen levels. This can happen if you've burnt up calories way faster than you've replaced them, and it doesn't take a genius to work out that cycling 20 miles this morning without breakfast was the reason I had it now. It's the most awful feeling. I felt weak, dizzy and my hands shook, and I knew from past episodes that even after eating, it may still take me a while to recover. Thankfully, I was less than a mile from Stratford town centre, and after veggie burger and chips I began to feel considerably better.

Now, though, I had myself a problem: I'd already noticed the pub across the road and, whilst I almost never went into pubs alone, it was either that or another three hours of Roger. Cautiously, I pushed open the heavy door. It was calm and quiet inside, with wooden floors and a long bar, and it seemed safe enough. I ordered a pint and took my seat in a corner, hoping to go unnoticed. But I should have remembered this wasn't the south-east, where strangers remain strangers, and I'd barely blown the froth from my beer before the interrogations started. First up was a husband-and-wife team: Charles and Mary. They had the veiny noses of hardened drinkers, but they were friendly enough, and so I asked them about their hometown. Amongst other things, they advised me not to visit the house of Shakespeare because, in their words, it was "a load of old crap the tourist board has made up". They gleefully said William's real house had been destroyed a long time ago. (Although, later, I found out there is strong evidence that the house on Henley Street is, in fact, the real deal.) Mary exited at this point to go get their supper ready and, left with Charles, I made the mistake of mentioning my ride to him. He spent the next hour trying to arrange me a lift to Glasgow in the morning to save me having to pedal there, and nothing I said could make him understand why I (or anyone else for that matter) would voluntarily choose to ride. In fact, it made him furious. Thankfully, Mary reappeared just then and dragged him away, and I breathed a huge sigh of relief.

Geoff, a thirty-year-old travelling salesman who'd been on the periphery of the conversation the whole time, now moved closer. He was intrigued by my accent, eagerly explaining how he found southerners far friendlier than the people around here, which was interesting because I held the opposite opinion. As I accepted another pint, we debated the topic keenly. After a few drinks, the conversation inevitably turned more personal and Geoff perceptively deduced that people don't change the course of their lives dramatically unless they have suffered some big or traumatic life event. Thinking back now, I realise that Geoff was the first person to whom I ever told my real reasons for making this journey.

DAY 14

(40 MILES)

*D*uring the night, I must have slipped into a deep despondency because when I awoke, I was clutching my sleeping bag and paralysed by melancholy. I remember thinking, *well, that's that then. It's only been fourteen days and 450 miles.* But I knew that something must be at the heart of my lacklustre attitude and I wanted to at least try to find out what it was. It was time for the pep talk.

'Now then, you,' I put a firm hand on my shoulder, 'care to tell me what is making you think this is anything less than a fantastic experience?'

I'm tired and I've got a headache.

'Well, what did you expect after a night in the pub? Don't worry, it will go.'

I can't ride forty miles.

'Yes, you can. You've done it before. And you're fitter now than ever before.'

It's forecast to be another really hot day.

'Good grief. Would you rather it rained?'

No.

'Would you rather be back in your old job, working twelve-hour shifts?'

No.

'So…?'

I know I should be relishing every day, but it's actually hard to be cheerful all the time, especially when the riding is so much harder than I'd ever imagined.

'Well, you've never done anything like this before, have you?'

But I feel guilty if I'm not loving every minute of every day.

'Ah, now I get it. Look, this is one of the hardest things you've ever done, physically or mentally. Some moments you're going to love and some moments you'll hate. On a long journey like this, no one can wake up every single day bouncing with enthusiasm. Go easy on yourself. You're doing just fine.' I thought about all this for a while before deciding I owed it to myself to give it my best shot, one last time. I got up and began packing my things away. And as I did, I found, to my relief, the gloom began to shift.

I had to run a few errands in Stratford and I was rather hoping that by the time I was done, my headache would be gone. My sister's comment about my lack of donations had been nagging at the back of my mind, and I thought this might be a good time to remind myself that as well as my mission to conquer the British Isles by bicycle, I was also on another mission to rid the world of landmines. I found myself a spot on the busy high street where I'd be visible, and with my collection tin in my hand, I tried to make eye contact with the passing shoppers. I often wondered if I just looked fit for nothing that morning, because my fundraising hour did *not* go well. I have often witnessed people collecting money for charity, standing on street corners and shaking their tins under people's noses with impunity. I don't know what kind of people they are, but my guess would be: ballsy and brazen. Characteristics I lacked. As person after person passed by, I found myself wanting to smile apologetically for even daring to ask them for money and each time I was ignored, it was kind of hard not to take it personally. In that hour, three passers-by stopped because they thought I would be a great place to rid themselves of their loose change, never even asking what charity it was for. About the only people to take a genuine interest were two elderly ladies. By the end of it, I had collected a grand total of six pounds and forty-seven pence, and I vowed *never* to put myself through the humiliation again. I guess it was just easier to entice donors whilst I was on the move. The town clock struck twelve as I left Stratford-upon-Avon, the hottest part of the day, and my head still throbbed.

The next circle drawn on my map was the town of Warwick, said to sport one of the finest castles in the whole of England. I have always loved castles for their turrets and fortresses, drawbridges and keeps. I could spend hours exploring every nook and cranny: huge inglenook fireplaces, kitchens where feasts of hog and broth would have been painstakingly prepared, dining halls large enough to hold banquets for a hundred. But as I pushed my way through the crowds and up to the entrance, I was disappointed to read the entrance fee was fifteen pounds. At more than twice my daily budget, I concluded that I couldn't really afford it. And yet, just a few miles up the road, I found something else to spend that money on. I opened the door of a cycle shop and sidled up to the counter to ask, 'Could you assist me in choosing a cycle helmet?'

Now, I don't think cycling is a particularly dangerous activity, no more so than, say, playing rugby or being up a ladder painting. Having said that, it is important to know that, in the event of a tumble, a cycle helmet has been proven to reduce head trauma by up to forty per cent. So, I am all for wearing them... I just shudder when people talk about making them compulsory... as if this is the only thing needed to make cycling safer. It isn't. Let's be clear about something: a helmet will only provide very limited protection if you should be hit by a moving vehicle, and in light of this, there are other, more glaringly obvious (and some might say better) ways to keep cyclists from harm. One way would be to increase cycling infrastructure, i.e., more designated cycle paths. Another would be a broader effort to make communities safer by lowering speed restrictions and demanding better driving standards from *everyone*. No cycle helmet legislation should ever be a substitute for safer streets.

How many times have I heard it said that "People who speed aren't *real* criminals"? Really? Well, what are real criminals then? I would define them as: *people who deliberately break laws that have been put in place to protect other people, their rights or their property*. So how about if I tell you that people

flouting road rules and driving like totally irresponsible bell-
ends are responsible for an average of 4,000 deaths in the UK
every single year. (For comparison, the murder rate in the UK
averages around 700.) That is 4,000 victims. Four thousand
heartbroken parents, husbands, wives, children and friends,
and 4,000 deaths that could easily have been prevented if
drivers paid more attention, didn't get so impatient and
didn't break the speed limit.

*

The next destination circled on my map was the pretty town
of Leamington Spa, a town full of historical interest, none of
which I saw. By now, it was past four in the afternoon and the
temperature was somewhere up in the dizzy head figures. In
the centre of town, I found a park and took refuge under its
trees, vowing not to move again until there was a significant
drop in temperature. Now and then, I trekked the few yards
to the kiosk and back to purchase sandwiches and chilled
sugar-filled pop, hoping it would bring me back to life. It was
nearly six o'clock when I finally accepted it wasn't going to
cool down anytime soon. And so, one by one, I arranged each
of my heavy limbs into position like a game of Twister, until
finally I was standing upright. *Okay*, I panted, *just six miles to
the campsite. I can do this.* Can you imagine how totally and
utterly exasperating it was when I realised the campsite was
on the *other* side of a dual carriageway? A road cut in half by
a 6ft barricade, meaning I would have to cycle a further mile
up the road to a roundabout, and then a mile back down the
other side. The language I chose that evening would have

made Beelzebub blush. Rule number seventeen of cycle touring: beware of getting directions from car drivers.

But the road gods must have decided I had endured enough punishment for one day, and I was greeted at the campsite by a kindly woman and her grown-up son. They ushered me into their cool, dark farmhouse and presented me with glass after glass of chilled homemade lemonade, until the thirst of an army would have been quenched. Despite its rundown appearance, the farmhouse was lovely, with paddocks and stables, and it would have been right up there in my dream house fantasies had it not been for the busy dual carriageway out the front. (I suspect the farmhouse was built over one hundred years ago, when the road would have been no more than a quiet lane.) If you didn't count all the cute ducks running around and gently quacking amongst themselves, I had the camping field all to myself. The following, in order, is what went through my head next.

Mmm, this is so peaceful, I'm just going to lie here in the grass for a moment and not move. How lucky I am to have this place all to myself. It's heaven. But… uh-oh, what's that? (Sits up). *Oh no, why is there a car driving across the field towards me? Shit, shit, shit.* All silence was broken as a battered Ford Escort wheelspan into the field, complete with stereo booming out house music at full volume. It halted not far from my tent and out sprang its two young male occupants. Bye-bye bliss.

After dinner and a shower, I decided, *what the hell*, and I went over to say hello. Now, I digress for a second, but when I was at college, I studied with two guys called Tom and Barry. From the outside, they appeared to be on the opposite ends of the social spectrum. Tom was well groomed and loved his clothes and jewellery and spent his weekends in nightclubs. Barry, on the other hand, was the polar opposite. He lived in a squat, wore second-hand clothing and was covered with tattoos and piercings. But, nevertheless, the two of them were the best of friends. The reason I mention them here is because these two guys reminded me so much of my former fellow students: Tom the lad about town and Barry the punk rocker. And just like Tom and Barry, despite appearing to have nothing in common, they were clearly very good *amigos*. It turned out these two guys at my campsite had jobs in nearby Rugby, working as painters and decorators, but realised they could save far more of their wages if they lived in tents rather than shelling out for a bed and breakfast. (I could relate to that.) They said they'd been as surprised to see me as I was to see them and they asked what I was doing there. When I told them, Tom turned to Barry (they never actually told me their real names) and said, 'We've got a right one here.' But I must have gained their approval because I was invited to sit with them.

As the sun began to set, I enjoyed listening to Barry's travel tales, particularly the one where he'd signed up to work on a cargo ship in order to get free passage to Australia. This epic voyage took almost eight months. I was dying to talk to him about coping for so long, alone in an infinite ocean of thoughts, and isolated from all that is normal. But by this time, it was rather late and the super-strength lager and cannabis had taken a hold of him. (It appeared this was how the pair of them coped with the discomfort of living in tents for months on end.) Still, I enjoyed my fair share of their goodies and once they'd both passed out, I made my way back to my tent. I lay awake for a while, my mind flipping between topics so quickly that I kept losing track of my thoughts. To my delight, I found my rock-hard camping mat had transformed and, for tonight at least, I was sleeping on the world's softest mattress.

DAY 15

(36 MILES)

*T*he patter of rain on canvas woke me up at five o'clock but within seconds I'd nodded off again, and I finally stirred at eight. The first thing I noticed was how much cooler it was. The rain had cleared the humidity and I looked forward to an altogether easier ride. Tom and Barry had already left. They'd forgotten their promise to give me a shout at seven, but after their substantial intake of mind-altering substances last night, I wasn't surprised. I went about my morning routine feeling at peace and when I was finally ready to leave, the woman who owned the farm wouldn't hear of accepting my money. Again, I placed the cost of the pitch into the collection tin myself.

Today, I was back on the Fosse Way, and I was about to reach the point where it crosses another ancient byway called

Watling Street. If you thought Roman roads were a good example of old roads then think again, because by the time the Romans came to Britain and discovered Watling Street, it had already been in use for centuries by ancient Britons. At 276 miles in length, it now forms the A5 from Wroxeter to London and the A2 from London down to Dover. The junction of these two byways occurs at a place called High Cross. There isn't an awful lot to see there, although I'm led to believe there was once a sundial, built to commemorate this important junction. But, sadly, it had long since been reduced to rubble. High Cross, like most Roman road junctions, was more elevated than the surrounding countryside: typical of pragmatic Roman architects. They simply aligned one high point to another and built a straight road in between. It ensured all the important crossroads occurred on high ground, where they could more easily see their enemies coming. As I cycled this straight road with the horizon ever far away, I tried to imagine what it might have been like for the many Roman armies who would once have marched this way.

Today, the generosity and friendliness of the people I crossed paths with never stopped. Through the village of Brinklow, a woman who lived along the Fosse Way stopped to make a donation, and I asked if she could tell me some more about the road. As we chatted, a man in his sixties, who'd spotted my charity tabard, also stopped to donate five pounds. He told me he was a former soldier and used to cycle until a few years ago, but when his knees became too painful, he switched to a motorbike. I remember this man best because he had thought to ask me if I had all the essentials: enough food, water and a place to stay. Aside from other cyclists, there weren't many to do this. His time in the army had taught him that kindness can be as simple as offering the bare essentials of life to another, and it left me humbled.

After Brinklow, the donations kept coming. Freewheeling through the town of Hinckley, I was so busy keeping an eye out for public toilets that I almost didn't notice a man who was stood in the middle of the road holding out three pounds for my collection tin. I almost mowed him down! I followed the A447 and then turned onto the B585. It was hard to believe I was cycling through the Midlands: Birmingham, Coventry and Wolverhampton to my left and Northampton, Rugby and Leicester to my right. Planning this section had been a bit of a headache because, whilst there were a few cities I wanted to visit, I had no intention of enduring five solid days of conurbation. And yet, ironically, here I was, cycling on some of the quietest roads I'd so far found in England. There was barely a car, the air smelt clean and I could hear the birds chirping. I spent all afternoon watching large, grey cumulonimbus clouds assembling themselves overhead. The flat lands of the Midlands were big sky country, and cloud-watching became my favourite pastime.

Along one of these quiet roads, my curiosity was piqued when a rather expensive open-top sports car pulled up. The man driving it sported a black jacket and bow tie, and the woman wore sunglasses and an elegant headscarf. They looked rather like caricatures from a 1960s Bond film and were clearly wealthy. But it didn't deter them from stopping to talk to a scruffy urchin like me and then making a handsome donation into my collection tin. As they sped off, I totted it up in my head. They were the seventh and eighth people that day to stop specially to make a donation. I thought back to my collection failure in Stratford yesterday and realised my hunch was probably right; donations were more forthcoming when I was on the move.

There was nothing special, however, about my next encounter: a cyclist called Rodney. He'd approached rapidly from behind and then slowed down to keep me company for a few miles. I was rather amused to find that I had to pedal downhill to try to keep up with him, whilst he had to keep braking on the flat so as not to creep ahead of me. As Rodney had cycled the End-to-End twice, I thought he might offer me some encouragement but, sadly, he was only full of criticism. I soon realised he was only asking questions about my ride so that he could then tell me what I was doing wrong: which way I was heading, what I'd had for breakfast, the bicycle I was using and the places I wanted to visit were all wrong in his eyes and before long I was grunting back single-syllable replies to his questions. Fortunately, my average cycling speed of 10mph was far too slow for such a pro and after another mile he left me behind.

My destination was a youth hostel in a place rather cutely named Copt Oak. Remember those cumulonimbus clouds I mentioned? Well, not two miles from the day's end a deluge fell, so hard it stung my hands and made foot-deep puddles in the road in just a few minutes. I imagined the passing motorists thinking, *oh, that poor cyclist caught out in this awful weather*, as they then simultaneously drove past at 60mph, spraying me thoroughly.

Similarly, as I cycled past houses, I caught glimpses of faces at windows. Although I couldn't hear what was said, of course, I bet I could have guessed their words. 'George, come and look at this girl on her bicycle. Fancy cycling in this weather. She'll catch her death.'

If I'd been in a car, I would have missed Copt Oak. I only noticed the broken sign, rusting away in an overgrown hedge, because I was travelling at 10 miles an hour. The village consisted of a church, a closed pub and just a few houses, and if there ever had been a village shop, it was long gone. The whole place had a sad aura of an almost deserted community and in light of this, I thought it was peculiar to even find a youth hostel here. I was dismayed to find the hostel didn't open for another two hours. Damn it, I had forgotten most of them are closed during the day. Never mind, they had thoughtfully provided a wet weather shelter, or the creepy-crawly shed as I soon renamed it, and it was here I retired, soaked to the bone and growing colder by the minute. At least my teeth chattering together helped scare away some of the spiders.

The first hour felt like an interminable length of time, but just as I was wondering how I was gonna survive a second hour, the door was unlatched and my jaw dropped open as a handsome, smiling man entered. Jack was about my age, Australian, and was very smartly dressed. (I, on the other hand, looked as though I'd just crawled out of a washing machine.) I wondered if I'd dropped into a parallel universe or something... I mean, how does a young man from downtown Sydney come to be here in this godforsaken shed? Don't young backpackers head for the bright lights of London, Edinburgh, Stonehenge; anywhere rather than Copt Oak? But Jack insisted that, to him, this place was a cultural extravaganza. I smiled wryly. I was suddenly feeling inexplicably warm again (maybe something to do with Jack's dazzling smile) and as we chatted and laughed, the second hour passed swiftly. Bang on four o'clock, the hostel doors swung open. As Jack had already spent the night here, he forewarned me about the warden whom Jack said was rude and surly. However, when it was my turn to check in, I found the guy was rather genial, if a bit cheeky. I forgave Jack his harsh misjudgement of the warden's character, since he'd only just arrived in the UK and probably hadn't got to grips with the British sense of humour yet. And besides, anyone who thought Copt Oak was a cultural extravaganza clearly still had a *lot* to learn about this country.

DAY 16

(37 MILES)

*S*taying in a youth hostel should have streamlined my morning routine, what with there being no tent to take down or anything, but for some unfathomable reason, it still took me the usual amount of time (more than one hour, not quite two) to get my butt into gear. What can I say? It was a mystery.

There was a lovely long descent out of Copt Oak, and as I coasted on down the hill, my nose picked up some wonderful scents as the sun began warming the foliage, still wet after a night of rain. The road steamed, raindrops on grass verges sparkled, and every blade of grass, every flower and leaf smelt sensational. It was one of those rare moments in life when I felt lucky just being alive... until a pothole in the road brought me back down to earth with a literal bang. I was going quite fast at the time with a queue of cars behind me, all patiently waiting to overtake. When I hit the pothole, it jarred my bike and body so hard that it snapped my right-side pannier clips, and my bag was flung into the middle of the road. Since it was the bag that contained my Calor gas stove, I hastily retrieved it before anyone could run it over, and I fastened it back on my rack with string.

In Loughborough town centre, I made a call to Orbit Cycles in Sheffield, the company from whom I'd purchased my bicycle. I knew it was their policy to offer a free six-month service on all new bicycles, something I'd never gotten around to arranging. I was rather hoping that if they heard about my charity ride, they might still be willing to service my bike anyway, even if it was eighteen months too late. I spoke to a friendly woman with a strong Yorkshire accent who said if I popped in Saturday morning, she was sure they could fit me in, *no bother*. I replaced the receiver grinning happily, but twenty miles later, I realised with dismay that I'd left my address book back at the phone box. I'd had this book for years now and not only did it contain contact details of everyone back home, it was also full of new contact details of friends I'd met backpacking around Europe this summer. I stood by the roadside in a quandary. Should I ride the 40-mile round trip to go and retrieve it? It would be 40 miles on top of the 20 miles I'd already ridden. Was 60 miles worth it considering it might not even be there now? Then I remembered I had the appointment to keep with Orbit Cycles the day after tomorrow. I couldn't mess them about when they'd shown me such generosity and so I sighed and conceded I must keep going. On my trip, I only ever lost three things. Unfortunately, they were all very precious items: a watch given to me by a friend who'd now passed away, a penknife from my ex-boyfriend (the only useful thing he ever gave me) and now my address book, filled with names of people who'd think I had gone away and forgotten about them.

*

Entering Nottingham by way of an A road doesn't sound like the best thought-out plan for a cyclist, but I couldn't think of another way to ensure I didn't get hopelessly lost and for a while, my gamble seemed to pay off: because this road was pretty quiet. Once again, the Midlands (the place I'd expected roads to be most murderous) was serendipitously the place I kept finding unexpectedly quiet roads. Here I was only a few miles from the city centre and yet my surroundings felt semi-rural. I spied a magnificent heron, fishing in a lake but, sadly, as soon as it caught sight of me, it spread its wings and flapped away. Whilst cycling is one of the more environmentally friendly forms of transport, I discovered it is not the best way to watch wildlife. Most of the time, animals will scarper when they see a bicycle but annoyingly, take not a blind bit of notice of the cars that zoom by; the vehicles that pose a real threat to their existence.

The peace didn't last long once I'd entered the real suburbs of Nottingham, and the contrast was jarring. The traffic was awful, overflowing bins stank, car horns and police sirens screeched non-stop and groups of noisy teenagers congregated on street corners, yelling and spitting.

Thankfully, I spotted a cycle path marked *City Centre* and, rather relieved, I followed it. It took me up quiet residential roads and across parks. But then, right in the middle of some random housing estate, the signposts abruptly halted. Without them, I had absolutely no idea where I was or in which direction I should head. I pedalled around for a while until, thankfully, I spotted another sign for the city centre and again, I followed the breadcrumbs. But just as before, the signposts eventually petered out. After wasting an hour of my day doing this, I gave up and headed back to the main road. Whilst I applaud Nottingham City Council for their "greening" efforts, there were major flaws in their cycle network. They needed better signposts for a start. But worse still, all the cycle paths were concentrated in the south and centre of the city. When it was time to leave Nottingham and head north, there were none and, as you'll see in a moment, that was a real safety concern.

You may be wondering why I risked my neck at all, cycling through a big city like Nottingham when I could just have easily gone around it. Well, the answer is that I wanted to visit Nottingham Castle. I've already explained my love of castles and this one, as well as being featured in every Robin Hood film ever made, has a long and interesting history. I cycled right up to the entrance gate and ate my sandwiches whilst staring up at the magnificent construction, but out of nowhere, I suddenly lost all enthusiasm to go in. The day was now terribly hot and having had an awful time fighting my way into Nottingham, all I could think was, *I've got to go through it all again when I leave*. And like all of life's difficult tasks, my motto was: the sooner I get on with it, the sooner it will be over.

As I headed north for my long slog out of the city, I kept seeing posters demanding the government should be taxing the rich. It seems Robin Hood was still very much an icon in this part of the world. Somewhere in the city's northern suburbs, I noticed my back tyre looked a little flat and I stopped to pump it up. But within a few miles, it looked flat again. I had a slow puncture. *Fuck it*. Today, I'd learnt the hard way that busy cities, cycling and heatwaves are a very *bad* combination. I also discovered that the A6, rammed with HGVs and with no provision for cyclists, was one mother of a dangerous place to ride. Not for the first time, I found myself thinking that what this country sorely lacks (in terms of cycling infrastructure) were safe passages between one town and the next. And I'm not talking about some complicated route either: like the mountain bike trails that lead you uphill and down dale, over gates and through the mud. What we need are direct, safe commutes between one town and the next. I thought wistfully about the cycle paths I'd seen in the Netherlands that run alongside most of its main roads: smoothly paved cycle lanes, separated from the traffic by a fence or hedge, with their mileage and destinations clearly marked. Surely this kind of visible alternative to the motorcar would be the best way to encourage people out of their automobiles and into the saddle?

There was a campsite marked on my map 9 miles north of Nottingham and once I'd turned off the A60, the contrast was astounding. As I rode along the back roads towards the village of Calverton, it was so quiet that I thought I'd developed a hearing problem. It was bliss after riding through the city for most of the day, and I could feel my shoulders physically relaxing… but it didn't last… because all hell broke loose when three police cars appeared out of nowhere, lights flashing and sirens blaring. I barely had time to get out of their way before they shot past me, far too close, then disappeared out of sight around the next bend. The world went so quiet in their wake you could have heard a pin drop.

I turned left at the next T-junction onto an even narrower road and with only a mile left, I started daydreaming about the next campsite: I longed for power showers, an onsite bar and maybe even a handsome male cyclist in the next tent. But my daydreams were shattered when the same three police cars reappeared, tearing past on blues and twos. Again, my eardrums were assaulted for a few seconds before they disappeared around the bend out of sight.

'Well, at least they weren't after me,' I said out loud, but when I finally rolled into Calverton, there they were again. Before the paranoia could creep over me, the campsite proprietor filled me in on the gossip. He said the police had spent the entire afternoon chasing armed robbers who, after a bungled attempt at a stick-up in a petrol station, had made their escape across the fields.

'The Merry Men have got themselves armed now, have they?' I joked, but the proprietor had already moved on to the next arrivals, repeating the same story. This was scandalous stuff for small-town Nottinghamshire.

I pitched my tent up in the corner of the campsite (a bare field with a chemical toilet; not quite the facilities I'd hoped for) and started up conversation with my neighbour for the night. He was a motorbike rider who went by the rather kooky name of Slalom Steve (not quite the handsome cyclist I'd been hoping for either). But he was a friendly guy who helped me locate and then remove a tiny slither of glass wedged into my back tyre: the cause of my slow puncture. Once the operation was over, I flopped into the shade, utterly exhausted, and Steve placed a can of beer into my hands. We chatted whilst I made myself some sandwiches and afterwards, we decided to make a trip together to the local hostelry. I was all for blotting out the many mistakes I'd made that day: not seeing the pothole, losing my diary and then thinking it would be a good idea to cycle through a city in a heatwave.

Turns out, gin and tonics are a great soother of nerves, and every time Steve went to the bar, he brought me back a double. I knocked them back whilst listening to his light-hearted tales about the rivalries between Yorkshire and Lancashire. (Steve was a proud Yorkshireman.) Ordinarily, I'd be a bit suspicious of a man I'd only just met plying me with alcohol, but I didn't get that vibe with Steve. I felt as comfortable with him as I would any of my other male *amigos,* and the reason, I think, was because we had something in common: we both worked (or in my case, had worked) for the railway. And that meant we were a part of what railway workers refer to as "The Railway Family". Steve didn't know this at first, since I hadn't let on straightaway, and I hid a smirk when he asked, 'I bet you've never met a train driver before.' Did I detect a hint of flirtation? In the last three years, I'd often exchanged pleasantries with *many* train drivers, in the café outside the station where we'd all worked. So, I'm afraid, if it was a chat-up line, it was a dismal failure.

DAY 17

(30 MILES)

I was beginning to feel trapped in my very own version
of Groundhog Day: one where I woke up each morning
at 6am, determined to get cracking before it grew too
hot, and then didn't get on the road until 10am. Or maybe
a naughty little imp would wind the clock forward an hour
when I wasn't looking.

I made Steve a mug of tea to thank him for helping me
mend my puncture yesterday. I was surprised he didn't bother
carrying a camping stove, but, as he explained it, when you
have 110 horsepower at your fingertips, you are never more
than an effortless ten minutes' ride away from breakfast. He
said not carrying a stove freed up room in his motorbike
panniers for more important stuff, and by that, I rather
suspected he meant for carrying cans of beer. Of course, a

camping stove isn't necessary for a cycle tourist either. You could be the disciplined sort who can make do with a quick muesli bar and a cup of water in the mornings, in order to get on the road early and get 60 miles done by lunchtime. But that wasn't for me. Once I'd realised I couldn't afford to eat out every day on this trip, I brought my stove so I could have hot food and tea at least once a day. And I didn't regret it, because sitting in the tent entrance each morning, swaddled in my sleeping bag, mug of tea in hand and watching the world come alive soon became my favourite part of the day. So, the extra weight was well worth it in my eyes.

I pedalled back through Calverton village and passed the pub where much merriment had been had last night, and made for the A614 northbound. I was joined briefly by the local postwoman, who cycled along beside me and put forward the best case I had *ever* heard for packing up my bike and never riding it again: 'Gosh, you're not planning on cycling the A164, are you? What, really? But it's so dangerous. They say more people get killed on the A614 than on the M25, and it's always the cyclists. Just the other month there was that accident where the cyclist got killed. People always have a blind spot for bicycles, don't they? It's been voted Britain's most dangerous road two years in a row now, especially in August when the tourists flock to the area. Oh, it is August. Well, you mind how you go now.' *Help.* And what she didn't do either was offer any local knowledge about how I might bypass this section of road. From my maps, I couldn't figure out a way around it either, and with this message of doom ringing in my ears, I reached the T-junction and turned right, out onto the Highway of Certain Death.

If you are at all baffled by my route-planning techniques, can I just say that these were the days *before* the internet, when trying to find cycling information outside of your own locale was tricky to say the least. As a member of the Cyclists' Touring Club (now called Cycling UK), I had spent many months scouring back issues of their magazine, hoping to find information on the areas I wished to visit. But in the main, articles were limited to already popular cycling spots, and that left the rest of the UK as a big unknown. Even educated guesses as to which roads might be safe for a cyclist was a hit and miss affair, because as already mentioned, some A roads are astonishingly quiet, whilst B roads can be busy. My only option was to go ahead and just plan my journey. Circle each destination on a map and try linking them by roads that I hoped were quiet, but at the same time trying not to make my route so complex I would end up lost. It was not an easy balance to pull off, and sometimes, like in the Midlands, it worked out pretty well, whereas other times (such as Cornwall), my strategy failed miserably. I learnt that it was best to stay flexible. Plan wherever possible but be willing to change route if necessary.

But on this occasion, I had messed up big time because just as the postwoman forewarned, the A614 was treacherous. For 10 miles I held my breath and prayed I wouldn't get hit by the giant trucks thundering by, and at the first opportunity I had, I got the hell off that road. I had been lured to this part of the Midlands because I wanted to see the famous Sherwood Forest. For anyone coming here to visit, be warned: blink and you might miss it. During the 1200s (around the time of the Robin Hood legends), the forest covered around 10,000 acres and was used for hunting, farming, building monasteries, peasant smallholdings and animal grazing. But by the time industrialisation came along, human activity was, as ever, having a severe impact on the forest. Materials and space were eagerly sought out for roads, railways, coal mining, housing, crop growing, grazing, military training and even for shipbuilding materials. You name it, they required this wood and this land to build it. Which is all well and good, but I continually wonder *why* it never occurred to our forebears to actually replant some of these trees.

By about the 1900s, it had become a well-known joke that if Robin Hood were still alive, there was only enough forest left for him to hide out for a week. Fast forward to today and the saying goes, "A group of schoolchildren could track him down in twenty minutes" ... which gives you a very clear, very depressing idea of just how little of the forest is left. The official country park covers an area of 448 acres, although not all of this actually has trees left on it. And positioned as it was between the A60 and A614, it already felt to me like a "drive-thru" forest. Maybe it would be more accurate to now refer to it as Sherwood Copse rather than Sherwood Forest.

Thanks to Nottinghamshire Council, the small surviving area of forest had been turned into something more closely resembling a children's play area than an ancient forest, but determined to see something authentic, I went on a recce to find the Major Oak. Now, prepare to be blown away, because this oak tree is thought to be around eight *hundred* years old. That means that this beauty was here when the Magna Carta was signed. It was here when Henry VIII was making his way through six wives and all the monasteries were being dissolved, and it was here as Oliver Cromwell's armies fought the English Civil War. Was its survival sheer luck or was there something special, something enchanting, about it that made people want to preserve it? I don't suppose we'll ever know, but I like to think it was the latter.

"Ere, John, see this big fellow 'ere, be a shame to cut him down just yet. Shall we give him a reprieve and see how big he gets?'

'All right, Richard, we'll do just that. But I'll wager thee half a pig's head it will blow down anyway, come the winter winds.'

What we do know is that the Victorians first took an interest in the tree as a tourist attraction in the 1800s, when it became centre stage for cock-fighting competitions, calling it Cockpen Tree. Only later did its name change to the Major Oak. The tree is a very awe-inspiring sight with a circumference of 33 feet, branches that spread over 92 feet and a weight of around 23 tons. But the poor old thing has been struggling this last century, and conservation measures had to be brought in in 1908. When I was there, it had specially made stilts supporting some of the branches; its very own tree-sized Zimmer frame.

In the tourist literature, I read that the Major Oak was a place frequented by Robin and his Merry Men on a regular basis, but where exactly does all this "Boys from the Hood" stuff originate? The answer is that nobody really knows, and there is very little evidence that Robin was a real person. During those times, the people who travelled the roads of Sherwood Forest were at real risk of being robbed by highwaymen, and whilst there are literary references and ballads from the 13th century that refer to the legend and his sidekicks, still nothing concrete was ever proved.

I didn't linger in Sherwood Forest for long. I should have known by now that, being a tourist attraction, I would be on the receiving end of some rather unpleasant staring. That afternoon, in a bit of a grump from the heat and the traffic, I gave up trying to smile at people and instead kept my eyes fixed firmly on the path ahead. But still, I could feel people's eyes boring into me as I passed. The one and only thing to cheer me up was when I overheard a little boy asking, 'Look, Mummy, why does that lady carry all her things on a bicycle?'

I felt like telling him, 'Because I can.'

Thank heavens for towns like Worksop. I liked to think the road gods decided to smile on me that evening, and three pieces of magic occurred. The first was when a casual glance at my milometer revealed I had come 550 miles. Oh my... I was *halfway* to John O'Groats and the realisation was exhilarating. The second was Worksop itself. As I sat in the high street nibbling malt loaf, I realised with immense relief that I had finally left behind the land of Arctic stares and I was now surrounded by an altogether friendlier breed of people. These were pleasant people. Normal people, who didn't stare rudely but if you did catch someone's eye, they had the good manners to nod, or smile, or just say good evening. After the tourists of Sherwood, such simple old-fashioned courtesy made me want to weep in relief.

In Worksop, I was faced with a logistical dilemma. According to my map, there were only two campsites: one some 10 miles in the wrong direction (no, thank you) and the other on the far side of Sheffield. As there was no way I wanted to cycle through an unknown city on a Friday night, the only other option was a youth hostel, some 30 miles distant in the Peak District. Don't worry, I had no intention of cycling there. According to my map, it looked possible to catch a train there and then return to Worksop in the morning to carry on. But it did sound like an awful lot of hassle, and ever mindful of the all-important bike service tomorrow, I wondered, would there even be trains running that early on a Saturday morning? Feeling rather beaten, I went into the tourist information centre. The woman behind the counter listened patiently as I gabbled through all the various but imperfect options that I thought I had. When I paused for breath, she said, 'Why not stay at the campsite here?' Here, it turned out, was an unmarked campsite only a two-minute walk away. Weak with relief, I could have hugged her. Praise the road gods for my third dose of serendipity that evening.

Just like the town, the campsite was also friendly, and as I pitched up my tent, everyone who passed said hello. As ever, my first job was to put the kettle on. When I'd first started out in Land's End, I'd made do with black coffee, as a small jar of instant was easier to lug around than a box of tea bags and a pint of milk. But very quickly, I drifted back to my tea. Aside from gustatory reasons, I began to suspect that more than one cup of coffee a day depleted my energy levels. This might just have been my imagination, but the reward of a hot, sweet cup of tea every morning and evening made carrying all the tea-making paraphernalia around worthwhile. As the campsite was right in the middle of town, I decided to make the most of the location and I wandered around Worksop looking for something novel for supper. In the end, I chose takeout Chinese stir-fry because I could eat half for dinner and save the rest for the morning. (Cold stir-fry for breakfast is delicious… *trust* me.) As I sat eating in my tent porch, I found myself casting my eyes around the campsite every now and again, on the off-chance a kooky Yorkshireman on a big motorbike might arrive.

PART 3

UP NORTH

Chaotic packing every morning

DAY 18

(23 MILES)

*F*or once, I was ready to leave by eight o'clock, but as I made my way out of Worksop, I heard an ominous clunking noise coming from the bike. Uh-oh. As anything other than simple puncture repair was beyond my expertise, you could say this was perfect timing: on my way to get my bicycle serviced. And yet my anxious mind still found things to fret over. Had the woman at Orbit Cycles said they *should* be able to fit me in this morning, or did she say they could *definitely* fit me in? What if they couldn't, then what? It would be foolish to continue if my bicycle was about to develop a cataclysmic fault (the clunking noise did sound pretty dramatic), but equally, I didn't fancy spending the night in Sheffield whilst I tried to find someone else to fix my bike.

I stopped to think for a moment. It seemed the best course of action was to present myself at the Orbit factory as early as possible and then pray they could make my bicycle good again in no time. It was now 08.20. With the Nottingham nightmare still clear in my mind, I realised that if I wanted to get there *this* side of lunchtime then there was really only one thing for it. With uncharacteristic decisiveness, I about-turned and headed for Worksop's train station. I was disappointed to be missing out 18 miles but I wasn't going to beat myself up over it; by the time I finished this trip, my overall mileage would be far in excess of the minimum 874 miles that is Land's End to John O'Groats. And besides, I'd already more than made up 18 extra miles when I'd gone the wrong way in Cornwall many times over.

Down on the platform I was surprised to find myself enjoying this sudden change to my schedule: surprised since I'd never have put *waiting for a train* down as an enjoyable activity. I realised, what I was actually enjoying was being back amongst people again after a long period of solitude, and just for this morning, I was ordinary again: I was waiting for a train like everyone else and not isolated by my own unique quest. From the conversations around me, I gleaned people were on their way into town for a spot of shopping, happy the weekend was finally here. Their merry chatter turned a mundane activity into something more closely resembling a social occasion, and I was included in several conversations. I don't want to keep banging on about "friendly northerners", because it is such a cliché, but nevertheless, it was a phrase that would pop into my head regularly over the next week.

An old diesel train, just two coaches long, pulled up

and everybody clambered on. Once aboard, I got talking to a couple roughly the same age as my parents, and they mentioned an old canal path which runs between Worksop and Sheffield that is sometimes used by cyclists. This highlighted nicely the problems I had back then, finding out cycle-friendly information; information which these days can be found with the click of a mouse key. Whilst asking locals was admittedly more fun than searching online, it wasn't much use if you couldn't find out what you needed to know until it was too late. Once we'd arrived in Sheffield, I found the lifts to be out of order. Luckily, my new friends were on hand to help carry my bicycle up and over the footbridge.

Sheffield: a city in the county of South Yorkshire which played a vital part in the British Industrial Revolution thanks to its local steel industry. Today, it spans 40 square miles and has a population of over half a million inhabitants. They say it was built on seven hills, just like Rome, although others think that's a myth. The seven hills bit. Or, was it the bit about it being like Rome? I'm not really sure. Anyway, what wasn't in any doubt was that Sheffield is very hilly, and, surprise, surprise, Orbit Cycles was located at the top of the longest, steepest hill of all.

Inside the Orbit factory, I was like a kid in a sweet shop: everywhere I looked there were shiny new bicycles of varying kinds. My worries (as always) had been unfounded, and in the end, I only waited twenty minutes to see a mechanic. Garry secured my bicycle by a clamp so it was up at eye level and the inspection began. I tried explaining in layman's terms about that strange noise but typically, despite him spinning wheels and twiddling with other bits... silence.

'Perhaps it was your knee,' he suggested kindly. In desperation, I got hold of the front wheel myself and span it furiously and the clunking noise sprang back into life. Garry diagnosed the problem as the front wheel bearings and showed me. They were dirty and corroded and some were missing, and I thought back to when I'd dragged my bicycle through the flooded roads of Somerset and felt extremely guilty. I stayed to watch the entire service. I was secretly envious of how easily Garry could find his way around a bicycle, and whilst cycle mechanics was something that I'd been meaning to learn for a while now, I kept putting it off. Deep down, I know I lack that all-important skill when it comes to fiddling with inanimate objects: *patience.* And to this day, it is still my firm belief that any bicycle I try to fix will ultimately end in a far worse state than before I started, and therefore, I should leave it well alone.

As he worked, Garry told me it was nice to have an *ordinary* customer to deal with, but before I could take this the wrong way, he explained he'd had several customers already today who'd been snobbish and rude. This was sad to hear. I'd always thought, or hoped, cyclists were one big happy family. Once the wheel bearings were done, Garry stripped and replaced the brake and gear cables, adjusted them to perfection, pumped up my tyres, then slipped a spare chain and two spare inner tubes into my pannier bag for good measure. With my bicycle as good as new, I was mightily relieved, not to mention blown away that it was all for free, but I thought I'd better check on this.

'How much do I owe you?' I ventured, and immediately wished I'd kept my mouth shut because now, Garry looked peeved.

'You don't owe me anything,' he said, sounding almost hurt. (I think I'd offended his generous nature.) It was an important lesson in the art of accepting kindness gratefully and so I thanked him and then quickly changed the subject.

Before leaving, I was given a tour of the factory. Amongst all the bicycles on display, my favourite was an Audax; a slimmer, lighter version of my own expedition bicycle with 700c wheels in stunning bright blue. I ran my fingers over the frame longingly before remembering I was jobless, technically homeless and fast running through my life savings, which had to last me until the end of summer, and so reluctantly, I moved on. Another thing I love about Orbit Cycles is their policy of donating ten percent of profits towards the building of cycle lanes, and I wondered if I dared suggest some better ones in Nottingham?

I said good morning to all the other customers as we went around, but two people on the second floor, hotly debating which bicycle they would buy, totally ignored my greetings. From this snub, I deduced they were probably the snobbish customers Garry had mentioned and I decided not to let this show of rudeness go. I did something I wouldn't normally do: and in my best, but so obviously put-on, posh BBC English voice, I butted right into their conversation.

'You know, you really should try the Expedition bicycle. It's such a splendid machine.' One of them grunted something and then turned her back on me, but I wasn't finished.

'I've ridden my Orbit bicycle here from Land's End.' Ah ha, now that got their attention. They asked me a few questions and passed on their congratulations. Now was the time to go in for the kill.

'One is doing this for charity. Landmines Clearance International. Yes, that's right, one of Princess Di's friends.' Ka-ching went the donation into my collection tin. I winked at Garry.

Pretty soon, I found negotiating Sheffield's streets much less of an ordeal than Nottingham had been, and I wondered if the lack of chaos was anything to do with its newly working tram system. I say new, but actually, this is not the first time Sheffield's streets have hosted trams. Horse-drawn trams first appeared in 1873, extending across the city and multiplying rapidly, and by 1902, the whole fleet had been electrified. The system reached its heyday in 1951 when it extended some 48 miles, but sadly, the trams only made it to October of 1960, after which they were relegated to museum pieces. During my travels around mainland Europe this summer, from stoic Warsaw to cosmopolitan Amsterdam, I saw that many countries had kept their trams operating all this time and I often wondered why Britain had so rashly abandoned hers. I mean, it's pretty obvious why: the increasing popularity of the motorcar, of course, but I am inclined to think the cuts were rather short-sighted. Because fast forward thirty or forty years, and the futility of individual car ownership for city residents is now all too horribly clear in the perpetual traffic jams and smoggy air. But, at least now, trams are making a comeback in several cities across the UK. I stopped a while to watch fascinated at what is known as the Sheffield Supertram. I loved the noise they made as they glided off, and that quaint ding-a-ling.

Before I was through the city, my stomach began to cry out for attention, and so I stopped at a shop selling baked potatoes. Delicious, hot, fluffy potatoes, oozing with carbs and dripping with melted butter and cheese: can there be any food finer for a hungry cyclist? Even out here in the city suburbs, everyone wanted to know where I was from and what I was up to. (There was no disguising my foreign southern accent now.) And everyone called me *lovey* or *pet*. For the past week, people from the surrounding countryside had continually warned me against Nottingham and Sheffield because, according to them, cities up here were highly dangerous places. I'd heard this said so often that their fear had started to infect me, and I'd arrived here expecting trouble. But whilst the traffic had indeed been horrendous, I'd found the people were as genial as anywhere else I'd been, so why all the scaremongering? I mulled over this conundrum a while until it eventually dawned on me that people probably viewed me as a vulnerable and naïve young woman. But what they didn't know was that up until recently, I'd been living in a rather unsavoury suburb in the biggest city of them all (London), where I'd had no choice but to become streetwise *very* swiftly. But even then, I'd never felt so afraid that I wouldn't walk or cycle around the place on my own, so, for me, these northern cities didn't feel any different from being in London. In fact, if anything, I was finding them a damn site friendlier.

I was deep in thought about all this as I headed slowly north-west when all of a sudden, I rounded a corner and stopped in amazement; Sheffield was no more. In place of the factories were green rolling hills and empty space. Only 10 miles from the city centre and I was slap-bang in the middle of the Peak District. After a day spent in urbanisation, the contrast hurt my eyes and flooded into my heart. I was back in the place I felt most content. Somehow, I just *knew* I would be giving serious consideration to moving here. I imagined living in a tiny cottage in the Peak District and taking a trip into Sheffield once a week. But the road gods must have been sniggering at me that afternoon, because I was so caught up in my joy of "discovering" this new and beautiful area (well, it was new to me) that I totally failed to register the significance of a sign I passed which read: *Scenic Area Ahead*. Rule number eighteen of cycle touring: when you see such a sign, it means the area you are about to ride through is *really* hilly.

For the time being, though, I could remain in blissful ignorance. I didn't have much further to go today and although the A616 was a long uphill climb, the gradient was shallow enough that I could ride it quite comfortably. On my left, the old industrial factories were behind me now, leaving only views of the empty moors below, whilst to my right I was barricaded in by steep cliffs that stretched up to the sky. It was a blissful ride, except after a time I needed to take a leak and there was nowhere to go. Either side of me was a sheer up or a steep down and there was neither bush nor wall to hide behind. I carried on for a few more miles becoming uncomfortable, until finally I came to a break in the cliffs. A gorge had been cut out by rainwater and the little clearing was full of lush greenery and framed by a viaduct. It was a beautiful spot, almost too nice to answer the call of nature in, but I was desperate and scrambled through the fence.

At first, I thought it was just the contrast between the bright sunny road and the shaded gorge that caused me to shiver, but as I looked around, I could feel the hairs on the back of my neck tingling. Now I could see this place for what it was. From the roadside, I hadn't realised it was a fly-tipping spot, nor had I noticed the mosquitoes that whined over stale puddles, or smelt the unpleasant stench. I thought I could sense a bad atmosphere which prevailed in this place, as if something very sinister had happened here. And I felt like someone was watching me. Cautiously, I pulled down my shorts, eager to be finished as fast as I could. It may sound crazy, but I was genuinely scared, and all I wanted was to get back to the safety of the road. I pulled my shorts up and made a dash for the bright spot of sunshine through the trees. Bursting back out into the open again, I'd never felt so relieved. I picked up my bicycle, but before heading off I glanced back at that clearing and once again it looked picturesque, and back to a scene of serenity.

I arrived at the Langsett Youth Hostel an hour before it opened and, as ever, my thoughts were focused on my stomach. It was good to see the village shop had so far survived the onslaught of supermarket chains and I came away with three large cheese and mayonnaise rolls, or bread cakes, as the people in the shop had corrected me, which is apparently what they call round bits of bread in these parts. I ate them on the steps of the youth hostel enjoying the afternoon sunshine, but by the time the youth hostel opened, I had sunk into extreme lethargy. Not for the first time, I wondered if these unexplained dips in energy could be linked to my consumption of dairy produce, in the same way I'd linked them to too much coffee. I openly admit my diet on this trip was atrocious. If it was cheap, vegetarian, tasty and filling, then I ate it with no thought about how it might affect my performance. I had opted for a vegetarian diet at the age of thirteen, which was all well and good when I'd lived at home, and our mother, who was an exceptional cook, made sure we all ate healthily. But when I left home, I subsisted on sandwiches, pies and too much cheese; a bit like a student but without the university bit. With regards to the dairy produce, there may have been some truth in my hunch, because sometime later, I read that our bodies need energy to digest protein and fat, and so, for someone like me, completing a long ride each day, it is best to stick with carbohydrates during the daytime and save the protein and fat for the evening meal.

I was the only guest at the youth hostel that night. My room, which I had all to myself, was only four pounds; cheaper than most campsites. I chose the top bunk bed so I could lie with my head propped up by my elbow and watch the horses playing in the field outside, and I spent the evening poring over a stack of old Cyclists' Touring Club magazines. My peace was spoilt only by the roar of traffic passing on the road outside.

DAY 19

(SECOND DAY OF REST)

For someone who has written an entire book extolling the virtues of the bicycle whilst frowning upon excessive car usage, I actually come from a family who relied pretty heavily on their motorcar. We'd lived in a semi-rural location which was served by only three rather unreliable buses each day. And so, as my sister and I grew, our parents (like many parents) morphed into our taxi service. They frequently drove me to see friends in the nearest big town (a 30-mile round trip), and when I eventually flew the nest, they insisted on delivering me home after each weekend visit (a 70-mile round trip). And once, after my father dropped my sister at Portsmouth University for the start of term (a 130-mile round trip), he arrived home in time for a phone call saying she'd been taken ill and could he come and fetch her right away? And bless his heart, he did it.

During my breakfast, I chatted to Sandra, the hostel's manager and when I told her my parents were driving up to see me, she was flabbergasted.

'Driving here from Sussex? Just for the day?' I could understand her surprise, considering the mileage was… well, let's just say it made a double trip to Portsmouth look like a breeze in comparison. But I guess travelling far and wide to visit one another is part and parcel of family life now, and the days when children always opted to stay within their hometown is largely a thing of the past. It was hard to convey how much it meant to me to see my parents arriving; those two faces more familiar than any others on this earth. That they should arrive here in this new reality I'd created, smiling and radiating normalcy, felt like a magic trick of the universe. No matter what the continent or how large the crowd, to spot those two faces was like exhaling a long-held breath.

'Ah, there you are.' Familiarity, comfort, acceptance.

Because the great weather had continued on from the last time we'd met, our idea to go for a picnic seemed a good one; however, seating me *next* to the food in the car was maybe not such a great idea. I rummaged through the picnic basket gleefully as we drove: sandwiches, crisps, pasta, salads, pies, cakes, desserts and fruit. After three weeks of the same old pre-packaged, pre-cooked food, it was more than I could bear, and I found myself reverting back to an almost childlike identity.

'Mum, can I have one of these? Pleeeease.' Just as before, both of my parents were tickled pink by how much I could eat. (And it is interesting to note that once I'd finished my ride and returned home, this voracious appetite did not instantly disappear. The constant hunger took months to subside.)

The Peak District easily earned its name as an Area of Outstanding Natural Beauty, and it was a rare advantage to be getting a sneak preview of my upcoming route. Why I then chose to sit back in the car admiring the scenery like a passive observer, rather than thinking like one who had to cycle these hills the next day is beyond me. I should have been preparing myself psychologically and making the connection between today's scenic drive and tomorrow's agony.

Up until this point, the only other cyclists I'd encountered were either shoppers or cycle tourists, so it was interesting to find the Peak District full of another genre of riders: weekend racing cyclists. These super-fit, Lycra-clad creatures drove out to convene in a car park, then headed out in groups on lightweight racing bikes. They would complete a predetermined circuit of set mileage before dumping their bikes back in their cars. I was intrigued since, for me, cycling is all about exploration at a steady pace and a proud independence from motorised transport, whereas for these guys, it was about light and fast and smashing one's personal record. It's hard to imagine two styles of the same sport being more different. Racers didn't have to carry luggage on their bicycles, they didn't have to find food and shelter at the end of a hard ride, nor, I suspect, did they venture out in inclement weather. I'm certainly not knocking their style of riding – each to their own – it was just that we were so chalk and cheese that it was hard for me to get my head around it.

At one car park, I observed one rider slapping another on the back, congratulating him in a loud voice.

'I say, Charles, great run.' I certainly wouldn't have wanted to give one of these guys a race, but I'd wager most of them probably wouldn't be willing to give my style of riding a go either.

We stopped to look around the pretty village of Holmfirth, not realising to begin with that it is the film set for the BBC television series, *Last of the Summer Wine*. On discovery of this fact, my mother and I went into full, unashamed tourist mode: taking in tea at *Sid's Café* and posing for photos upon *Nora Batty's Steps*, whilst my father lurked in the shadows looking uncomfortable and embarrassed. At the end of a hot and sunny afternoon, we returned to the youth hostel for a cup of tea with Sandra and my parents promised to visit for a bit longer next weekend: the August bank holiday. Oh, how the summer was racing by.

I was joined in the hostel lounge that evening by another cycle tourist, a middle-aged man on a charity ride of his own. Simon was a knowledgeable cyclist who had completed his own End-to-End last year, and he shared some insight into potential routes in the far north of Scotland. He advised me to take the less direct inland road, rather than my planned coastal route which, he said, would be heavy on traffic. We spent a pleasant hour conversing until we reached what felt like the natural end to the conversation (when all information and advice had been exchanged). I began gathering my things ready to head upstairs but Simon had other ideas, and he began another conversation which basically involved him repeating everything he'd already said. Perhaps he had been starved for company lately. Whilst I could empathise, on this occasion I was dying to be alone so I could mentally replay the lovely day I'd just had. I stifled a few yawns and shifted bored from one buttock to the other. After another hour, Sandra entered the lounge to say hello and I used her as the distraction I needed to flee. Only later did I understand she had been listening for some time, realised I was being held captive by my own politeness and had surreptitiously come to my rescue.

In the sanctuary of my dormitory, in which I was the only occupant again, I delved into the goodie bag my mother had left with me. It contained fresh clothes, another water bottle, some expensive, sweet-smelling hair conditioner to tackle the dreadlocks accumulating at the back of my head and another one of my favourite books. She'd also brought a stack of my mail, mainly letters from friends, but there was also a postcard from Les whom I'd met in Wells. On it, he wished me well, told me how his trip was going and ended by saying he thought I had a fantastic arse. I groaned out loud. *Why* would you write something like that on the back of a postcard where anyone could read it? (And knowing my mother, she would *definitely* have read it.) How embarrassing.

I lay on the top bunk again, pushing the window wide open so I could watch the horses in the next field. They were galloping around, bucking and snorting and playing in that frisky manner equines do when they sense the electricity of an approaching storm. The air was so humid and sticky as I wrote letters back to my friends, and I sweated as I wrote. Finally, the long-awaited breeze blew in through the open window; nature's way of warning you the rains are coming. I switched off the light and lay in the dark, listening as the thunder approached.

DAY 20

(37 MILES)

*T*he guest numbers had doubled overnight, and in the hostel kitchen, I met two men on a hiking holiday. Did I say I *met* them? Because it is actually quite hard to meet someone when your polite and cheery 'good morning' is ignored. I am always intrigued by the loosely defined etiquette here in Britain when it comes to acknowledging others. For example, on the London Underground, nobody acknowledges anyone... period, even when, or *especially* when, you find yourself in that awkward position of your nose in their armpit. Likewise, when walking through an urban environment late at night, should a stranger approach and try to strike up conversation, the general rule is to simply pretend you are deaf and carry on walking... as quickly as possible. The rules become a little more blurred in a rural setting. If you pass another human whilst out hiking, particularly where there aren't many others around, should you say hello as you pass? I think most people, myself included, consider it good manners to do so.

So, when we are talking about a youth hostel (places which pride themselves on welcoming youngsters), and there are only two people in an otherwise empty kitchen, one might consider it daft to not, in some way, acknowledge the other person's presence. As I hunted around for bowls and cutlery, I glanced surreptitiously at the two men. I don't think they'd expected me to be staying, and now they realised I was, it meant them having to keep up the charade, pretending I didn't exist, or it would be like admitting to ignoring me in the first place. I wanted to laugh at the absurdity: being in a 10-foot by 10-foot space whilst trying to ignore someone. Sometimes the reserved British nature is so tiresome. Luckily, Sandra entered the kitchen just then and without any awkwardness, began addressing us all as though we were already friends. As I made my breakfast, I could hear her discussing my bike ride with the two men, sounding as though *she* was the proud parent discussing her own daughter, and I was rather touched. The two men congratulated me on getting this far and in return, I asked them about their hike, and by the time we all left, the atmosphere had become quite convivial.

The first 20 miles across the Peak District that morning was relatively painless. The mist blocked out the sun and kept temperatures at a cool twenty degrees Celsius. It also hid the hills. I passed a sign that welcomed me into West Yorkshire: *Working for Peace* it declared, but peace with whom it didn't say, Lancashire perhaps? Freewheeling into the next valley, I arrived once more at Holmfirth, this time pausing only to buy a loaf of bread. Now a Monday morning and with weekend tourists gone, the place seemed ordinary again, as if it were disguising its celebrity status.

It had been a valiant start to the day, but as the clock struck ten, my probation period in the Peaks was up. The mist cleared, the temperature spiked at just south of thirty degrees and by the third torturously steep hill of the morning, I understood all too horribly clearly what I was faced with. Those hills and valleys that looked so beautiful in the car yesterday were today *killing me*. My legs turned to jelly and my lungs burned. The morning consisted of short sharp bursts: struggling to cycle up each hill or getting off to push, which was almost as difficult. Downhill was no fun either because, I kid you not, some hills were almost vertical. Down I would come, hanging onto my brakes for dear life, hands aching. I found myself thinking wistfully about those super-slim racing bikes I'd seen yesterday and understanding now why they preferred to ride *sans* panniers.

Hang on a sec… doesn't this sound all too horribly familiar? Familiar as in: Cornwall and Devon? Only now it was worse, for now, after 600 miles, I'd have expected to be tackling these hills with proficiency and ease, but nothing could have prepared me for this.

As I was struggling to push my bike up my fifth near-vertical climb of the morning, I heard the *vroom* of a motorbike approaching six o'clock. Blinded by the sweat in my eyes, I was totally unprepared as the biker came alongside me and blared the horn. I jumped in surprise and my bicycle fell to the ground.

'Fucking *idiot...*' I began and then, to my amazement, I saw it was Slalom Steve from the Calverton armed robbery.

'I don't believe it,' I said.

'I don't believe it,' he concurred, and we stood there for a second, both panting and sweating, me in my sunhat and him in his leathers. I don't know who was hotter, but we agreed we should try to find somewhere a little cooler to catch up.

I set out first but had not got far when I heard Steve's frantic shouts for help, and when I turned back, there was his motorbike, on its side in the road. Now, I'm led to believe that dropping a motorbike whilst manoeuvring at slow speeds is somewhat embarrassing for an experienced biker (and hence why Steve's real identity will forever be kept secret), but knowing just how heavy *my* bicycle is with all its panniers, I could sympathise. The weight of a loaded 1200cc motorbike is immense, and unless you're Arnold Schwarzenegger, it's going to need two people to pick it back up. A sudden window of opportunity flashed through my mind... *if* I dared to ask.

'So,' I ventured as I helped Steve heave his motorbike upright, 'as I've helped you out, how do you fancy returning the favour?' and I asked my new friend if he'd consider becoming my backup rider for the day. This isn't quite as audacious as it sounds. My gut feeling told me that, having unexpectedly met again, it was unlikely we would just wave goodbye after a five-minute catch-up. (And Steve's first question had been, which campsite was I headed for, rather implying we would be hanging out together again later.) Thankfully, he willingly accepted my proposal, and five minutes later, all my heaviest items were strapped to his machine. Without a tent, sleeping bag, books, gas stove or tins of food, my bicycle became magically lighter and now I was ready to do battle with the hills.

Today's route was a labyrinth of back roads that were a navigational nightmare (again, just like Cornwall), but I thought they would still be preferable to using the main road through Huddersfield. Steve's help couldn't have come along at a more valuable hour. With 110 horsepower at his fingertips, at each poorly signposted junction, he would go ahead to scout out the route whilst I waited in the shade for him to report back. This saved me untold miles where I'd no doubt have sped off down the wrong road a few times before struggling back up again in order to take the other turning. But, despite the luxury of a backup vehicle, the day was as long as it was painful, with sweltering heat and bodily pains my constant companions. Even with Steve's help, I still got lost, *a lot*. In hindsight, I now wish I'd stuck to the main road and braved the Huddersfield traffic. Rule number nineteen of cycle touring: as a rule of thumb, main roads tend to be built *around* the hills or mountains, whereas back lanes traverse up and down each and every one. It took me the rest of the afternoon to cover a mere 17 miles, making my average speed less than 5 miles an hour. Talk about frustration. I think Steve must have wished a few times he'd just left his motorbike laying in the road! But his patience was saintly and his dedication to helping me unequivocal. It was a day when that shadow of doubt I thought I'd left behind in Cornwall came creeping back into the periphery of my mind, crushing my spirit. *What the hell are you doing this for? You'll never make it and you're certainly not enjoying yourself. Why not quit now and save yourself all this pain?*

What a relief to reach Sowerby Bridge. It was like stumbling through the door that released me from the maze. Now I had only to follow this one road and the hell would be over. The humidity, which had been building up all afternoon like steam in a pressure cooker, finally broke when I pulled over at a shop. Luckily, I was able to take shelter under the canvas awning and watch, mesmerized, as the thunder and lightning crashed overhead, whilst deep puddles appeared in the road within minutes. But the pageant did not last long and after five-minutes the deluge slowed to a trickle and stopped. And by the time I'd finished my chocolate bar, the sun was out again and I was cycling on in temperatures that were as hot as if the rains had never come. (When I met up with Steve just 2 miles further up the road, he had asked me, what rain?) Those final 5 miles to Hebden Bridge only took me twenty minutes; it was the fastest I'd moved all day. Now this was the kind of road I'd been dreaming of all day: one simple flat road that required no map-reading, and I kicked myself when I realised it was the very road I'd gone to all that trouble to avoid. (I refer you back to rule number nineteen.)

But the hell wasn't quite over. Steve's last instructions to me were to head for a campsite located 2 miles north of Hebden Bridge, and consulting my map, I could see it meant traversing another one of those pesky 1:4 gradients and so I resigned myself to walking. About halfway up the road, I passed through the village of Heptonstall. It was a pretty West Yorkshire village with original stone setts paving its streets and cast-iron gas lamps. But all I could think was, *who in the hell would want to live at the top of such a steep hill?* But as a dozen cars and then a bus passed me with all occupants' eyes on the poor sod with the pushbike, I had my own question answered: this was the age of the combustion engine and it was here to stay. Rather than wallowing in self-pity, I instead thought about the working horses which would have once pulled carts up this same lane. Lost in reverie, the pain and the traffic faded to the sweet pleasure of daydreaming as I imagined myself in a bygone era, when four-legged friends were kings of the road. But I would have been a considerate owner, who would have walked with her horse up the steepest hills. I thought then about the novel *Black Beauty*. Many people mistakenly believe it to be a children's novel, but the author, Anne Sewell, wrote this book to educate her fellow Victorians on how to better treat working horses. Much cruelty went on in those days, often due to ignorance, and in a small victory, it was thanks to her writing that the cruel draw rein was finally made illegal in the UK.

During today's 40 miles of excessive heat and hills, I may have felt like I was dying, but if I had, then I'd surely died and gone to heaven... for this campsite was paradise. Positioned on the side of a small but beautiful valley, I lay down in the cool grass and felt instantly soothed by the sounds of the river rushing below and the sheep bleating on the hillside opposite. I wondered: *is this wonderful place my reward for plodding on all day, despite wanting to stop early numerous times? And if I had quit, what sort of place would I have found to spend the night?* I bet it wouldn't be a patch on this little Eden.

Interestingly, in the years that followed, I would often

remember this moment; the image captured in my memory with the precision of a photograph. Time and again, I would recall not just the beauty of the place, but also how I'd felt as I'd lain there, and it became my go-to happy memory. In that moment, I'd finally started to really believe in myself, and to like myself for who I was. And in the future, if ever life dealt me with a blow, I would return to that moment in my mind, like an antithesis to the bad times; a reminder of how magical life could be.

Once my wingman and I had both showered, we strolled back into Heptonstall for a glass of beer, but none of the pubs were offering what we really wanted, which was a hearty meal, and so we took a taxi to Hebden Bridge in order to find somewhere to sate our appetites. It was after dark when the taxi dropped us back at the campsite and we sat in the entrance of Steve's tent, drinking and laughing until he dozed off. But I couldn't sleep. This was a trait which began during my depressed teenager years, when on the rare occasion I'd had a good day, I wanted to prolong it by staying awake as long as possible. Kind of like a child who can't sleep in anticipation of an exciting day, but in reverse. I wrapped my sleeping bag around me and sat listening to the rushing of the river somewhere in the darkness and recalling the triumphs of my day. I must have dozed off eventually because when I stirred it was four in the morning. I was still slumped in the tent entrance with spilt beer soaked into my sleeping bag and I was badly dehydrated. I found the water canister and drained the contents, but this then led to a full bladder. Three times I had to unzip the door to go to the bathroom, and on each occasion, the temperature inside the tent plummeted to that of a refrigerator. It was the first time I'd noticed a change in night time temperatures, from summer humidity to autumn chill, and it was another indicator of just how far north I'd come.

Steve and I awoke to the blaring of trumpets signalling our hangovers. I sat squinting in the bright morning sunshine, mug of tea in hand, and silently craved the one thing I knew would make me feel better: a fry-up. And then an extraordinary thing happened... someone *did* make me a fry-up. Last night, after a few pints, I had foolishly tried to explain to Steve the whole "died and gone to heaven" analogy but, judging by his raised eyebrows, I realised I shouldn't have bothered. But when Julie in the neighbouring caravan offered to make us a fried breakfast each, even he had to admit that this place had some connotations of heaven.

DAY 21

(29 MILES)

I set off fully laden once more. I thanked Steve for his assistance, but I got the impression he'd rather enjoyed himself. It was certainly an unusual story to tell his mates down the pub. Steve had told me about the motorcyclists' bed and breakfast he ran back home and I was invited to go and stay anytime as an honorary, non-motorised guest. As I was about to stray over his home turf anyway, we made plans to rendezvous the day after tomorrow and as I rode away, I caught myself feeling excited about the prospect.

Given that today I'd be accompanied by the three H's – hills, heat and hangover – I decided 30 miles was quite far enough and I headed for the village of Slaidburn where I knew there to be a youth hostel. Today's route was mercifully simple, almost in a straight line and would take me across hills which, after weeks of sun, had faded from lush green to yellowy brown. Without a detailed map, it was difficult to decipher exactly where I was at. Was I in the Pennines or the Peak District? The Bowland Fells or the Yorkshire Dales? But the land didn't care for such artificial boundaries or human labels, and was unwavering in its geographical features: wild heather moors, dry stone walls, river valleys and hilly plateaus. Wherever I was at, it was all beautiful to me.

There was something mesmeric about cycling across a landscape where everything, including myself, blurred into a heat haze, and I paused to take a photograph. Looking along the road ahead, I saw nothing and no one, not even a sheep. I looked back and again saw nothing but the dry grass, incessant hills and a shimmering heat haze wavering above the tarmac. I suddenly became aware just how much I wanted to flop into a ditch and sleep for the rest of the day. But my mind was set on my daily goal and if I had learnt anything yesterday, it was that stopping sooner than I meant to reaped no rewards.

As the sun tried its hardest to frazzle my skin, I mulled over everything that had happened to me over the last twenty days. I thought I'd remember it all in a neat and orderly timeline, but it seems memory doesn't work that way. I found I could only recall the most prominent events (mostly in the West Country), and the rest were just sketchy memories. In fact, I could almost believe I'd skipped straight from Somerset to Yorkshire without all the bits in between and it was only much later that I realised why: in the beginning was the West Country. With its terrible weather and tough hills, it would be hard to forget such times. But once I'd built up my fitness and learnt the ropes of cycle touring, I had a much easier time of it through the Midlands, where the traffic was more challenging than the physical riding. But just when I was beginning to think, *so, cycle touring… I've got this; it's a cinch,* then boom: along came Yorkshire, my biggest challenge yet. And everything I thought I knew about cycle touring was turned on its head. I consoled myself with the thought that once I was through here, things would be easier. Next up was the Lake District, with its simplified road network and after that, Scotland. Now Scotland was a place I was eager to reach, for I had cycled in the Highlands many times and I was sure there would be no nasty surprises… If I could only make it over these never-ending, goddammit, hills.

I want to pause here because I'm sure you're now thinking: *the Lake District and Scotland? Duh, doesn't she know they are full of hills too?* So, to clear this up quickly then, yes, of course I *knew.* But for me, it is the *type* of hill that can make or break a cyclist. Those I encountered in the south-west and north-west were short and steep. These are the ones I struggled with, since the downs didn't last long enough for me to recover sufficiently before pedalling up the next one. They were exhausting and demoralising and an entire day on this type of topography ensured my average speed stayed in the low single digits. But in the Scottish Highlands, I'd always found that when it came to cycling over a mountain pass, whilst it was still hard going, it was at least possible to establish a pace I could maintain over the miles (even if it was only 5mph). This compared markedly to the constant changing of pace on the smaller, steeper hills: rocketing downhill one minute then crawling slowly up the next. There was no chance of establishing a rhythm here, and for me, it was far more exhausting in the long run. (And, of course, the bonus on reaching the top of a mountain pass is the rewarding run down the other side.) Give me a mountain pass over a series of shorter hills any day.

The small hamlet of Roughlee was memorable for a kind, elderly local man, who came over as I pored over my maps.

'Can I help tha, lass?' He took the map in his wrinkled hands and studied the line I'd drawn across it, and after a moment's consideration he advised me to take a 2-mile detour instead. This, he said, would save me toiling up and over a particularly steep hill. I thanked the man and followed his advice. And sure enough, when I got around the other side and saw just what a steep (and unnecessary) hill he had saved me from, I whispered thank you again. It was my second day struggling across the Pennines/Peaks/Bowland Fells/Yorkshire Dales, and I swore that if I ever had children, I would *never* bring them here on a cycling holiday.

It was a day for falling into conversation. I met a young woman, Mary-Anne, out hiking and we stopped to talk. She pointed to a towering mass in the distance and said it was her favourite hill and she was off to hike up it for the sixth time this year. It looked more like a mountain to me and I really hoped the road snaked around it. As she seemed to be enjoying her solo hike, I was a little surprised that she asked me if I got bored or lonely on my own. Alone, alone, alone… It was the one word which cropped up again and again. But I didn't think of myself as being alone; it was more that I was *enjoying the solitude*. Without wanting to sound too new-age about it, I've always believed a person can benefit from short spells of solitude. I looked upon it as a time to gather one's thoughts and reflect on life. Moreover, I have found that whenever I've travelled solo, it has not only helped me to build up my confidence, but in a final irony, it's also the best way I know to meet new people.

All this had been demonstrated to me earlier that year when I'd chosen to solo backpack around Europe, even though the very thought of it made my knees knock together in fear. To start with, I had begun in places I was familiar with, such as France and Germany, but I also wanted to visit other places and after some deliberation, I headed for Poland. I am sorry to say that, as an inexperienced traveller, I found the bureaucracy of post-communist Warsaw (at the time in its infancy of independence) was a challenge too far for me. After wandering around all day, failing to find anywhere to stay, or to find anyone who would cash my traveller's cheques, or to make my attempts at Polish understood, I once again found myself back at the railway station. With the hustlers and perverts closing in on my bag and backside respectively, I lost my nerve and fled, on the first train back to (what felt like) orderly and familiar Germany.

In my haste to leave, I mistakenly hopped onto a regional service that took fifteen hours to reach Frankfurt. The carriage was hot and crushingly busy and I slunk in the corner feeling apprehensive. But as the train clickety-clacked its way out of the capital, the inhospitable streets of Warsaw were left behind and the true warmth of the Polish character was finally revealed to me. The strangers in my coach talked convivially to each another and shared out their food, and a few turned their attentions on me. They didn't care that I couldn't speak their language (we communicated using pidgin German). They seemed concerned for this young foreign woman travelling alone and offered me some of their food and drink. As the hours went by, I stared out of the window at the countryside passing. I thought how surreal this situation would have seemed to me only months before: I had just turned nineteen, I was travelling alone in a far-off land, surrounded by strangers I couldn't speak to, and no one back home knew where I was or what I was doing. But it was okay because I felt safe and at peace. The whole situation was very humbling. For the first time, I noticed a new door opening. One which was previously locked by my fear of the unknown, and I vowed to make full use of it.

But if the universe was on a mission to teach me a few things that day, it wasn't done yet. As the hours went by, more and more people alighted at their stops until seven hours later, I had the coach to myself. I took off my shoes, lay down on the seats and dozed off. Sometime later, the train jolted to a halt in the middle of nowhere and I awoke with a start. Doors slammed and heavy footsteps filled the corridors. I barely had time to raise my head when the carriage door crashed open and about a dozen men in military uniform piled in. I was immediately fearful. Would I have to spend all night alone with this rowdy bunch? Could I move to another part of the train? (Alas, it was an old train without interconnected coaches.) I tried creating a psychological barrier by tucking myself into the corner and hoping I'd go unnoticed. Fat chance. Before long, the soldiers all turned their attentions my way, firing incomprehensible questions at me. In an effort to appear confident and not how I really felt (which was terrified), I fired questions back at them. Did they speak English? No. German perhaps? No. Okay, so just Polish then? Again, surprisingly, no. The lead guy kept repeating a word to me: *Russkiy,* and eventually the penny dropped. These guys were Russian military.

Being able to finally communicate *something* was like dropping a coin into a slot that unlocked a whole new perspective: one where fear and mistrust fell away to fascination. They'd never met an English person before, nor I Russian, and avid attempts were made at communication. With no common tongue, we relied on sign language, drawings, and maps from my guide book to convey where we were from, where we were going and how many people were in our respective families. It is astonishing how much can be communicated in this way. There was a lot of laughter and the guys even managed to convey how the short bald fellow was the butt of their jokes because he spent so much time on the lavatory. Their commander pointed at me and said, 'You... Rocky.' And he flexed his muscles like Sylvester Stallone and then held up a finger to denote that I was solo and that he thought I was brave and strong to be travelling alone. As we approached the German border, they alighted from the train, but before they went, they ripped their badges from their uniforms and presented them to me as something to remember them by.

As the train rumbled on, I let out a long, held breath. Those twelve hours had been like a crash course in confidence-building: gain it or lose, sink or swim. I'd arrived in Warsaw frightened of my own shadow. But as time and again my fears were proved to live only in my imagination, another self-limiting belief fell away, and I emerged in Frankfurt a lot more confident and bit more worldly-wise. I mention all this here because it is my firm belief that none of this would have occurred (or at least, not felt so intensely) if I'd been travelling with a companion. People engaged with me more when I travelled alone and as such, you'll rarely hear me complain that solo travel is lonely or boring. (And yes, I did return to Warsaw a month later and this time I stayed a while.)

*

In a Lancashire village, I was practically ambushed by a group of locals who fired questions at me and then shovelled great handfuls of spare change into my collection tin, blowing me away with their enthusiasm and generosity. And yet, only minutes later, I witnessed the opposite end of the spectrum, when a café proprietor of the same village refused to fill my water bottle. The man told me that the local authorities had placed all residents on to a water metering system, much to his chagrin, and they were now charged per cubic metre used rather than at a fixed price. He said, because of that, he couldn't afford to fill my bottle up unless I bought something first.

Water metering was a subject I am familiar with since, in the last three years, my home county in the south-east of England had seen one too many hot, dry summers and cool, dry winters. We had been in the middle of an official hydrological drought for some years now and this idea of water meters had been bandied around for quite some time, although nothing official had yet been decided. But why would they impose metering up here in the cooler, wetter climes of the north-west of England? Was there a drought in Lancashire? I asked the café owner. He gave a grunt that could have meant either yes or no. I wondered if the authorities were using this area as a sort of testing ground, before deciding whether or not to roll water meters out across the rest of the country. Either way, I wasn't going to get my bottle filled up here. I was too embarrassed to say, but I only had seventeen pence left in my purse and I doubted there was a cash machine in such a small village. I felt he was being a touch pedantic; it would have cost him less than a penny to fill my bottle for me and he could see I was on a charity ride. (I thought of all those campsite owners who'd waived their fees for me in support.) So, I shrugged and left, but for the rest of the afternoon I found myself surreptitiously watching as people watered their gardens or hosed down their cars, whilst liberal doses of water ran off wastefully across the road. They didn't seem particularly concerned with the cost.

Seven miles before Slaidburn, a refreshing shower fell, signalling an end to the oppressive heat. I propped my bicycle up against a field gate and stood in the rain until goosebumps covered my arms. At the top of the next hill, I thought I might catch a glimpse of Slaidburn, but as far as my eyes could see there was nothing even remotely manmade on the now mist-covered hills, not even a barn. At times like these, when I was getting a bit weary, it always helped me to play a psychological game with myself. I would turn my bike computer upside down so I couldn't read it and then say to myself, *okay, that last signpost said there was still umpteen miles left to go*, and I'd convince myself I'd only come three or four miles since then. At some point, I knew I'd pass another sign with the correct mileage on it, and of course, it would be a lot less than the distance I'd told myself it was. The whole point of this strange exercise is that I've found there's nothing better than thinking you still have 10 miles left to do, then discovering it is really only about three. The joy always gave me a surge of energy, which then helped to get me through those final few tiring miles.

Slaidburn was a picturesque village and so well hidden amongst the hills, it felt a bit like stumbling across hidden treasure. But when I went into the local shop to buy provisions and was more or less blanked by the server, I quickly understood it to be a tourist hotspot. At the youth hostel, I dumped my belongings on my bed and took a much-needed shower, washing away the sweat, grime and booze from the last few days. Then I went to the kitchen and made myself some pasta with tomato sauce and cheese; the *de rigueur* of youth hostel meals. Unlike the Langsett youth hostel, this one was busy with plenty of people to chat to. I was thoroughly impressed with one guy, who was able to deduce which county people were from by their accents and on occasion, he even guessed the exact town. (If you are wondering why I was so impressed by this, then let me tell you how I once confused an Irishman for a Canadian and a Welshman for a Norwegian. What can I say; accent identification is *not* my strong point.)

I noticed people were smirking at my plate, piled high with food. I thought it was a bit rude but then a woman asked me how far I was cycling each day. I assumed she'd seen me arriving on my bicycle but then she told me that this youth hostel was located on the most direct and popular End-to-End route, and therefore, if anyone was seen stuffing their face, it was generally assumed they were doing the challenge. I laughed. She also mentioned we were 400 miles from Land's End. I didn't tell her I'd clocked up 650 by this point.

Then I met Ian, a Scottish lad about my age. He told me he was hoping to make John O'Groats during his two-week summer vacation. He said he'd started out with a companion but they'd quit only two days into the Cornish roads. I found myself nodding knowingly. Ian said that in order to finish the End-to-End in two weeks, he had to cycle 60 to 80 miles each day. My jaw dropped open: 60 to 80 miles? Good grief. I was pretty sure I wouldn't be capable of imposing such a schedule on myself, no matter how fit I was. And my mind flashed on all the serendipitous meetings I might have missed out on if I'd been unable to stop whenever I wanted. Eighty miles a day? No wonder his companion had thrown in the towel in Cornwall; I probably would have too. During our conversation, I was shocked to hear Ian say that, since setting out, he hadn't seen one *single* thing he thought worth photographing. But as I thought about it more, it made a kind of sense. Pushing himself as he was, he wouldn't get a chance to appreciate either the places or the people. Restricted by a deadline, the whole experience was reduced to nothing more than an endurance test: head down, cover the mileage. Maybe that's the way some people like it, but for Ian, he said he couldn't wait for it to be over, which kind of proves the point. To have this opportunity to see so much but to not *really* see it; it was such a shame for him. With all these revelations swimming around my brain, I wished Ian all the best and went upstairs to my dormitory.

There were ten beds but only two were occupied, mine and one other, and I made myself at home. I was really looking forward to a relaxing evening: writing postcards, reading my book and wallowing between clean sheets. But the moment the other female occupant entered the room, I knew immediately that all chances of relaxation were over… I liked to think of myself as someone who can get along with almost anyone, but even I was unsettled by the way this young woman breezed into the room and *immediately* began sharing with me (a total stranger) the graphic details of her troubled relationship with her parents. I sat with my now redundant book in my hands and listened nervously to this aggressive diatribe. I kept nodding my head and making appropriate uh-huh noises, but what I was actually thinking was, *I've had two days' hard riding in a heatwave… please, God, just fuck off and leave me alone*. But there was no chance. Then this woman, (I'll call her Julie) told me she'd been kicked out of this particular youth hostel twice already for using drugs, returning each time under a different name. That in itself didn't bother me. What bothered me was her aggressive and volatile nature. I felt scared of her. Twenty-one-year-old me was lacking the confidence to deal with this situation. These days, I would have told Julie to leave me alone, or at the very least, I'd have gone and asked to be moved to another dormitory. Instead, I was as patient and polite as I knew how to be, and even played a game of chess with her at her request... as if everything about this situation was perfectly normal. But it wasn't. Something was terribly wrong.

The evening ended abruptly when, without warning or consultation, Julie snapped off the main light, plunging our dormitory into darkness. I had been in mid-sentence writing my diary, but decided not to challenge it. I sighed, put down my pen, pulled up my sheets and politely called out, 'Sleep well,' into the darkness. It was met by a stony silence. About twenty minutes later, on the verge of drifting off myself, I was suddenly snapped back into full consciousness by a hostile voice raging through the darkness.

'What did you mean by that?'

Unsure whether Julie was talking to me or to herself, I chose to ignore her, but her voice came back in an alarmingly threatening tone.

'What the fucking hell did you say that like that for?'

Puzzled beyond belief how anyone could misinterpret a simple 'sleep well' as something sinister, I adopted a gobsmacked silence. But this paranoid bitch was determined to get an answer out of me and I was now receiving threats that she would 'give me a good hiding.' I heard Julie leap from her bunk and storm over to flick the light back on. I, in the meantime, sprang up too, as I had no intention of being attacked whilst lying in bed. I couldn't believe what was happening. I faced Julie, trying to remain calm despite my racing pulse, and calmly explained what I had meant by 'sleep well.'

Finally, she seemed satisfied by my explanation and retreated back to her corner, though not without warning me to: 'Keep it shut from now on.' I lay back down in the dark, my heart beating wildly and stupidly hoped it was over. I must have been too nervous to see what was coming next.

Two minutes later, the light was on again and this time Julie was screaming something about me stealing her soap and toothpaste. Again, I pacified her. But when the lights flicked on for a third time and she began rifling through my bags and making threats to 'Lay me out' I couldn't take it anymore and fled downstairs. Seconds later, I was banging on the door marked "hostel warden". Through a combination of anger and tears, I relayed to George the commotion that had just occurred. He listened compassionately but didn't seem at all surprised.

'Stupid woman,' came his reply. '*I* cleared her toiletries out of the communal bathroom earlier. I'd told her three times already not to leave them there.' He said he'd sort this out, and back up the stairs we went.

As quickly as I could, I gathered all my clothes and panniers together, only stopping to yell back at Julie now that I had George to protect me. (Later, he said he'd only felt brave enough to tackle her since I was there to cover *his* back.) Downstairs, I was given a private room and a glass of brandy to calm my nerves. George confessed to needing a shot himself most evenings. His hope that running a youth hostel in this rural idyll would cure him of anxieties had not panned out, and his nerves had grown steadily worse since he'd arrived. I smiled wryly, for I could see a similar irony in it for me too… I had wandered through inner cities and camped alone in semi-deserted spots, and never once had I smelt even a hint of trouble. I stay the night in what is thought to be a safe family establishment and end up meeting a terrifying individual who threatened to beat me to a pulp as I lay sleeping in my bed. As we finished our brandies, we heard Julie storm out through the hostel's front door, slamming it so hard behind her that all the windows shook. Heaven only knows where she was headed this late at night, but I don't know who was most relieved she was gone, myself or George?

DAY 22

(16 MILES)

*W*hilst breakfasting on leftover pasta, I was questioned repeatedly about the night's events: news which had spread like wildfire amongst the other guests. I didn't appreciate having to relive the scary (and somewhat humiliating) events ten times over, but I was momentarily comforted by the words of a little girl. She confided in me how glad she was the strange woman had gone, as she'd felt frightened of her. Well, that made two of us.

It was a relief to get into the cool air outside. I took a few deep breaths and began loading my bike, but my dour mood was made worse by the resident Mr Know-it-all. I spotted him standing a few yards away. He was staring rudely and although he didn't say anything, I could tell he was dying to.

After a few minutes of feeling his eyes boring into my back, I could bear it no longer and I turned my glare upon him.

'What?' I snapped.

'You're a bit overloaded, aren't you? Why don't you carry less?'

(I'm on a month's cycle and camping tour and am only carrying the bare essentials.)

'Why don't you get yourself a lighter tent? They're only a couple of hundred pounds.'

(I don't have a couple of hundred pounds.)

'Your saddle's a bit low, you should be able to stretch out your leg and level your ankle bone with the pedal.'

(I can.)

'Your bicycle frame's too big for you.'

(It's not.)

'Why don't you buy yourself a new bike?'

That was the final straw. Without another word, I swung my leg over my saddle and rode away, raising my middle finger at Mr Know-it-all's back as I went. I would not be in a hurry to return to Slaidburn.

This was to be my third and final day struggling across the Pennines/Peaks/Bowland Fells/Yorkshire Dales. Before I'd left Slaidburn, I'd asked George if the road to Bentham was a particularly hilly one, and he had asked if by hilly, did I mean 'was it very up and down?'

'Well, yes,' I'd replied. To which he'd said, in that case, no, it wasn't hilly… it was just one long up, all the way. Ho-hum.

I was happy the heatwave had ended, but it had been replaced by a gloom to match my mood, and a heavy drizzle fell. I found myself cycling warily around the narrow lanes, keeping an eye out for any movement in the hedgerows. Perhaps I was being paranoid but I had a genuine fear that Julie might be waiting for me somewhere, keen to exact retribution for her swift departure from the hostel last night. Her voice was still etched into my brain. *I'm gonna get you for having me slung out of the youth hostel.* Besides, it didn't make any sense; where could she have gone, leaving in the middle of the night like that with no car and no public transport? The chances of her still hanging around were not beyond the realms of possibility. The warden had been right, of course, and for 13 miles I went at a snail's pace up the steadily rising road. In another time and place, I might have enjoyed this ride. The road ran through a remote valley with high cliffs lining either side and, save for the sheep, it was deserted as far as the eye could see. But I wasn't happy. The towering cliffs made me feel vulnerable and hemmed in, and every time the wind blew through the crags, which was often, it made an eerie wailing noise. I regularly had to get off to push up the ascent, even though the road didn't look particularly steep. In fact, it appeared flat in places, so I couldn't understand why I was struggling so much.

It is time to relay rule number twenty of cycle touring: gradients can be very deceptive. This is an important point to note since *not* recognising it can lead to a lot of frustration. What I was experiencing that morning was an optical illusion known in the cycle racing world as *false flats*. False flats come after a particularly steep ascent, when the road *looks* as though it has flattened out, but really, it is still going uphill, only not as steeply as it was. The upshot of this is you'll think you've reached the top of the hill when you haven't, and you'll start wondering why the hell it isn't getting any easier. A good tip here is to stop and look behind you, and that will give you a truer picture of the gradient. I'm told there is also a more welcome optical illusion known as a gravity hill, where what appears to be a slight uphill is in fact downhill. This will result in the feeling you are magically freewheeling *up* the road. Sadly, I've yet to come across one myself.

So, anyway, because I hadn't realised that I was encountering all these false flats, I grew fed up because no matter how far I'd come, I never seemed to get any fitter. Mr Morale, meet Mr Floor. In all honesty, though, if Bentham had been 13 miles of all-out down, I still wouldn't have enjoyed myself. Nothing could erase the drama of last night from my head, which played over and over like a videotape on a loop. Being threatened with violence whilst laid in bed would surely leave anyone feeling despondent. I was especially sad about how this might affect my ride; whilst I stand by what I'd said previously about *most* people not meaning you harm, I wasn't going to get away totally unscathed. There would be an inevitable shake-up in my world: a displacement of my firm grounding. What I didn't know was that this trust in strangers would be tested far sooner than I'd bargained for.

With a bit more effort, I finally made it to the top of the pass and I stood panting for breath and gazing at the 360-degree views. But there was barely time to marvel, for in the distance I spied a strange vision that made me rub my eyes in disbelief. It appeared that a Knight of the Round Table was heading towards me on a big black horse. As the vision came nearer, I deduced that horse and rider were indeed real, and when they were close enough, the rider called out, 'Hail there, fair maiden,' and he introduced himself as Sir Hellingwell and his gallant steed as Oliver.

Actually, the knight's real name was David and they were homeward bound after a trekking holiday around the castles of Cumbria. They'd cut their trip short when the unexpected heatwave became too uncomfortable for them both. David explained he'd slept in hedges or barns, whilst Oliver was stabled and fed by the kindness of local farmers along the way. We chatted for a while and David admitted he was stuck in a different century. He asked if I too was a traveller, so I proudly introduced him to my steed, Loopy Loo, and we exchanged tales of being on the road. He lowered his voice and speaking softly, he confided in me how he'd realised long ago that he lived in a world all of his own and asked, with all seriousness, if I did too. I ummed and aahed and said, 'Well, maybe just a little.'

Still shell-shocked from last night, my usual faith and confidence was shattered. This extraordinary meeting with an unusual character would normally have been a source of great excitement for me. Now, though, I found I had to keep taking a step backwards to leave an unusually large gap between the two of us. It was almost as if I expected David to bludgeon me over the head at any minute. I need not have worried, though; he was perfectly safe and if I am honest, probably one of the sanest people I met on my entire trip. Being a horse lover and a hopeless romantic myself, I was quite envious of his lifestyle. It was the sort of trip I'd dreamed about as a girl; still do, come to think of it. When David announced his way of life was an objection to the motorcar and to modern life in general, I felt nothing short of admiration for him, and I knew we were definitely on the same wavelength.

David let me have a quick ride on Oliver (who looked thoroughly unimpressed when I tried to point him in the opposite direction to home). They hailed from Sowerby Bridge, which I had passed through in that torrential downpour a few days earlier, and I was given an open invitation to visit any time. We shook hands and the eye contact between us made words unnecessary. There was a mutual understanding that passed like lightning, backwards and forwards. A sense of recognition: *I know you and I know your way. Good luck to you.* I waved to Sir Hellingwell and Oliver until they were out of sight and then I turned to face in the direction of Bentham. I felt on top of the world, and as well I might, for I'd made it 1,300 feet to the top of this very long road, concluding what I believed was the most difficult part of my trip. I had also met a wonderful character who'd been sent by the hand of fate to reinstate my faith in people. All I had left to do now was to enjoy three glorious miles of downhill, before taking my first proper break, in the company of my new friend Steve.

*

Studying the timetable at Bentham station, I would once have felt dismayed to learn I had a two-and-a- half-hour wait for the next train, but these days I was well into the swing of my new nomadic lifestyle and simply saw it as a time to relax. I ate the final bit of last night's pasta and then settled back on a bench in the sunshine and got out my diary.

What with my parents' visit and then meeting Steve again, and then the Julie saga last night, I had a lot of writing to catch up on. But just as I poised my pen over the page, out of the corner of my eye I spied a shady-looking character enter the otherwise deserted station.

Oh, cripes, I thought nervously, *who's this now?* The old man pootled about the station, clearing twigs and sweeping leaves. By his actions, one might assume he was the gardener, but he wasn't wearing any form of railway uniform. I felt him surreptitiously watching me, which kept my nerves on edge. As he didn't look as though he would go away anytime soon, I thought it would be best to try to ignore him. Fat chance. The second I put pen to paper and... *pounce* ... he was sat right next to me.

'You're not from around here, are you?'

Never have I been subjected to sit and listen to such an enormous pile of drivel in my *entire* life. By the end of the first hour, once the conversation had progressed to how he thought the royal family had been taken over by aliens, I found myself seriously contemplating cycling to Skipton just to get away from him. I looked at the station clock and sighed. My instincts had been correct: he wasn't the gardener. He did odd jobs around the place because there was no one to tell him not to, and pretending to be the gardener meant he could be on the scene in a jiffy when some poor unsuspecting traveller appeared. I assumed he kept a regular watch on the station from his house; how else could he have appeared so quickly after my arrival?

What felt like eons later, I arrived in Skipton. With half an hour before Steve arrived, I found a bench where I could finish writing my diary. Again, fat chance. Another nosy parker sat down next to me.

'You're not from around here, are you?' Later, over a round of beers, I relayed all this to Steve and he laughed his socks off.

'People around here saw you writing and probably thought you were a journalist,' which helped to explain all the sudden interest in me.

DAY 23 & 24

(THIRD & FOURTH DAY OF REST)

*I*t's hard to pinpoint the most enjoyable part of my mini-break. It may have been sleeping in a proper bed with real pillows and sheets (and was why I slept in past ten o'clock *both* mornings). Equally fantastic, though, was access to a washing machine. But I think my favourite part was wandering around the town exploring all the shops and hostelries. None of this would have been possible without Steve's generosity. I realised his home was more of a casual bed and breakfast affair, where out-of-town biker acquaintances could come and stay for a nominal fee. Downstairs he'd built a bar in the living room and, judging by all the handpumps, I guessed most of his regular guests were beer drinkers. Myself, I prefer something a little sweeter and I discovered an as yet unopened bottle of Baileys Irish Cream at the back of the drinks cupboard and kept it company of an evening. I only meant to stay one full day, but when Steve suggested a ride out to the Lake District on the back of his motorbike, I couldn't resist, and I ended up staying another. But I probably wouldn't have been so keen if I'd realised the psychological consequences of all this recreational time.

DAY 25

(25 MILES)

Staying in one place long enough that it starts to feel like home was the polar opposite of what this journey should have been about. Sure, I was hoping to identify a few places along the way I might revisit afterwards, with an eye to staying permanently. But that was for later... this was now, and now meant keeping up the momentum and mental discipline in order to get to John O'Groats which, incidentally, was still 600 miles away. (That's the same distance I'd already ridden *all* over again.) Why then, I wondered, had I allowed myself to get so comfortable in Skipton, and start to think of it as though I was already home?

I guessed it had something to do with feeling so rootless these last few years. Since I'd left home, I'd changed jobs a number of times and even when I'd found an employer

I wanted to stick with, *they'd* changed my work location frequently. Coupled with the choppy time I'd had in my personal life, this meant having to move frequently; not only between homes but towns as well. I went from a shared house to a crummy bedsit, then on to a friend's sofa. From there I spent the winter in a dilapidated caravan before moving back into another shared house. But not one of these places had felt remotely homely or like somewhere I even *wanted* to live. Either the landlord was an arsehole, or I was escaping a bad relationship, or a flatmate turned violent. (On one memorable occasion, a housemate broke into my room in the night and punched my boyfriend.) Or I was forced to move simply because it was impossible for me to get to my new job from where I lived.

So, for a few magical days, Skipton had become an antithesis to all of that. For the first time in three years, I could actually imagine myself living somewhere and liking it. As I'd wandered around the town of a morning, chatting to shopkeepers or café owners, I daydreamed about this place becoming a permanent fixture in my life. I'd already made one fabulous friend and been introduced to several others. It had been a tantalising glimpse of the very thing I'd been searching for. But allowing myself to believe I might already have found it, even for a second, was a grave error, because when the moment inevitably came to move on, it was harder than I could have ever believed.

I only just made it in time for the 07.20 train. Rather than return to Bentham, I decided I would start in Settle. It meant an extra 10 miles to ride but the road this way wouldn't be quite as hilly. The train deposited me in the tiny town and what started out as a drizzle soon turned into a heavy downpour. Although I hadn't lost any physical fitness during my few days of indolence, the road I returned to felt different… or maybe it was *me* who was different. Prior to now, the journey had been everything, and I'd greeted each day with enthusiasm. But now, all I wanted to do was head back to Skipton and pick up where I'd left off.

I was well prepared for the realities of travel and knew I was bound to experience some low points. I knew, because studying travel literature had been my number one hobby for some time now. Over the years, whenever I'd felt fed up with life, I'd taken solace in my local library and absorbed myself in traveller's literature, or read *Lonely Planet* Guides from cover to cover. I'd become an expert armchair traveller. What I'd gleaned from those who'd gone before me was that exploring the world wasn't always easy or fun. Travelling was as likely to be about negotiating difficulties as it was pleasure-seeking, and it was the overall experience that mattered most. I also came to realise that the difference between "going travelling" and "being on holiday" is that the traveller hopes the experience will change them in some way. My travels this year were certainly changing me, and I believe that was no bad thing.

After fifteen wet and miserable miles, I came to Kirby Lonsdale and took refuge in a bus shelter. As I unwrapped my sandwiches, out of nowhere, a voice popped into my head and in a very frank manner it said: *you were here with Steve yesterday, and you were really happy*. And there it was again… that same flicker of emotion I'd felt the morning I left Heptonstall: an acknowledgment that my feelings towards

Steve were not entirely platonic. Denying feelings in order to protect myself was a skill I'd honed to perfection over the years, and I realised now, I'd skilfully (and subconsciously) played out this very charade the whole time I'd been in Skipton. Whilst there'd been no outward signs of attraction (no love at first sight with stars lighting up the sky), there had been an undeniable connection between myself and Steve. A sense of *simpatico*. It was how attraction always started for me; not by how someone looked but by the words that came from their mouths. I was undeniably attracted to a person's charm. But as I flicked crumbs into a puddle, I acknowledged the futility of all this… What was the point in giving myself permission to have feelings for Steve now when it was too late? Even if I was prepared to risk looking a total idiot by telling him any of this, maybe by letter, I wouldn't get the opportunity to do anything about it. I had an End-to-End to finish and straight afterwards I had a four-week tour of Scotland planned with my friend. It would literally be *months* before I would see Steve again. I told myself I should forget the whole thing, because being hung up on someone was a complication I could do without. But just *knowing* that the timing of our meeting like this sucked, made me want to put my head in my hands and weep.

I arrived at Kendal station an hour before my scheduled rendezvous with my parents and stood forlornly in the rain like some ill-fated character from a Dickens novel. I pulled the cord of my hood up tight, but telltale patches of damp on my back suggested this latest coat had also failed the test. I'd always wanted to visit the Lake District, especially since I'd been told so many times how beautiful it was. But as I looked around the ugly station car park in the grim, grey weather, I laughed hollowly.

At last, they were here: my parents' blue Ford estate car pulling up on the other side of the road. I wish now I'd better expressed how happy I was to see them and had shown them more gratitude. Not just for them coming all this way to see me, but for the fact that *they* were my parents. But, as is often the way of parent/offspring relationships, we didn't do gushing declarations of love. And besides, the cold had frozen my face in its frown, and all I could muster was a weak smile. My bicycle, along with all of my panniers, was dumped unceremoniously into the back of the car and off we drove in search of accommodation for the next few days.

Sat thawing out in the back of the car, I noticed the exceptionally high volume of cars on the road, and a part of me was glad not to be riding any further that day. It looked as though people were driving aimlessly around and soon enough, I realised a good proportion of them were probably looking for a place to stay. Finding somewhere was nothing short of a nightmare. Bed and Breakfast establishments were out of the question, unless you could afford to spend a fortune (we couldn't) *and* were willing to stay for a minimum of three nights (we weren't.) We walked around every town and drove around the surrounding countryside, but to no avail. Everywhere we went, unscrupulous and scheming proprietors told us the same story. Feeling like Joseph and Mary arriving in Bethlehem (was I the donkey?), we were given the same answer again and again: that there was no room at the inn.

Eventually, my father and I persuaded my mother that camping (something she'd always vowed she'd never do) might be the only option left open to us, and we discussed how she and I would sleep in the tent whilst my father would sleep in the car; we were getting that desperate. But even the campsites were full to bursting. I stood outside the reception of one site, pleading with the young man on reception that he could surely find room for one teeny-tiny tent. But even flattery and then bribery didn't work. I was relieved not to be here alone on my bicycle: if I'd arrived after 40 miles' hard pedalling, only to be turned away from every campsite in a 30-mile radius, I think I would have sat down and wept. The only campsite willing to take us in offered pitches in a dung-strewn field, with a cold tap and a hole in the ground for the loo. And for this, the farmer wanted thirteen pounds per person per night for a minimum of three nights.

'Are you *serious*?' I asked the farmer, but his smirk said it all. It was an *obscene* amount of money and he knew it. But hey, this was the Lakes on August bank holiday and it was open season to fleece visitors. Their cash cow weekend had come and they were going to milk it for all it was worth. After this, I suddenly found myself back in my mother's camp (so to speak). At those prices, camping was also out of the question.

We eventually drove 30 miles outside of the Lake District before tracking down a Bed and Breakfast that was both affordable and available, in a place called Carnforth. Here we hired what was more like an apartment than a family guest room, and all for just thirteen pounds per person per night; the same price Farmer Dung Field had wanted to charge us. Over dinner in the cosy hotel bar next door, we discussed Carnforth. It was a pleasant enough town, though clearly not a tourist attraction, so we wondered who all these other guests were at the hotel. Perhaps they were here visiting friends and family, or maybe, like us, they'd stumbled across the town by accident. I learned Carnforth did have rather an intriguing claim to fame, though. In 1945, its railway station was the setting for a scene in the famous film *Brief Encounter*. Who knew?

DAY 26

(27 MILES)

*A*t our lodgings, our host Louise served our breakfast and did her utmost to force-feed us as much fried food as we could manage, beaming with delight when we accepted another sausage or one more tomato. I quickly developed an affinity for her, not only because of her catering ethics, but by the way she interjected when her husband started telling me how brave I was. She waved all that nonsense aside and instead gave me a knowing nod of the head and said that I was just fine, that there was nothing wrong in me choosing to travel alone and that I should be proud of being an independent young woman. It was fantastic to hear her words of validation, especially since many others had looked upon me as peculiar or eccentric (even if they hadn't actually said so out loud).

We loaded my bicycle into the car and my parents drove me back to Kendal so I could continue on from where I'd left off. It felt wrong to be cycle touring in this way, but what other choice did we have? At least I could travel light. Everything, except for a bike pump and puncture repair kit, was left back at the B&B, and that was just as well considering what was in store today. I planned to follow the A591 to Windermere and then the A592 to Penrith. It was a nice, straightforward route which wouldn't require me to stop and look at the map 300 times a day, like I'd had to in the Pennines/Peaks/Bowland Fells/Yorkshire Dales. There was, however, a slight blip in my plans. Not so much a blip actually, but a mountain… the Kirkstone Pass. It rose up from Lake Windermere to a towering 1,500 feet and comprised of gradients as steep as 1-4 in places. But after nearly a week honing my leg muscles across Yorkshire, I was ready for the challenge. By the time I reached Windermere, I was grateful to get off the traffic-laden A591. Although the rain had gone, the cloud cover kept the humidity high and before I'd even started on my ascent, the sweat was pouring into my eyes. A sign for the Kirkstone Pass emphasised its seriousness: *1500ft and winter conditions are hazardous*. But I felt excited rather than daunted. As far as mountain passes go, at 1500ft, the Kirkstone was a tiddler on a global scale and thus making it a good one for a beginner.

If you've never cycled up a mountain pass before, I will try and describe how it feels to go against gravity for many miles at a time. How easy you find it will depend upon your fitness levels, but even if you are in good shape, as I was, there will be no escaping some pretty unpleasant sensations.

During the hour it took me to reach the top, I was aware of only four things: that my breathing was laboured, that my heart thudded like a bass drum, that my face burnt red hot and that the sweat poured off me in rivers. Two things helped. Firstly, I followed rule thirteen and after the steepest sections, I would stop to catch my breath. But the main way I tackled the long ascent (and particularly as I didn't know how far it was to the top) was by taking it easy: using the minimum amount of energy possible and stretching out my reserves in case the last bit was the hardest.

It was during this climb that I first noticed the most extraordinary thing: I had missed this. (And by "this", I mean the cardiovascular workout: you know… those sensations I've just described as being *unpleasant*.) Despite the fact I'd just grumbled and complained the entire way across the Pennines/Peaks/Bowland Fells/Yorkshire Dales, I'd come to know these sensations so well by now that, although I wouldn't go so far as to say I welcomed them, I did greet their return as one might an old but comfortably familiar adversary. That's not to say it wasn't still a relief to get to the top, and in under half the time I'd expected, I made it. The views were spectacular, if a little hazy, and in celebration I bought a half pint of shandy from the Kirkstone Inn, the third highest pub in the country. I had an hour to wait for my parents, who were off on their own sightseeing adventures that morning. For a while, I enjoyed watching other cyclists arriving at the top of the pass. They all had pride written across their faces, as I'm sure I did too. But before long, I began to shiver uncontrollably. Sweat dries quickly at high altitudes and my bare arms and legs were soon freezing. I attempted a few star jumps to keep warm but by the time my parents arrived, we had to eat our picnic in the car with the heating on and me wrapped in a blanket.

The descent was every bit as enjoyable as I'd hoped it would be. With a jumper borrowed from my mother and my cycle helmet on firmly, I shot off, perhaps a little too keenly. Tempting as it was to go like a contestant in the Tour de France, a nasty scare halfway down involving some uneven tarmac put paid to that idea, and I reduced my pace to a much safer speed for the rest of the descent. Back at ground level, the clouds had cleared and it was hot again. Now my main challenge was over, I could relax and have an easy ride the rest of the way. I was enjoying the atmosphere in the Lakes that afternoon. People were swimming, sunbathing and picnicking on the shores of Ullswater Lake and I was almost tempted to take a dip myself, except I had no spare clothes with me. Even car drivers were exceptionally courteous today. I suspect this collective good mood was down to us all experiencing that rare phenomenon: a hot and sunny British bank holiday weekend.

There were a lot more cyclists on this side of the mountain, mostly going in the opposite direction. From snippets of their conversations that I picked up as I passed, I gleaned that most had hired bikes in Penrith. It was a good route for an impromptu novice ride, since the road was neither busy, nor hilly, and ran pretty much flat around Ullswater Lake… until, that is, the daytrippers spied the Kirkstone Pass looming in the distance. I have to confess I was somewhat amused by the looks of horror that befell otherwise happy faces.

'Holy shit, look at that hill.'

'*Noooo waaaaaaaaaay* am I cycling up there.'

'I'm heading back to Penrith, is anyone else coming?'

As I passed, I tried to shout encouragement, but words such as *it's not as bad as it looks*, or, *it'll be worth it when you get to the top* fell flat against their resolute fear of physical discomfort. I guess it takes a long time to realise that the uphill bit is really the best bit in disguise.

DAY 27

(20 MILES)

*B*efore my parents began their long drive home, we spent a few more precious hours together, sightseeing some of the places not on my cycle route. During the course of the morning, we passed a sign for the Hardknott Pass: a single-track road that winds its way up and over towards Eskdale and reaches a height of 1,280 feet. Originally built by the Romans, by the early 1900s it had become popular with cyclists and early motorcar owners, who wanted to challenge their skills on the steep and winding unpaved road. Whilst the pass isn't as high as the Kirkstone, it is steeper, and on the most extreme sections, I'd read that the gradients are 1-3. This gives Hardknott pass (along with its adversary, Rosedale Chimney on the North York Moors) the title for the steepest road in England. I wasn't sad to have missed out on it, though. One mountain pass in a weekend was enough for me.

At Penrith station I said goodbye to my parents. This would be their last visit; by next weekend, I would be well into Scotland and out of daily visiting range. The 20 miles from Penrith to Carlisle were a doddle. The road was almost flat and there were barely any cars. Well, actually, I could see and hear plenty of traffic, but thankfully it was all confined to the M6, which ran parallel to this road, and I was left in peace. The world around me was flooded in afternoon sun and I was mesmerised by the views in all directions. To my left were the peaks of the Cumbrian mountains, to my right lay the Pennines, and ahead of me loomed the hills and mountains of Scotland. By tomorrow, I would be over the border and into the land of heather, whisky and mountains. The very thought made my insides dance with excitement.

Lost in a dream world as usual and enjoying the empty road, I jumped out of my skin when I heard a man's voice booming right in my ear.

'So, you're heading for John O'Groats too?'

It was a fellow cyclist called Pete, who had crept up on me unawares. I listened as he explained that he was riding as part of a team (although where the rest of that team were, wasn't entirely clear). But it all sounded very well organised. They cycled a set mileage each day and stayed at pre-booked accommodation. They had motorised backup with nutritionists and physiotherapists aboard. And it goes without saying that none of the cyclists were carrying their own stuff.

'Why would I want to cycle with all that on my bike?' Pete said, casting an eye over my bicycle and trying to humour me. I wondered if I should try explaining that I'd found independent travel liberating and maybe even a bit more interesting. But before I could say anything, one of the group's many backup cars slowed to check if Pete needed anything before speeding off again. Apparently, they did that every 5 miles, which I thought was a teensy bit ostentatious and unnecessary.

At the end of the day, though, we were both cyclists with a common aim, and despite my initial wariness about Pete's scathing remark, he turned out to be quite friendly. As there were barely any cars around, we rode side by side and exchanged tales of the road. (Cornwall sucked, Devon was wet, not looking forward to the Scottish midges, etc., etc.) As often happened when I met other cyclists, I found I had to pedal far faster than my normal pace just to keep up with them, whilst Pete had no doubt slowed his own pace to match mine. The next few miles whizzed by and before I knew it, we were on the outskirts of Carlisle. Pete suggested I stick with him to Lockerbie, the team's destination for the day, and come and meet the others. I mulled it over for just a few seconds and then dismissed the idea. As much as I loved a bit of company, especially from fellow cyclists, I knew I couldn't bear to let someone else's itinerary steer my own. At the next set of traffic lights, I turned right towards the city centre, yelling and waving Pete goodbye. After trying to keep up with him, it was quite a relief to get back to my usual snail's pace.

Because I'd wanted to delay leaving my parents for as long as possible, I'd had an unusually late start. Normally, I'd be settled into my tent by four o'clock, so it was slightly disconcerting to find that at six o'clock, I'd only just reached Carlisle and I still had no idea where I would spend the night. To my relief, the Tourist Information Centre was still open and the woman behind the desk smiled in greeting.

'Oh, we're a friendly lot up here,' she quipped. I'm not sure if this was the standard patter they gave all visitors, or she genuinely wanted to reassure me. Maybe I sounded vulnerable and a long way from home. Either way, it had the desired effect. I got all the information I needed and then decided as I was here now, I might as well take a walk around the city centre. I bought some sandwiches and ate them on a bench in the sunshine, whilst a couple from Cornwall, who'd spotted my charity tabard, came over to chat and donate a few pennies. Once the last rays of sun had disappeared behind the tall buildings, I set out again. The campsite was 3 miles from Carlisle and only 10 miles from Scotland. I'd already decided to have a mini celebration that night; toast my last night in England with a cup of tea and a cigarette.

It's funny, isn't it? Those occasions in life you think *should* be momentous or memorable often turn into a damp squib. No sooner was my ride over for the day than the depression descended; a blanket smothering the event. I was no stranger to the black dog. I could sense its unmistakable crushing presence, and its timing was no coincidence. Since I'd left my parents in Penrith, I had kept myself afloat by riding resolutely on and pretending I didn't have a care in the world, whilst depression lurked in the bushes. Knowing. Waiting. It knew how much I would miss them, and the minute I was no longer preoccupied by physical activity, it saw its opportunity and pounced. As I curled up in my tent, I wondered sadly if it were at all possible to outrun it. But what depression also knew was that my parents weren't the only ones I missed. Despite my resolve not to, my thoughts had returned to Steve. I couldn't stop myself thinking about the fun we'd had together and how happy I'd been in his company. I wanted to go back to that point in time we'd shared, with an insatiable longing.

Whilst I still maintain that journeying alone was the right decision for me, I also recognised that it could be the best and worst of both worlds. On the one hand, it made things easier because I was master of my own destiny, and free to come and go as I chose with no conflicts. But by equal terms, it could make things harder. There was never anyone to fall back on for support when times were tough. Like it or not, I was on my own now until I got to the end. There would be no more familiar faces dropping in on me to take the edge off my raw emotions. It felt like a big sign was hanging in the air saying: *From now on, Dawn, you are on your own.*

Sir Hellingwell: my knight in shining armour.

The viaduct which wasn't what it first seemed.

PART 4

SCOTLAND

My favourite place

DAY 28

(60 MILES)

*A*s the sun came up on the horizon, it brought with it a renewed sense of optimism. This was a new day and the chance for a fresh start in another country. And for now, at least, I could leave the black dog behind. I was on my way by seven thirty, which must be my earliest start ever. The sky had been stained with crimson since first light and it reminded me of a book that I once found in the library called *The Old Bastard's Book of Country Lies*. The gist of the book was to change old country proverbs into something more practical and amusing: *Red sky at night, shepherd's delight, red sky in the morning, someone's set the barn alight*. As I pedalled north, the troposphere lost no time morphing from stunning red to arresting pink, before degenerating into the inevitable grey. A stiff southerly breeze started up, pushing me out of

England and into the arms of Gretna. My eyes searched for the sign I had been longing to see, and there it was: *Scotland Welcomes You*. I had expected to feel ecstatic at this point, not least because I loved Scotland. (Does anything say adoration like twelve visits in four years?) But instead, an uneasiness settled over me and I wasn't entirely sure why. Was it the melancholy from last night still lingering in the recesses of my mind?

Gretna Green doesn't exactly deliver the wow factor as you enter Scotland, but the Blacksmith's Shop has an interesting history. Its story dates back to Lord Hardwicke's marriage act of 1754. This new law for England and Wales meant people under the age of twenty-one could no longer marry unless they gained their parents' consent first, whereas over the border in Scotland, boys as young as fourteen and girls as young as twelve could marry without any parental consent. The difference in ruling opened up the floodgates for young couples to head over the border if they required a quick and easy, non-parentally approved marriage. The no-frills ceremonies were carried out by blacksmiths, who didn't pull any punches.

'Are you currently married?' (no)

'Do you wish to marry?' (yes)

'Okay, I declare you married.' Bearing in mind this was the latter half of the 18th century, so it wouldn't have been an easy journey to Scotland. There were no motorcars, autobus, or train. Even bicycles didn't exist until the 1800s, and it was ages before they resembled the bicycles of today. (Can you imagine doing the Pennines/Peaks/Bowland Fells/Yorkshire Dales on a penny farthing?) So, that left private pony,

Shanks's pony or, if you could afford it, a seat on a horse-drawn stagecoach. But even these were neither speedy nor comfortable, taking up to ten days from London to Scotland.

But before we go all misty-eyed over how brave and in love these young couples must have been, let's remind ourselves that Hardwicke's law was meant, above all else, to help stamp out clandestine marriages (also known as secret unions). These were marriages performed without the formal rites and banns of public ceremony, and far from the family parish. People went into secret unions for all sorts of reasons, and it wasn't exclusively for romantic young couples who couldn't wait for their parents' approval. It may have been ladies or gentlemen wanting to marry above or below their class. It could be men who'd made one wife pregnant, then abandoned her to marry again. It could have been couples hoping to conceal a pregnancy, or even people in incestuous relationships. So, these days, whilst the tourist office is busy making Gretna Green sound like the most romantic destination in the world, this wasn't necessarily the case. I like to imagine Gretna as an olden day version of Las Vegas, where dubious ceremonies could slip more easily under the radar. But despite my cynicism, these anvil priests, as they became known, performed some 5,000 ceremonies for runaways from England and Wales, and they continued on until 1856 when, after much pressure from south of the border, Scotland agreed to introduce a rule whereby runaways had to take a twenty-one-day cooling-off period before they could marry. (This would have been a great business opportunity for the locals, to start offering lodgings.) Finally, in 1940, anvil weddings were outlawed, and the blacksmiths passed their duties over to licenced registrars, and the age of marriage consent in Scotland was finally raised to a more sensible sixteen.

I sat outside the Blacksmith's Shop writing postcards to my friends, telling them I'd just cycled all the way to Scotland and whilst I did so, I placed my collection tin on the wall beside me, always hopeful of attracting more donations. But the other tourists were only interested in the bored-looking bagpiper, and the bored-looking bagpiper looked only interested in going home.

Although I'd wanted to plot my entire route out in advance, whenever I'd got to the bit between Gretna and Glasgow, I'd been stumped for what to do, since my road atlas made it look as though riding main roads was my only option. In the end, I'd given up. I decided I'd wait and see what emerged when I got here. Then yesterday, in Carlisle's tourist office, I'd stumbled across the perfect solution: The *Sustrans Number 7 Carlisle to Glasgow cycle route*. For six pounds, I got a small plastic wallet containing a beautifully detailed foldaway map and a booklet full of cycle-friendly tourist information. The Sustrans group (short for sustainable transport) is a leading cycle campaign group and registered charity in the United Kingdom who create long-distance cycling networks all across our Isles. A quick glance at the map told me this route wasn't designed with speed in mind and was about the longest route I could take to Glasgow. But as the booklet promised scenic rides and traffic-free routes, I decided the 100 extra miles would be worth it.

My spirits rose as I hit the road again. Maybe it was possible to outrun depression after all. Or should I say outride it? As excited as I was to be in Scotland, I also remembered that it is 56 miles longer than England, so rule number twenty-one of cycle touring is: the further you travel, the further away your destination feels. Route 7 headed west out of Gretna. Remember that back in Somerset, I'd wondered if there was such a thing as perfect cycling weather? Well, now I'd found it. I had both warm sun and a stiff breeze on my back, keeping my body at the perfect temperature and pushing me forward, and I easily motored through the first 40 miles. The Sustrans map was easy to follow and was far more detailed than the photocopied maps I was used to, and they hadn't lied when they'd stated it would be traffic-free. I barely saw a car all morning, and the few drivers I did see waved in greeting. I was now in *a' Ghalldachd* or the Scottish Lowlands (as opposed to the *a'Gháidhealtachd*: the Highlands). *Ghalldachd* refers to the non-Gael speaking areas of Southern Scotland and translates as: *place of the foreigner*, no doubt referring to all the English, Welsh, Picts, Anglo-Saxons, Romans and other non-Scottish people that have lived here over the centuries.

I cycled through the villages of Annan, Ruthwell and Glencaple, before turning north-west towards Dumfries. In Ruthwell, I found a museum dedicated to the world's first Parish Savings Bank. Back in the early 1800s, Ruthwell's most famous resident, one Dr Henry Duncan, returned home after years spent working in the banking system in Liverpool. He was unhappy with what he described as an unjustifiable poverty trap for the working class, and his answer was to try to give people a hand up by opening the world's first Parish Savings Bank. It differed from other banks, since people only needed sixpence to open an account (instead of the usual ten pounds), for which the investor would receive a substantial five percent interest. Duncan's vision was that even the less well-off should be able to earn interest on their meagre funds. The good doctor saw to all the administration himself and instead of pocketing the profits, he used them to build a new school in the parish. Records say that by the end of the first year, over £150 had been deposited, and the idea began to spread across the British Isles. Within ten years, the amount of savings deposited in all Parish savings accounts was around three million pounds.

I personally feel it is a sad twist of fate that today's Ruthwell is now devoid of not only a bank, but it doesn't have so much as a post office or shop for its residents, forcing them to drive miles into Dumfries for amenities. Progress, huh? I spent an hour browsing through the museum's collection of 200-year-old home savings boxes, coins and banknotes from various parts of the world. Then a sparrow flew in through the open door and couldn't find its way out again, causing great consternation amongst the staff. Amid a chorus of Scottish flapping over what to do with the intruder, I made my own exit.

I began to encounter more cars again as I entered Dumfries. The giant clock in the town square read a quarter past one, and so I found a bench in the sunshine where I could rest up and eat. I was thrilled with my progress and relaxed, knowing I had all afternoon to do the next 20 miles. I became engrossed in my book but a while later, when I glanced at the clock again, it still read a quarter past one. Uh-oh. A woman on the next bench confirmed it was actually a quarter to four already. Just hearing this was enough to bring on severe lethargy. I flicked through my Sustrans booklet, hoping there was another campsite closer by, but there wasn't. I was about to find out that rule number twenty-two of cycling is that: no matter how capable your body might be, if the mind isn't willing… then you're screwed.

According to my Sustrans guide, the next 5 miles were a gentle climb up towards the intriguingly named village of Lochfoot. (Presumably at the foot of a loch.) It soon became clear that *my* definition of a gentle climb and other people's definition were two totally different concepts, and I had to push my bicycle up some of it. Today would be my longest ride yet; I would have done well over 60 miles by the time I reached Castle Douglas, and my thighs and backside voiced their grievances about the sudden increase in mileage. To distract myself, I practised saying *Lochfoot* over and over, trying to perfect a Scottish accent. Whilst the English pronounce loch like *lock*, the Scottish pronounce it with the emphasis on the *och*, but more drawn out, like gargling water. Since I adored the Scottish accent, you can imagine my raptures of delight when later I came across a place called Loch Lochy. (I practised that one for weeks.) The satisfaction of learning to say these things correctly was similar to the joy I experienced when I first learned to roll my R's in Italian, where for weeks, I repeated aloud words such as *erratico* and *irregolare*.

My joy at reaching Castle Douglas was marred when I found out the cost for a tent was ten pounds a night. The price, the women on reception explained, once I'd finished spluttering, was based on up to four people sharing. For a split second, it was tempting to think, *wow, Scotland must be a really conformist place if they can assume everyone goes on holiday as a family of four*. But then I realised it was simply an ingenious scam. Lone travellers and couples had to pay over the odds, whilst a family of five had to pay an extra ten pounds for their thirdborn. I briefly tried voicing my opinions on the unfairness of this system, especially since I was on a charity ride. But the woman just shrugged and said I was welcome to find another campsite if I didn't like it (knowing full well there weren't any others). I slammed my fee down on her desk, hoping this wasn't a typical rule of thumb in Scottish campsites, or things could get mightily expensive this side of the border. But worse was to follow. As I set up my tent and went for a shower, I couldn't help but notice a lot of people staring. I sighed wearily; not this again. I had read travellers can experience culture shock when transitioning from one country into another, but I hadn't expected to feel it so markedly between England and Scotland.

I remembered my unease as I'd entered Scotland that morning and felt it more acutely than ever. After twelve previous visits, I couldn't for the life of me work out the cause. Was it just this campsite? Was it that, having just come from the land of chatty, in-your-face northerners, the Scottish seemed more reserved? I worried they might hate tourists, or cyclists... or English people. Maybe they'd just hate me. Thankfully, a few people around the campsite smiled and said hello and it helped stem the growing tide of anxiety (although it didn't escape my attention that the friendliest people were holidaying Lancastrians). I lit my only cigarette of the day. I knew it was crazy to have let this habit creep back into my life, but I enjoyed the soothing feel of nicotine flowing through my tired body, particularly after an arduous day; and the icing on the cake was to combine it with a mug of hot sweet tea.

DAY 29

(47 MILES)

*A*fter riding more than 60 miles, I had expected to get a good night's sleep but my waterworks had had me back and forth to the toilet block half the night, and now I was bleary-eyed and irritable. I put it down to all the water I'd drunk yesterday during Scotland's mini heatwave; something which was unlikely to be a problem today. The only liquid that concerned me now fell from the sky in a never-ending deluge. I know Scotland isn't exactly famous for its Hawaiian-like climate, but the weather that morning had me zipping the tent door closed and crawling back into my sleeping bag. The wind was so fierce I could hardly hear my radio, and eventually I gave up hoping it might pass. At half past ten, I was packed up and in a phone box, relaying my weekly report to my mother, whilst outside, my sodden bicycle looked as though it too wanted to be inside. But there were only so many ways I could describe to my mother Castle Douglas, the awful weather and how wet I was about to get, before it was time for the inevitable replacement of the receiver and my exit into the gloom. The dim light made it feel more like dusk time in November than mid-morning in August and huge drops of rain fell from the sky (were they bigger in Scotland?) and found their way down the back of my coat.

What with sore legs and shite weather conditions, one thing was for sure: my leisurely ride down leafy country lanes was over, and I eagerly abandoned the Sustrans route in favour of the A713. This road cut directly north-west across the Southern Uplands towards the town of Ayr and would shorten my journey considerably. It's funny that yesterday I'd enthused about having time to take the scenic route and today, I gladly cut out the extra mileage. It was a good example of how volatile emotions can get when cycle touring. It rained and it rained and just in case I didn't quite get the message, it rained some more. It rained with an intensity that said, *Look, lady, playtime's over. You are in Scotland now, and if you thought the weather was bad in Cornwall and Devon, you ain't seen nothing yet.* At least the gale force winds were behind me.

The morning dragged. There would be ten minutes of pedalling, ten minutes of getting soaked. Then I'd foolishly glance at my bike computer and look away again, dismayed at the mileage not yet done. The scenery, when it was visible through the gloom, was nothing to write home about, and I was surprised there were no hills. I mean, they must have called this area the Southern Uplands for a reason, and I wanted to find them. Just a few, since I was now of the firm belief that hills are a good thing. They brightened up the view, gave me a challenge I could get my teeth into, and they relieved the monotony. The thing about hills is that they can be the best *and* worst part of your ride. They can be extremely slow going and uncomfortable, and make you grumble and whinge: *I can't do this. It's too hard.* But once you accept the discomfort and realise it's only temporary, then slowly, very slowly, as your summit gets closer, you begin to feel the excitement: *Just another few hundred yards... fifty... twenty... ten,* and you're there. Elation. Pride. Personal victory for having conquered another ascent. And then it's time to stop, regain breath, survey the view, and then look forward to a thrilling ride down the other side.

Imagine if life was like this road: flat, dull and easy. Monotonous and without challenges. No ups or downs. No good times to compare with the bad.

It didn't take me long to realise I'd been wrong about the A713; it wasn't at all busy. I hadn't taken into account that Scotland's population density is about four times lower than that of England, even lower in rural areas, and for mile after delicious mile I had the road all to myself. But my ambivalence about being in Scotland remained. On the one hand, I was in love with the silent emptiness of this land, but a part of me was daunted by entering such a desolate, wild place. Sometimes I actually believed the desolation was a living entity; a presence, beckoning me on with a long and bony finger. At times, it felt like a benevolent presence, but other times, I was afraid of it. And the further into Scotland I travelled, the more ensnared by it I felt.

I was beginning to understand the root cause of these feelings. Whilst many outdoor enthusiasts come to Scotland specially to enjoy this remoteness, on a bicycle it's very different. Having a car means you can enjoy camping and hiking but you know that at any time, you can retreat back to "civilisation" with a simple turn of a key and a press on the gas pedal; no planning or effort required. But on a bicycle, it isn't that simple. If you get tired, hungry, injured, or simply decide you've had enough, it could be hours to the nearest village or days to the nearest railway station. So, once you're in it, you're in it for the long haul.

In this state of ambivalence, I rode on, thinking how much I'd love a distraction right now: some music, maybe a comedy show; hell, even listening to *The Archers* would have been welcome. I experimentally put my radio on and put it in my coat pocket but I couldn't hear it over the wind. So, that left me with my usual two options: singing or thinking. After four weeks on the road, I'd discovered that the reliving of past events was a great way to pass the time; for what are our memories but an infinite library of story books, brimming with snapshots and tales from our lives? To say I did a lot of reminiscing on this trip would be an understatement. I thought about family, friends and boyfriends. I remembered the fun from my travels, and I smiled at the good decisions I'd made and cringed at the bad. Nothing was left out, no matter how painful. Each and every memory was hung up and aired out, replayed, examined closely, perhaps smoothed over a little, and then set free. And I left each one floating off behind me as I cycled onwards in the direction of my future. For me, the act of cycling made the memory banks a lighter, and much brighter, space.

*

During the first of many breaks that day, sat miserable and cold on a bench under the dripping wet trees, I was struck by a sudden brainwave. I'd realised some time ago how useful plastic bags are on a tour, especially since my panniers weren't entirely waterproof. (Showerproof maybe, but after three or four hours in the rain, the water *always* found a way in.) Plastic bags had become my saviour since I'd learnt to put everything inside my panniers into a plastic bag first, doubling up protection against the rain. So, on that bench, I got to thinking: *if plastic bags can keep the things in my panniers dry, won't they keep my feet dry too?* The sensation of water sloshing inside my boots had first become familiar in the West Country, but in Scotland, where temperatures are noticeably more frigid, it was potentially a more serious problem to get soaked right through. Surely a plastic bag over each foot would keep them warm and dry. And if my feet stayed warm, then the rest of me would stay warm too. I chided myself for not thinking of this twenty-nine days ago. I sat on that miserable bench, cheerfully peeling off wet socks. I rubbed each wrinkled foot vigorously with my towel until the circulation got going again, and then very carefully, I wrapped each one in a warm, dry sock, secured it into a plastic bag and stuck it back into its boot. In less than a minute, I could feel the warmth returning to my feet, a glow that soon extended out to all of my extremities. Oh, the joy. How happy I was at the thought of no more cold, wet feet. And it worked... for a while... until eventually my toes rubbed a hole in the plastic and the water got in again.

After lunch, the weather (and my mood) began to brighten. The sun appeared and I got my wish: to leave the drab flatness behind. The road began winding its way up and into the hills; I say hills but they were actually the mountains of the Southern Upland range. For years now, I'd been asking the question, when does a hill officially become a mountain? And it surprised me that no one knew. Later, once the internet came along, I finally found out *why* nobody knew: because there is no universally defined answer. In the UK and USA, a mountain used to be defined as: *a summit of 1,000 feet and over*, but that was abandoned in the 1970s. The official English Oxford Dictionary definition reads rather vaguely as: *a large natural elevation of the earth's surface rising abruptly from the surrounding level; a large steep hill.* In other words, the definition is left to be defined according to local wisdom, which seems a bit of a cop-out. I mean, by this definition, couldn't Glastonbury Tor be defined as a mountain?

The Southern Uplands were mesmerising. In every direction there were shades of purples, greens and browns that I attributed to the various types of heather growing there, carpeting the ground where only the animals walked. Pine forests grew in abundance as far as the eye could see, both below me in the valleys and above me on the mountain slopes. And stray wisps of cloud floated intermittently above them, giving the impression of a dozen smoldering forest fires all going on at once. There seemed no limit to how far and wide I could see that afternoon, and I certainly had no trouble spotting rain approaching, giving me ample time to pull on my coat. Despite frequent soakings, it never took long to dry out again, not once the giant radiator in the sky worked its magic. I simply powered along as the blustery wind remained firmly behind me at all times. It felt like Mother Nature was giving me a helping hand when I needed it most.

It became virtually impossible to be up this close with nature and not feel philosophical about the cyclic nature of the universe.

Life, no matter how much people try to ignore or reject it, always comes back to the same principles, that all of us, everything, is bound by the same cyclical process and the essence of those principles: the earth turns, we orbit the sun, even the stars are slowly revolving. Trees grow their leaves and fruits and at the end of the season, they die and drop and rot in the ground, which fertilises the earth and assists the trees' growth next year. This process repeats itself, round and round. You cannot fault it. But for some reason, the human race overlooks the simple premise of "what goes around comes around". We think we've evolved outside of our place in nature, believing there'll be no consequences. And we often treat each other with the same disdain.

I cycled past fields full of inquisitive cows who lined up along the fence in their dozens, silently watching me with their great brown eyes. Cyclists must make a rare form of entertainment for the cattle up here. I observed hundreds of sparrows, sheltering in the hedgerows and in the grass verges. They flittered from one side of the road to another, often right in front of me, almost as if they were playing a game of dare. Luckily, my brakes were in good working order and I became adept at slamming them on when needed. After seeing so much carnage on the roads of Great Britain,

I didn't wish to further add to it. My final 4 miles of the day were a fantastic descent, following the course of a mountain stream which bubbled and sang as loudly as I did.

In the next sizable settlement of Hollybush, I found a small shop inside a petrol station. It appeared to be the only retail outlet in the village and I gratefully bought a supper of two cheese and onion pies. With the ongoing closure of rural shops, I wondered about the impact for rural Scotland, where distances between towns could be an awfully long way, and I made a note to always stock up wherever the opportunity arose. Outside the shop, a cheery woman stopped to chat, but I'm embarrassed to admit that I struggled to follow the conversation, as my ears hadn't yet adjusted to the strong Ayrshire accents. I nodded and smiled through the exchange, hoping to appear neither rude nor dumb.

Some local children pointed me in the direction of the campsite and I found it where the houses stopped and the fields began. And *what* a campsite it was. I would describe it as a relic from a bygone era of British family holidays, circa the 1950s, and it was full of dilapidated static caravans as far as the eye could see. Right in the centre was a large, semi-derelict building which I assume had once been the clubhouse, where holidaymakers would have flocked each night to be entertained. As I poked my nose around the door, my mind flashed upon the happy evenings people must have spent here: dancing newlyweds, flirting teenagers, children competing in cutest kid contests with tipsy parents cheering them on from the sidelines. My own family had holidayed in these sorts of places in Cornwall during the 1980s and a wave of nostalgia washed over me. But now there was neither bar nor disco. Only the cobwebs and the dust remained, along with a strong musty smell. I wondered why the place had fallen into disarray. The most obvious answer, it seemed, was that people just didn't holiday here anymore, not since "exotic" foreign package holidays had taken off and become ever cheaper. I also got the impression that most visitors to this country head straight to Edinburgh, Inverness and the Highlands, and to what they consider to be the "real Scotland". It's certainly been my experience that these are the places people tend to gush about and go misty-eyed over. The Lowlands of Scotland rarely seem to get a mention.

I picked my way past dozens of cute semi-feral cats that appeared to be multiplying out of control around the neglected buildings. They dashed away when I first approached but came creeping slowly back in a true curiosity killed the cat manner. As there was no welcome reception desk anymore, I called in at the farmhouse located to one side of the site. The man who answered the door wasn't the most cheerful soul and I wondered if he ran this place alone. Maybe death or divorce was another reason the place had fallen by the wayside. I could hear his television in the background playing the theme tune to *Neighbours* and he waved me away with his hand, muttering *pitch anywhere* before slamming the door in my face. I found the spot where I thought tents should go and set up in a sunny corner where I could watch swallows swooping low over the fields.

After spending nearly thirty evenings living in my tent, I'd like to share a few tips with you; things I believe make for a better night's sleep. First and most obvious is that, when given the choice, always pitch your tent on flat ground. There is nothing worse than waking up in the night to find one's self and one's pillows have slid off the mat, and are now pressed up against the wet sides of the tent. Secondly, if I had to choose between a sheltered spot or a spot with a great view, I'd go for the sheltered spot *every* time, especially when it's windy. The less the tent flaps, the more sleep you're going to get. (Or remember to pack earplugs.) Thirdly, I like to pitch my tent where there's a fence, a post, a tree, or anything solid I can lock my bicycle to. Having one's bike right outside the tent means not only peace of mind but, if you want to, you can leave some of your panniers attached to it. And that means more room in your tent and a faster get away in the mornings.

And finally (and I make no apologies for suggesting this), unless I'm lucky enough to be positioned near the toilet block (which only ever happened the once), then I try to pitch somewhere a little secluded and near a bush or hedge, in case I need a tinkle in the night. Whilst I don't want to encourage turning campsites into urine stinking hell-holes, if you are miles from the toilet block and you get caught short, then I can't see anything wrong in a quick trip behind the bushes. (Number ones only, of course.) It became a great source of irritation to me when I realised that most campsites give their best pitches, i.e., those nearest the toilet blocks, to the caravanners. Why? Why do they do that when most caravanners already *have* a toilet inside their van? On the other hand, us peasants in our tents, have no such luxury. If we wake up in the night with a full bladder, we have to mess on: finding clothes and shoes and a torch, and then go on a ten-minute hike just to get to the toilet blocks. If you take all of that into account, wouldn't most of us prefer a discreet trip behind a bush, as nature intended?

DAY 30

(36 MILES)

*L*ate last night, I encountered the only other lone female cycle tourist of my entire journey. She turned up at the Hollybush campsite around nine o'clock and I managed to restrain myself for a whole ten minutes before skipping off excitedly to say hello. But despite a beaming smile from me as we met at the shower blocks, the woman barely grunted in acknowledgement. Clearly, there would be no sisterly conversations for us that night. I retreated back to my tent crestfallen, consoling myself with the thought that she'd probably just had a really shitty day, with sixteen simultaneous punctures or something like that. She did, however, stick a sleepy head out of her tent and wave me off this morning, so that cheered me up.

The rain held off as I cycled the 8 miles into Ayr to find breakfast, but my real interest in the town stretched beyond culinary need. A few years ago, I'd secured a place at the university in Ayr to study a four-year degree in Environmental Protection. I'd initially applied during an unhappy time in my life, thinking a fresh start in a place I'd never been before would do me the world of good. (This could more accurately be described as running away.) But as the time got closer, and I looked around at the bags and boxes packed up ready to go, I had an epiphany moment and I knew then: the student life just wasn't for me. As I rode into Ayr, it felt strange to have ended up here after all, only under totally different circumstances. I took a table outside a café in the high street and tucked into tea and toast whilst appraising the town. The streets were lively, bright and cheerful and the people seemed friendly, and I was rather pleased I'd chosen such a nice place to study. I was rather taken with the notion that, if there was such a thing as a parallel universe, then there was another me in Ayr right now, halfway through a degree and by the looks of things, enjoying myself immensely.

As well as having a good university, I learnt some other interesting facts about Ayr. It was the birthplace of the much-celebrated Scottish poet Robert Burns. It was also home to one of five citadels built by Oliver Cromwell's English army in 1652, after they defeated the Scots and declared a Commonwealth between the two countries. The fortified posts were allegedly built to "control" the still very angry Scots, and its ramparts remain today. Another interesting thing I'd read was that Ayr had continuously elected a Conservative MP for ninety-one years, from 1906 to 1997, the year I was there. By then, the good people of Ayrshire finally decided they wanted a change and elected a Labour MP instead. (Labour would then remain in favour another eighteen years until 2015, when the Scottish National Party would take over.) I think it safe to say that the population of Ayr isn't too keen on change.

The next place I wanted to see was Glasgow and as I was craving some social interaction, I phoned ahead and booked myself into Glasgow's backpackers' hostel. I'd stayed in these places before and they do tend to be incredibly sociable. With my bed secured, all I had to do now was decide the best way to get there. As the crow flies, Glasgow was only 35 miles away, but that was on main roads. Now that the weather had improved again, I thought it might be nice to pick up the Sustrans cycle route again; it turned out to be a good idea, and I meandered north through peaceful western coastal towns such as Prestwick, Troon and Irvine.

In Troon, I sat on the breaker wall eating a pie and watched as a faint sun tried to burn its way through the clouds. If I squinted, I could just about make out the Isle of Arran, floating on the wave tops across the bay. The clean sea air tingled my nostrils and I could taste the salt on my lips. Troon's beachfront is magnificent, with its carpet of clean sand as long as it is wide. But the thing I found peculiar was, aside from a few dog walkers, the seafront was deserted. It was the school summer holidays, and it was the weekend, so where were all the daytrippers? How come the place wasn't full of noise and litter, with the smell of fried chips hanging in the air? I'm pretty sure that a beautiful sandy beach such as this on the south coast would be *packed* with daytrippers the entire summer. Maybe it was an unusually quiet day. Or perhaps Troon's charms just aren't well known outside the local area. (If you weren't familiar with this part of the world, a casual glance at a map could lead you to wrongly assume Troon was just another Glaswegian suburb.) Or maybe, just maybe, it is protected from tourist hoards by a little thing I like to call hypothermia. Either way, it reminded me of the beautiful beaches in North Wales during the winter months, once all the holidaymakers had gone home.

Heading north from Troon, I had the pleasure of bumping into Archie, a local cyclist who agreed with me that, from time to time, the Sustrans route did get unnecessarily complicated. For example, it would detour off through a muddy field (somewhere you won't want to ride when loaded down with panniers), when there was a cycle friendly road running alongside it; a road you would then be directed back onto anyway at the end of the field. Archie and I cycled side by side for a few miles. He had just returned from a cycle tour around the Highlands and wild camped every night. Wild camping means pitching up in a non-designated camping spot. It could be in a wood, on a moor, a beach or even up a mountain, and unlike England this is actually lawful in Scotland. I told Archie I thought this sounded fantastic, and romantic images swirled around my mind of sleeping in ditches under the stars, a bit like Laurie Lee in *As I Walked Out One Midsummer Morning*. Surprisingly, though, Archie expressed some concern, saying wild camping might be a bit risky for a woman on her own. Rather than this rankling my feminist side, I was actually quite touched by this show of protective, chivalrousness. (Perhaps I'm more old-fashioned than I'd realised.) And anyway, I wasn't about to start an argument with someone who'd gone out of his way to show me a better route to take *and* made himself late for work in the process.

Incidentally, I never did try wild camping. To be honest, my indecisive nature means it probably wouldn't suit me. I like having a definite destination to aim for. This is how I imagine wild camping would go for me: *That looks a good place to pitch a tent, but it is a bit close to those houses. Perhaps I'll find somewhere more isolated further on.* Then a bit further on and I'd be thinking, *Well, it looks okay to pitch here, but there aren't many trees to hide me. Maybe they'll be better coverage a bit further ahead.* And later still, *Okay, I could pitch here, but it's not very flat. It might get flatter if I keep going.* And on and on it would continue until it was almost dark, I was out of options and forced to pitch on the side of a dual carriageway.

Further up the coast and I had reached suburbia. Near Ardrossan, I went into a shop to buy a sandwich and as I sat on the wall outside eating it, a middle-aged couple rocked up. I would usually say that we "had a chat" but that would indicate a two-way conversation took place and it was nothing of the sort. What actually happened was that they talked whilst I nodded… but barely understood a word they said. I know you'll be thinking, *here she goes again, not understanding Scottish accents.* But this time I had good reason not to… because these two were as drunk as skunks and slurring their words accordingly. Between the spittle and the alcohol fumes, I did manage to decipher the odd sentence. The woman, whom I identified as Rachel, disappeared into the shop to buy cigarettes whilst I sat outside with her husband, who told me what I'm sure was a very interesting story. He was definitely the drunker of the two and when Rachel re-emerged, she'd bought me a Mars bar as a thank you for looking after her drunken husband. Some of the conversation I managed to understand was pretty much the standard stuff.

'Ye never cycled all this way alone? What d' y' parents think about it?'

Rachel gave me their telephone number and said, *'Give us a wee tinkle when ye get there, let us know ye all right.'* I was meeting a lot of friendly Scots today. I watched them stagger off supporting each other as they went, and I have to admit, I was rather impressed that anyone could get themselves into such a state by only 11.30am.

Slowly, though, the Sustrans route began to lose its appeal. Between here and Glasgow lay a lot of suburbs; a concrete jungle of ever-increasing traffic. Having thought it'd be nice to come the long way, I realised now that if I kept going, I'd end up having to ride 75 miles. It would take me *ages…* much longer than ages, especially since getting lost was an inevitable part of city cycling. I thought about my booking at the backpackers' hostel, about the comfy bed and the socialising I was hoping to do tonight. I was winding myself up pretty badly, and so when I spotted a sign for Kilwinning railway station, I had a bit of a "to hell with it" moment. I decided there and then I would take a train the rest of the way into the city. Did I feel guilty for skipping 30 miles? A bit. But my conscience smoothed it over quick enough. *This was my trip,* I told myself. No one was monitoring me, and I would never *claim* to have cycled every inch of the way.

I'd happily tell everyone who'd sponsored me how, owing to practicalities, I'd missed out two small sections totalling 50 miles, but that I had still ridden 1,205 miles overall. And you know what: no one ever cared. As the train chugged towards Glasgow, I stared transfixed out of the window at the never-ending sea of housing estates, roads, factories and tower blocks, and I went cold at the thought I'd ever *considered* cycling through it all. I tried to work out where, for example, Paisley ended and Glasgow began, but like London, it was just one thick conurbation from one end to the other.

It is time for me to confess something. Call it a preconception if you like, but as keen as I was to visit Glasgow, I was also scared of it. Before anyone laughs (or gets offended), please let me explain. I was still quite young and naïve. I didn't personally know anyone from Glasgow, or know anyone who'd ever visited Glasgow, and these were the days before the internet, when information was not so easily accessible. There was only this over-reliance on rumour and I'm afraid that when I was growing up in the '80s, well, let's just say Glasgow didn't have the best reputation. (I still remember listening in horror as some boy in the school playground gleefully explained to me the intricacies of a Glasgow smile.) Throughout this trip, I'd grown accustomed to people's scaremongering about city dangers. But there was something more alarming about Glasgow's reputation back then, and in this cautionary frame of mind, I stepped off the train and headed out into the sprawling metropolis; with all the anxieties of a new inmate arriving on the wing. I kept my head down and made eye contact with no one... So, I was completely thrown when I entered the tourist information centre and met Gordon.

'Welcome to Glasgow,' he beamed at me from behind his desk, instantly relaxing my every muscle. Glasgow tourist board certainly picked its people well. I'd only gone in to get a city map, but all around me I could hear other tourists being told there was no accommodation left anywhere in the city (apparently there were several big conferences going on), so I felt both smug and relieved to have had the foresight to book ahead.

With my map in my back pocket, I recited the directions Gordon had given me until I knew them word-perfect, then I crossed my fingers and set out. It was a very enlightening 3 miles through the city centre. Firstly, I was surprised by how little traffic there was, considering this was the largest city in Scotland. But the architecture was the biggest eye-opener; it was beautiful. Although there is little left of medieval Glasgow, the city centre and West End comprise of breathtaking Victorian architecture, built out of red and blonde sandstone. (I'd half expected it to be all 1960s tower blocks and dark, gloomy streets.) Instead, I found the main thoroughfares wide and spacious with pavements to match, and it gave the place a very cosmopolitan, European feel. But the best was yet to come. As I pulled up at a set of traffic lights, two men in a white transit van (having presumably spied my collection tin) wound down their window and yelled across to me in heavy Glaswegian accents.

'Whit urr ye collecting fur?'

'Is this yer first time in Glasga?'

'Och, th' youth hostel? Gang left 'ere, left again at th'neist set o'traffic lights.' Friendly locals indeed. A little further on, I suddenly panicked, thinking I'd gone the wrong way, and pulled over. As I sat astride my bicycle studying my map, approaching six o'clock, the driver of a double-decker bus tooted his horn and drew up alongside me. He opened his doors and asked if I needed help with directions.

'*Och, th' youth hostel? Caw left up 'ere, ye cannae miss it.*'

Can you *imagine* a London bus driver doing that? (I can't.)

It had been a *fabulous* introduction to the city. I'd arrived expecting the worst and been shown the best. Whilst I am no expert, I think either Glasgow's reputation is exaggerated or the city has mellowed, if that's possible. Certainly, there was a lot of investment in Glasgow during the '80s and '90s, to tackle poverty, unemployment and poor housing; major contributors to social problems everywhere. Aesthetically speaking, reconstruction started in the '70s. The last tower block was constructed in 1978 and the restoration of those beautiful Victorian and Edwardian sandstone buildings became a major project. 1983 saw the birth of the *Glasgow's Miles Better* campaign, and its purpose was to change negative stereotypes about the city (although it clearly bypassed my school). But it did encourage more tourists to visit. I can only go on personal experience, but from what I'd seen in my first hour, Glasgow's residents seemed a most friendly crew, perhaps they always had been. Maybe, as usual, the media's representation of the city was about as far removed from reality as it's possible to get.

Once I'd checked into the backpackers' hostel, I left my things and went in search of some food. Just when I was beginning to think Glasgow wasn't as frightening as I'd first thought, I turned a corner and right on cue, I spied a newsagent's billboard that, no word of a lie, read: *Attacks on English grow.* I stopped dead in my tracks. I felt at that moment like Glasgow had given me a big welcoming hug… and then spat on me, all in one afternoon. For the rest of my shopping trip, I kept my mouth firmly shut. I avoided speaking and when I had to communicate in shops, I kept my responses to *"Aye"*, the only bit of Scottish I could confidently mimic.

The backpackers' hostel was a converted students' halls of residence for the summer. It stood in Glasgow's West End where huge Victorian terraces, with rooms large enough to house several double-decker buses, sat in grandiose style in perfect cream-coloured crescents. It was cool, light and welcoming, and within five minutes of my arrival I felt right at home. Just as I'd hoped, it was full of young, fun, chatty backpackers and after weeks of sporadic meetings and intermittent conversations, I couldn't get enough of the never-ending supply of people to chat to. A group began arranging a night out. Some time ago, I'd read in the *Melody Maker* that Glasgow offered some of the best nightlife in the UK and although eager to experience it, I would never have *dared* venture out alone. But in amongst our group of nine: five Australians, three New Zealanders and myself, I felt cocooned and safe and, even better, my English accent would be drowned out by their southern hemisphere tones.

Around nine o'clock, we went to a bar that played the sort of *indie* music I'd spent my teenage years listening to obsessively, and after two pints of lager, I was up on the dance floor with the rest of them, wondering why I'd ever felt apprehensive. The club was no different from any other

1990s club I'd been to. The women wore the same ripped jeans and danced to the same Nirvana songs, whilst the same groups of men prowled the club using the same old chat-up lines. I was approached a number of times, but I found an easy way to deal with unwanted attention.

'Sorry, I'm English,' I'd say, which in these parts seemed to have the same effect as saying, 'Sorry, I'm gay.' Either way, they nodded, disappointed, and moved on to try their luck with one of my more exotic companions. I spent most of the night chatting with the only male member of our group, a New Zealander by the name of Matt, who'd come to Glasgow a few months ago and then landed a job at the backpackers' hostel. He gave me a lesson on the differences between New Zealanders and Australians, and I finally began to hear the variation in the accents. I'd become intrigued with New Zealand ever since I'd met Les back in Wells, who'd told me (all of) his stories from his four years living there, as well as a bit about the country's history. I decided that night I'd definitely like to go cycle touring there some day.

DAY 31

(FIFTH DAY OF REST)

*N*ext on my *must-see* list was Loch Lomond and Glen Coe, but when I awoke to heavy cloud and misty rain, I knew it wouldn't be worth moving on today, not if I wanted to see those breathtaking views. I decided to take my fifth day of rest. I loved that I could stay or go as I pleased. I loved that no one dictated what time I got up, how far I should ride, or how I filled my time. Just before I'd come on this trip, an ex-boyfriend, perhaps in an effort to rekindle our relationship, had tried to persuade me to let him tag along. But I'd been *adamant* that I was going alone. I can't even begin to imagine the type of journey we would have had together, but I suspected arguments and misery would have played key roles.

I decided to volunteer my services at the hostel. The price of a bed for the night was two hours cleaning toilets and showers. I set to it with gusto and by the time I'd finished, the manager expressed her amazement at the gleaming taps and spotless floors; strongly suggesting they hadn't been done properly for quite some time. That night, a fresh group of backpackers arrived, mainly from New Zealand, and we spent the evening together, chatting and swapping stories. There was something remarkable about these young twenty-somethings. I don't like to generalise, but the majority of New Zealanders I've met travelling in Europe seemed to possess an inordinate charm, confidence and sense of humour. I thought New Zealand must be one hell of a country to produce so many fine, well-rounded individuals.

Matt was stationed on reception tonight. It must have been a good gig: getting pay and free accommodation to essentially do what the rest of us were willing to pay for. (Visit another country and hang out with fellow travellers.) Tonight, though, was an exceptionally good gig for Matt, as he sipped Scotch whisky in between answering phone calls.

'This is my dream job,' he slurred at one point. I was happy to chat with him again, until it dawned on me that he'd taken a shine to me and, with the help of alcohol, was working up the courage to make a move. At around ten o'clock, the proposition finally arrived. Or at least, I *think* that's what it was; Matt was so drunk by this point that it was hard to decipher his words. He was nice enough, but I had no inclination to become involved, and so the next time he answered the phone, I scuttled off to the safety of my female-only dormitory.

DAY 32

(51 MILES)

*W*hen I woke up at seven, I felt chilly and as I cast bleary eyes around the room, I noticed all the other dormitory occupants were still sound asleep. I shut my eyes and the next thing I knew; it was ten o'clock. Everyone had gone and I hadn't heard a thing. I was astonished. Back in my "ordinary" life, I was *never* able to get back to sleep. For me, it was a case of: once awake, stay awake. I'm not sure if this came from my working two jobs (meaning free time was squeezed to the point of strangulation), or my powerlessness over my own thoughts. Natural-born worriers, such as myself, will always find it difficult to control the ceaseless whirling of our minds, especially when trying to sleep. I can tell you now that when my brain is in overdrive, it regularly defies fatigue. It has defied all my attempts at meditation. And I wouldn't mind betting it could defy gravity itself. But that morning, not even the other women packing up and leaving had disturbed me. Was it a sign of some fundamental change within?

Out of the dormitory window I could see a thin blue line of sky over the city, signalling it was time for me to move on. I packed up my things whilst humming the theme tune to *The Littlest Hobo*, a cheesy '80s animal show I'd loved as a child. Downstairs, Matt, looking hungover and sheepish, gallantly carried my bicycle down the hostel's steps and we hugged goodbye. In fact, quite a crowd had gathered to wave me off. The urban sprawl of Glasgow lasted for 10 rather unappealing miles, but it was Saturday and so the traffic wasn't too bad. Or, at least it wasn't… until the A82 turned into a dual carriageway, whereby vehicle speeds suddenly increased by three hundred percent. It was all too reminiscent of Nottingham. Thankfully, in another 5 miles, I knew there would be that most sublime of all things: an off-road cycle path. I'd read that it was 15 miles long and would take me from Dumbarton and out all the way to the shores of Loch Lomond.

As I said goodbye to Glasgow disappearing over my shoulder, I thought cheerfully that I was leaving civilisation behind for a while, at least until Fort William or maybe even Inverness. My sojourn in the city had fulfilled all my desires to reconnect with people, but now I was ready to get back out there and greet the wilderness head-on… alone. Before leaving the city, I'd decided to stock up on food, since shops would be rare where I was headed, and interesting vegetarian food even rarer. In my experience, a typical Highland settlement (if large enough) will consist of a hotel with a public bar and a petrol station that doubled up as the village shop. These I would come to rely on for my food, although I knew they wouldn't offer much in the way of variety. I had a sneaking suspicion my diet would consist mainly of cheese and onion pies from now on, as these were the one vegetarian fast food you could be sure to find in any UK shop. In preparation for this culinary blandness, I'd found an artisan food store and spent the equivalent of two days' budget stocking up on a wide range of snacks. My plan was to stop for a picnic on the shores of Loch Lomond to celebrate my arrival in the Highlands, but it didn't turn out that way because I couldn't get food off my mind. Like a woman possessed, I ran through the names of each item in my panniers a dozen times, mentally tasting each one: *Spicy Jamaican vegetable pie, chocolate macaroons, organic strawberry yogurt, chocolate-covered Brazil nuts, yogurt-covered peanuts, fresh tomatoes, falafels, red apples, chilli-flavoured crisps, humus dip*, and on and on until I was in danger of drowning in my own drool. In the end, I made it within 2 miles of Loch Lomond before my willpower gave out, and I stopped on a bench and wolfed down over half of my supplies.

All too soon, I'd reached the end of the cycle path and was spat back out into the murderous traffic. The A82 followed the shoreline of Loch Lomond, but it was a further 15 miles before I could join less busy roads. For weeks now, I'd been dreaming of this moment, when I'd finally enter my beloved Highlands.

"O ye'll take the high road and I'll take the low road..."

I'd pictured myself cycling on roads that twisted their way across majestic landscapes of mountains and lochs.

"And I'll be in Scotland afore ye…"

But, in reality, there was only this dull, flat road stretching endlessly on, with cars racing past just inches from my elbow and at speeds far in excess of the limit. It felt as though I'd never left the city.

"But me and my true love will never meet again…"

I found myself blinking back tears of disappointment; would there be no Highland dream for me?

"On the bonnie, bonnie banks of Loch Lomond."

Can I be brutally honest now? Bonnie just wasn't a word I'd use to describe most of my time in Scotland thus far. The trouble, I think, was I'd allowed selective memories from previous trips to merge with this fanciful daydream I had of cycling off into the mountains at sundown, and the result was a sort of unrealistic nirvana. Forgotten were the everyday issues that blight any cycle tour, namely, traffic and more traffic. And the problem was, the more I'd "bigged up" this place in my mind, the further it had to fall. I began glowering at the constant stream of cars passing and thinking bitterly how not one penny had been donated into my collection tin since I'd crossed the border. And worst of all, I appeared to be back in a land of people staring at me. As the afternoon neared an end, so was my patience, my optimism and my humour. Was it my imagination or were car drivers becoming more aggressive by the minute? At one roundabout, an obnoxious bloke tried to wave me out of the way as I moved into the correct lane, and many others tooted their horns, not in greeting, but in a desire to display their disapproval of cyclists in general. At least seventy percent of traffic passed far closer than was safe (or necessary), and my range of four-letter words began to expand exponentially.

Many times, I've been a passenger in a car and witnessed the explosive reaction some drivers have as they come up behind a cyclist.

'*Damn, it's a cyclist,*' they huff in annoyance.

'*If I'm quick, I can just follow the car in front and squeeze past. Nope, too late, something's coming the other way now.*' And on come the brakes in a manner which makes you think that having to slow down for a moment is the worst thing that has *ever* happened to them.

'*Come on, come on, you shouldn't even be on the road, holding me up like this.*' Why are they totally unable to recognise that this whole process only takes about a minute?

'*Bloody cyclists,*' they say as they rev their engines pointlessly.

'*Right, I'm just going to go now.*' By this point, they are so hacked off that, despite not being able to see if it's clear coming the other way, they pull out. At that point, I'll shut my eyes and wonder what will happen if something does come the other way. Will we have a head-on collision or will we swerve back in and knock the cyclist flying? I think I can guess.

I have been trying my hardest not to sound at all: *it's them and us* or: *it's car drivers vs cyclists.* Or at least I *was* trying, until a few seconds later. Just when I thought things couldn't get any worse, a white transit van passed by too close. There was a brief pause, before a thick strawberry milkshake landed in my lap. Splashes dribbled down my face whilst hoots of male laughter could be heard through the open van window. That was *it*. I exploded in anger and pulled up so I could give them the middle finger with *both* hands. But inside, I was emotionally bruised. Was this the final sign that cyclists really were the underdogs of the road? The milkshake seemed to scream a resounding yes.

'*Who was that angry wee lassie with dairy produce in her hair?*'

Long before Lance Armstrong, Bradley Wiggins and Chris Froome made cycling as popular as it is now, I think cyclists were seen as a teensy bit, well... geeky and uncool. And I felt rather indignant about that, because the fittest, strongest and bravest people I knew all happened to be cyclists. The thing they all had in common was that they shunned convention. Whilst everyone else I knew was aiming for higher salaries, expensive cars and bigger houses, these individuals were bucking trends and rejecting the well-worn path of wealth accumulation in favour of more meaningful lives. And I really admired them for it. I'd always had trouble anyway, understanding *why* someone with a fancy car is envied, or is seen as having "made it" in life. For me, a car will always be just another mode of transport, and no matter what the price tag, the accomplishment (if you can even call it that) is the same: sit on your arse, press your foot down 2 inches and hey presto, you've made your machine go faster. *Congratulations, sir.* Some big achievement, huh?

But really, though, I know why they're envied. It's just that I'm with my geeky cycling mates on this one. Money for me will only ever be something I have to earn to cover my basics of living, and I *refuse* to define myself by how much of it I do *or* don't have. Sometimes I find it a little depressing. It's been 370 million years since fish first crawled out of the primordial mud with all that human potential tingling in their DNA. Against the odds, we survived and evolved to become these amazing beings that learnt to walk upright, discovered fire and colonised the planet. We have the ability to understand things, amazing things; we have language and music and science. We have begun to map the heavens and the human genome, and we have made amazing art and architecture. Most importantly, we have the propensity to care and love and understand, not just other human beings but for other species as well. Wouldn't it be a tragedy if the human story ends with the accumulation of bits of green paper, whilst we bury ourselves and our world under a pile of plastic trash?

*

Thankfully, the road split into two at Tarbet. Most of the traffic took the left-hand fork whilst I took the right, and instantly the noise ceased, as if someone had pressed a great silencer button on the world. Now that I no longer had to fear for my life, I was able to turn my attention to my surroundings. It was early evening and the sun began its descent behind the mountains. After all the knotted-up tension from the A82, I felt the calm wash over me, in the same way waves washed over Loch Lomond and gently rested upon its shores. How could I ever have doubted Scotland's magic? I pulled on a jumper. I couldn't remember the last time I'd cycled in anything other than a t-shirt (unless it was raining), and it symbolised how far north I'd come. I hummed one of my favourite songs, Dire Straits, *Brothers in Arms*. Whilst the song was written about the Falklands War, given artistic license, I have always associated this sad but beautiful tune with the Highland Clearances. These began after the final Jacobite rebellion ended in mass slaughter at Culloden in 1746, with Bonnie Prince Charlie fleeing in exile. The government, not wanting any more uprisings, started to crack down on the Highland clans and their way of life, with the wearing of tartan and the playing of bagpipes banned, and a law was passed to make it much easier for outsiders to purchase large areas of land.

But worse was to follow. For hundreds of years, Highlanders had had indefeasible rights to rent land, to live and farm within their clan territories, but this was never actually recognised by Scottish law. So, when landlords realised sheep grazing was more profitable than their tenants' rent, the unscrupulous landlords began to forcibly evict the Highlanders, a growing trend which continued throughout the 18th and 19th centuries. Highlanders were moved out to crofting communities on the coast, where they were expected to eek out a meagre living from the fishing and kelp industries. But as time went on, these communities suffered more and more devastating effects, firstly, from the collapse of the kelp industry, then with the growth and overcrowding in crofting communities, and finally from potato blight and famine. By law, landlords were meant to financially assist their struggling and often starving tenants, but most found it cheaper to simply pay for their passage to Australia or America. (And as we now know, this was no rosy option, since many died from disease before arriving.) It is thought that around 70,000 Scottish Highlanders emigrated during that time (and I'm guessing is one of the reasons so many Americans come here looking for their ancestral roots). This whole sorry episode takes its place in history along with far, *far* too many other examples of profit for the few taking priority over the welfare of the many.

*

One could be forgiven for mistaking the campsite in Ardlui for a battle scene. Marauding gangs of children ran amok, screaming and shouting, whilst their equally noisy parents hollered to each other between tents. And judging by their flushed and sweaty faces, I think many of them already had a full afternoon of boozing behind them. In between lingered a few souls like myself, wearing resigned faces and knowing their dream of a peaceful night under the Highland stars just wasn't going to happen here. Maybe Archie had been right; perhaps wild camping was the way to go. My defence against all this was to growl and hiss at any child who dared come near my pitch, a bit like a swan protecting her nest, and then chuckle quietly as I watched them scatter. Sometimes during the lonely hours of camping, I found myself focusing on the prospect of motherhood. Like most young women, I wondered whether I'd have a family of my own one day, and on occasion, I'd even known myself to get broody. But at campsites like this, I'd borne witness to the many harassed mothers: running around after the family, worrying, holding everyone together and never looking totally relaxed or like they were enjoying themselves. It was enough to put anyone off.

In amongst this scene of Armageddon, I noticed an older woman preparing food in the back of a Land Rover. As I struggled with my tent in the stiffening breeze, she came over and invited me to share a meal with her, and I accepted gratefully. I'd noticed her earlier when I was checking in at the campsite, and from the little I'd heard of her conversation with the receptionist, I'd believed her to be a well-spoken Englishwoman. My skills at accent identification must have been getting worse, because it turns out Margery was born and bred in Melbourne, Australia. In my defence, Margery admitted herself, her accent had mellowed during her travels; and *what* travels they turned out to be. As I tucked into a steaming hot bowl of pasta, I listened in awe as she told me about her life. As a girl of thirteen, she decided then and there she wanted to see the world, and resolved to never waste a single second of her life. She completed a spell in the army, and afterwards she'd continued to travel, living in many places on different continents. Right now, having just turned seventy, she was travelling around Europe and living out of the back of an old Land Rover. Her philosophy in life was that it was far more important to see the world than to make money from it. I couldn't agree more.

It was a particularly special meeting for me, not just because Margery's life sounded similar to the path, I hoped mine might take, but because I quickly realised that I was talking to a very intelligent woman. Wisdom radiated from her like a bright and comforting lantern on a dark and foggy night. Oh, it felt good to speak with and, more importantly, *listen to* someone so frank, wise and honest, and especially for that someone to be another woman. (Sadly, the majority of people who approached me on my trip had been men.) Margery asked me about myself, and I found myself instantly opening up to her. I told her of my hopes and dreams, my fears and doubts, and she counselled me without judgement. Her praise was particularly welcome. Whilst I'd not exactly been short of people encouraging or congratulating me, they'd usually ruin it by asking me why I was making my trip. People, it seemed, needed to file everyone into a category. *She did it because she was adventurous.* Or *she did it because she was eccentric.* Margery didn't ask why, though. She understood, no questions needed. Margery, Sir Hellingwell, Archie, John in Dartmoor and Peter in Exeter; they had all understood the longing to make a journey. To follow one's heart and explore the world; a rite of passage if you like. Journeying on until you find your true self.

Margery and I chatted late into the evening. I felt I'd met a person I think a lot of youngsters could do with; an elder who not only accepted them for who they were, but who could guide them too. Margery was a woman of substance and I devoured our conversation hungrily. I could have talked until dawn, but the sudden drop in evening temperature came as a shock, and despite wearing every stitch of clothing I had, I still shivered. I eventually had to bid Margery good night and dive into the depths of my sleeping bag to warm up. (In the morning, I found the five-pound note which she'd left in my collection tin.) As I lay in the dark, I heard excited shouts from the campsite's children; they had sighted bats up in the trees above. Despite loving these fascinating creatures, I was too cold to venture outside again.

DAY 33

(64 MILES)

*P*oking a frozen hand out of bed, I switched on the radio for my early-morning time check. The newsreader was talking about a car crash in France. Shivering, I pulled on my coat, which was cold right through to the lining, and waited for it to warm up. I wondered if this was the seven or eight o'clock news.

'And I am sure the nation will be shocked and saddened by the death of Princess Diana.'

Hang on… what? Was this an April Fool's joke? Blimey, how *long* had I been asleep? Listening intently now, I heard the full details of the paparazzi car chase and the resultant fatal crash.

I wonder how many people's first thoughts on hearing this news was that of a conspiracy theory. From what I understood, the favoured hypothesis was that the British state decided it too much of an impropriety to risk Diana's wealthy, non-British, non-Christian boyfriend becoming stepfather to the future king of England and staged the crash to look like an accident. In the years that followed, so many people made these accusations that in 2004, the Metropolitan Police were forced to launch Operation Paget, an investigation examining 175 alternative theories as to how the crash may have come about, and it cost twelve and a half million pounds. But all came back with the same conclusion: that Princess Diana's death was an unlawful killing by a chauffeur a little worse for wear whilst fleeing the relentless pursuing paparazzi.

I wondered if this would be one of those moments where people would look back and say, '*I always remember where I was the day that I heard about...* (insert world-famous event).' I certainly wouldn't forget this moment; shivering in a Highland campsite. Then I remembered Les, whom I'd met in Wells, cycling his way around the British Isles and raising money for the British Red Cross. Bringing the tragedy of landmine victims to the attention of world media would be Princess Diana's legacy, and Les had been adamant he would be meeting with his charity's patron after his ride. I distinctly remember raising my eyebrows at the time and thinking *in your dreams, mate*. Now I wish I'd placed a bet *against* it happening.

I desperately needed a cup of tea to warm me up. Whilst I waited for my saucepan to boil, a young Dutch backpacker, who'd pitched his tent beside mine last night and then diligently snubbed my every attempt to communicate with him, suddenly became as friendly as a puppy dog when he saw me making a brew. Feeling bemused by his sudden change in attitude, I offered to make him a drink whilst he hastily explained he didn't have a stove (*quelle surprise*). We drank tea and chatted… or rather, I chatted whilst he flat out patronised me: What I was doing, which way I was going, the time it was taking me and even my age (twenty-one was apparently far too young to be doing this) were all wrong in his eyes and *all* required a lengthy description of how I'd be better off doing things according to his own non-expert, non-cycling, non-stove carrying twenty-*three*-year-old arse. Just then a familiar face appeared out the back of her Land Rover.

'Margery,' I squeaked, and fled from this condescending young man.

*

I'd come to the end of Loch Lomond and, for a time, the road shadowed the River Falloch, one of seven tributaries to the loch. The heavens let loose one of those drizzles that doesn't feel particularly heavy but soon has you soaked through, and it was to last all day. In the cool morning air, the cycling was effortless and I felt as fit as a fiddle. My thighs were powerful; the wind had my back and I really believed I was invincible. Even as the road began winding its way up and into the mountains after Inveraran, I barely noticed; I simply changed down a few gears and was easily able to continue at the same steady pace. The scenery was spectacular and the mist, far from hindering the views, simply added to the eerie but mystical feel of the land. Only the occasional car splashing past me broke the isolation.

For the next 12 miles I was barely aware of the rising gradient, so it came as something of a surprise to see a sign informing me I was now at the peak of Rannoch Moor, 1,145 feet above sea level. (For comparison, the Kirkstone Pass was a 1,500ft climb in just 6 miles.) I stopped to brush wet hair from my eyes and stare out across the moor. Rannoch is known as the most inhospitable, wildest terrain in the British Isles; a vast expanse of peat bogs where one could be horrifically swallowed up and never seen again. Brimming with rare and important flora and fauna, Rannoch (which means bracken in Gaelic) was designated a *Site of Special Scientific Interest* on 5th January 1976, exactly one month before I was born, so we almost share a birthday. Stretching for 50 square miles, there are refreshingly few signs of man to be seen, save for the railway line, and that in itself was an amazing feat of engineering. As the line crossed many miles of bog, the men who built it had to float the track on top of tree roots, earth and brushwood. I'd once read a book written by a man who'd crossed Rannoch Moor on his horse, and ever since then, I'd been fascinated by this place. As I stood on the roadside looking out across the moor, for the first time on my trip I had the urge to go walking and to be a part of the landscape. I longed to wander across it with the wet ground beneath my bare feet and the smell of heather and peat in my nose. But at the same time, thoughts of being at one with such raw and unforgiving wilderness were met with a justifiable wariness. I believe being alone out here, with only the bicycle and my own energy to rely upon, made me appreciate all the more that nature commands the greatest respect. Even from my position of relative safety on the road: that narrow sliver of moor seized and tamed by man, I felt very vulnerable and I pedalled on with reverence.

Cycling through the Glen Coe Mountain Range that day, I experienced one of those rare moments in life when everything felt just right. I had an overwhelming sense that I knew why I was here and alive on this planet. And any past disappointments or heartache suddenly didn't matter, because now I had this: this moment, cycling in my favourite place. *The* most beautiful place, and feeling so fit and strong, it was almost a transcendental experience in itself. I was at the zenith of my life.

But just like a moment of bright sun on an otherwise overcast day, which floods the land in warmth and radiance before disappearing quickly again, my moment of clarity passed and everything started to unravel. When I'd set out from Ardlui that morning for my longest ride yet, I knew I was physically capable of riding 64 miles, but I'd failed to prepare myself psychologically. And without preparation, I allowed tiny niggles to escalate into major upheavals: *I'm soaked right through. My gloves are too thin. I have a swimming pool in each boot.* (The plastic bags had once again failed and I had to spend an inordinate amount of energy trying *not* to think about those freezing pools submerging my feet). Worse than any of this, though (and I'm ashamed to admit this), was that I was beginning to find the cycling boring. Yup, despite being in the place I had quite literally *dreamed* of riding, I was totally unable to prevent apathetic thoughts plaguing my mind. *What the hell am I doing this for? When will I get to Fort William?* And even worse, *I could be enjoying these views from the comfort of a warm hotel bar.*

Sometimes, when the isolation and seclusion ground me down, when I got bored of talking to myself and thinking just went around in circles, it was at times like these that I relied upon singing to keep my spirits up. I made a list of twenty happy or memorable songs and sang them out loud, one by one. Some of my more memorable cycling tunes included Lou Reed, *Perfect Day;* The Beautiful South (multiple songs), and a song I had heard often on the radio recently, with a woman telling me that I was free to do whatever I wanted to. I also regularly sang the entire *Simon and Garfunkel's Greatest Hits* album. Now these I knew off by heart because, as a child, whenever our family went on a road trip, it was guaranteed to get a play. And it was usually followed by *Abba's Greatest Hits* whilst my mother sang along in her rather off-key voice.

Further along the never-ending road, a minibus honed into view. It was parked in a lay-by and through the misted-up windows, I could see all the occupants staring out at me. Despite feeling self-conscious, I decided I would stop and play the role of eccentric stranger they no doubt perceived me to be. I knocked on their window and asked them for the time, something I couldn't have cared less about, but I just needed to hear another human voice. When I revealed to these twenty-somethings that I was heading for Fort William that night, I almost wished I'd kept my mouth shut, and I was bombarded by a string of smart-arse comments: *You'll never make it before dark. It's uphill all the way. The best thing you can do is to turn around and head back to where you came from.* But I had been to Scotland enough times now to know that this type of banter is part of the national character. The locals love telling unsuspecting cyclists that the place they are headed for is via a few mountaintops, or twice as far as they thought. From a Scottish perspective, I guess if you live with the isolation and less-than-clement conditions all year round, you are likely to conclude that anyone who comes cycling here *voluntarily* must have a few screws missing. Ergo, it is imperative to tease these cyclists mercilessly. I gave them an indulgent smile and gratefully accepted a mug of tea passed through the window. As I sipped the hot nectar, I received both looks of admiration and comments of *you must be mad*. I didn't appreciate it at the time, but I must have looked to them like a crazy woman; alone on her bicycle, atop a mountain in the pissing rain. No wonder they ribbed me.

I passed a sign: *F'aite don Gha'idhealtachd*. Or in English, *Welcome to the Highlands*. But my excitement didn't last and before long, I was enveloped once more in a blanket of melancholy. I was four hours into a six-hour ride and I had once again crossed that invisible line and gone from: *How marvellous it is to be cycle touring*, and over to: *God, I can't wait for this day to be over*. I was getting sick of being soaked and sick of having to make my feet go round and around whilst feeling like I was getting nowhere. I was in free fall, longing for hot showers, dry feet and stillness. I often think now that it was a pity I couldn't have charted my emotions on this trip and plotted them onto a graph. They were so up and down that I imagine they'd look something like the read-out from a seismic wave.

Just as I was reaching the end of my tether, where it seemed like the only way to release the built-up tension was to burst into tears, fate came to my rescue. It sent me a reminder to always appreciate how lucky I was to be here. It came in the form of 15 glorious miles of downhill. That was 15 miles where I could sit still and enjoy the rush of speed, feel the miles being eaten up effortlessly and watch the gorgeous views slipping by: the craggy clifftops, the rocky peninsulas and the waterfalls that thundered down the mountainside. Down and down I went, spiralling forever downwards. Through thick banks of low cloud where I couldn't see where I was going, then bursting out for a few seconds to catch sight of Glen Coe, before hitting another cloud bank. I felt as though I was falling into the arms of Fort William.

By the time I had to pedal again, I'd reached Ballachulish, where a welcome sign told me Fort William was only 14 miles further. I found a phone box and called the backpackers' hostel at Fort William (sister to the one in Glasgow) and secured a night's accommodation with my debit card. I wanted that comfy bed and hot shower guaranteed. I stayed in the phone box a little longer to shelter from the wind and eat a cheese and onion pie. I watched cars appearing out of the mist, having just traversed the same road I had, and I wondered if they'd enjoyed their journey. Had they ventured from their cars at all, maybe gone for a walk and really absorbed the atmosphere of Glencoe on a day like today? Ballachulish was a quiet village, stuck between the two major tourist attractions of Glencoe and Ben Nevis, and it seemed to have escaped a decorative glossing-over for the sake of attracting visitors. Two young boys played happily in a puddle whilst a run-down teashop offered hot drinks and cream buns. But I decided I would pass on the opportunity and I took up the reins (or should that be rains?) for the final leg.

I was glad to find my legs were still in fine working order after 60 miles but unfortunately, the same couldn't be said for my backside. My saddle was the same one I'd had for a number of years now. It looked plump and well cushioned and had served me okay up to now, but lately, I'd become aware that on rides of over 40 miles, things could get rather uncomfortable down there. Rule number twenty-three of cycle touring: when it comes to saddles, no one can give you the correct advice… *no one.* And if they try, I would take their advice with a pinch of salt. I can't tell you how many cycle shops and experts I would consult over the coming years about which saddle would be most appropriate for me. They would give varying advice and suggestions, from big sofa-type saddles to razor blade thin ones, and all would be convinced that their suggestion was the answer to my saddle woes. Well, I'm sorry to say, I eventually came to the following conclusion: finding your perfect saddle is a bit like finding your perfect partner. There are no set rules which, if followed, will lead to your perfect match. You simply have to endure the trial-and-error method until you find one that fits. And just like finding a partner, it is highly likely that, in the meantime, you will waste a great deal of time and money and suffer much pain before finding your soulmate.

Right now, though, finding "the one" was years away and right now, recurring waves of pain were crashing into my brain and making me feel sick. I resorted to walking for ten minutes at a time so I could give my posterior a break, and what should have been the final hour dragged out another two. A lot more cars were passing me now and judging by the hire stickers on the back, most were fellow tourists. I could see car occupants staring at me curiously as I pushed my bicycle down the road. Were they wondering why I was walking? Did it occur to anyone that I might need some assistance? If it did, not one of them stopped to ask whether I was okay. To keep my spirits raised, I thought of amusing quips I could give if (by some miracle) anyone did stop. My reply would be a cheerful, '*I'm fine, but my backside had an argument with my saddle.*'

Fort William was a lot bigger than I'd expected. It was a built-up town with lots of shops, numerous hotels, restaurants and car parks, and all built beside the lapping shores of Loch Linnhe and overshadowed by the mighty Ben Nevis, which, standing at 4,408 feet, is the highest mountain in the British Isles. It all came as quite a shock after the emptiness of the mountains, but there was no denying it; I was over the moon to be here. I arrived at the modest but comfortable backpackers' hostel and happily closed the door on the elements that had whipped and punished me. I took a hot shower to thaw out and then went down to the lounge and sat with my hair wrapped in a towel, boots drying by the open fire and helping myself to complimentary tea and biscuits. Once again, the greatest joys in the simplest things were always found at the end of the hardest days.

Later that evening, I headed out to find an off-license, complete with a long list of orders from the other backpackers. (Serves me right for saying out loud that I was off out to buy a bottle of beer.) On my way back, I stopped at a pay phone and called my mother, to dazzle her with my speedy progress since last we'd met. Engrossed in our conversation, I failed at first to notice a tragic drama unfold on the road outside. A wee lad of about six had been knocked off his bicycle by a car and lay quite still in the road. The ambulance arrived quickly on the scene, checked over the casualty and took him away. Sometime later, after making my statement to the police, I wandered back to the hostel in a daze. My elation at completing my longest day had gone, and I went to bed feeling the sadness choking me. The day had started and ended with a road traffic incident; one an international celebrity, the other a local lad, but both equally tragic for the families concerned.

DAY 34

(35 MILES)

*W*hen I saw the signpost for Inverness, 66 miles away, for a moment I forgot about my saddle woes and actually toyed with the idea of getting it all done in one go. The fact that I *wanted* to push on was rather telling. It forced me to accept that, for now at least, my love affair with this journey was over, and it had crept up on me unawares. I had started out *insisting* my trip would take me as long as it took. I had promised myself that I'd never rush through it or treat it like an endurance test. But somewhere in southern Scotland something had changed. After traversing hundreds of miles over endless hills, come baking sun or torrential rain, not to mention the emotional strain of living alone in a tent for five weeks, always the watched stranger, it had all taken its toll. Wanderlust had been replaced with a desire for stillness, familiarity and above all else, friendship, and I wanted to reach them as fast as my legs could get me there.

I thought back to six months earlier, when I'd gazed out of the window at work and schemed a way to make this dream happen, and I felt a bit guilty for wishing it over. Perhaps road weariness was something that befell all travellers eventually, a sort of saturation point. I think I realised that it wasn't so much the length of the trip which had left me jaded, but the emotional rollercoaster I'd ridden. It was as if my mental health was waving a little white flag and pleading, *'Whoa there, I've had enough of all these ups and down. Please return me to terra firma at once or we could be in big trouble.'* I decided not to feel guilty. I'd had a fabulous time and just because the magic of this particular tour was over for me, I knew in time I'd get my mojo back and there would be others.

*

After five minutes in the saddle with my posterior hurting, I shrewdly decided not to push for Inverness today. Instead, I implemented my well-worn formula for dealing with physical weariness, and instead of taking a rest day (which always made me feel depressed about my lack of progress), I instead planned a short, easy ride. I would head to Fort Augustus, just 35 miles up the road, and by the morning, I knew I'd feel as good as if I had taken a day off. (I pause for a moment here to proudly reflect upon 35 miles now being a short and easy ride for me.)

I was used to my cycling fantasies revolving around food, but today they'd been replaced with a desperate longing for a big, comfy, well-worn-in saddle. I'd heard it said many times that the ultimate in touring comfort comes from using a leather saddle… *but,* only once you get through the initial breaking- it-in stage. Breaking in a new leather saddle happens over time, as the leather stretches to fit the shape of your bottom perfectly and you end up with two little dips that your sit bones fit into nicely; a made-to-measure saddle if you like. But let's think about that for a moment… you have to mould this saddle *yourself,* using *your own backside* and ride at least 500 *miles* before it even begins to feel comfortable. Would you excuse me for a moment whilst I roll on the floor laughing at the very idea? I'm sure there are thousands of leather saddle fans out there who will tell me that it's perfectly true and that leather saddles really are the best thing since sliced bread, but for me, I'm afraid, it's a no. If you can grit your teeth through that much pain, then I admire you greatly. I briefly wondered if I should look for a new saddle in Inverness, since this one wasn't up to the job anymore. But one look at my rather forlorn bank account put paid to the idea. Besides, I wouldn't want to risk ending up with a saddle more uncomfortable than this one; it's not like I'd be able to take it back. (Do bicycle shops even allow you to return a saddle for a refund?) Rule number twenty-four of cycle touring: be absolutely certain your saddle will be comfortable over long distances. In other words, try it out before you go. Break it in and whilst you're at it, build up some fitness at the same time. Sometimes I think I should have called this book; D*on't Do this the Way I Did*.

I was still following the A82, and this particular stretch was the main thoroughfare from west to east or Fort William to Inverness, and it was busy, narrow and winding. I had become immune to the roar of cars by now, but the sound of a lorry coming up behind me always got my attention. I could hear it struggling and groaning its way through the gears as the driver tried to pick up speed on the steep gradients. I remember thinking that I would move off the road when it caught me up, but then I worried because with a steep drop to my left, there was no way of moving off the road. In a moment of bad luck, the lorry caught me up in the worst place imaginable: halfway around a blind bend. There was a screech of brakes behind me as I must have suddenly come into the driver's view; a terrifying sound. My heart skipped a beat and I closed my eyes, bracing for impact... but none came. I stopped to look round and saw that the lorry was not as close as the squealing brakes had sounded. The driver gave me a momentary hard stare, before crunching the truck back into gear and pulling around me. I pushed myself as close into the edge as I could without tumbling down the drop, and waited for the long queue of cars to pass.

In a lay-by, I stopped to calm my jangled nerves with a cigarette. The little picnic area was positioned above yet another stunning waterway, which according to my map was the aforementioned Loch Lochy, a beautiful name that rolled off the tongue like a line of poetry, and I repeated it over and over. Out of all the places in Scotland thus far, Loch Lochy had to be my all-time second favourite name (the number one being Kinlochleven). I don't know whether Loch Lochy has some other meaning aside from its literal translation. I mean, isn't it a bit like calling a place *the Woody Wood* or *the Hilly Hill*? This particular Lakey Lake is famous for being the site of *the Battle of the Shirts;* a battle which ended a 360-year-old feud between the clans of Donald and Fraser. The battle was named after a very rare phenomenon which occurred in Scotland that day: a heatwave; and it got so warm that the fighters were forced to discard their chain mail and fight in their underclothes. Perhaps a better name would have been Loch Shirty.

As I sat on a picnic table smoking, I surveyed the mounds of litter strewn about. Only the other day, I'd heard on the radio that Coca-Cola is now the biggest-selling soft drink in every country in the world (a rather depressing statistic in itself), except, that is, for Scotland, whose citizens prefer their national tipple of *Irn-Bru* (discounting, of course, countries subject to US trade embargos, where Coca-Cola isn't available to buy). Travelling through Scotland at a speed slow enough to observe every litter-strewn gutter, I'd say this claim by Irn-Bru at least appears to be true. But red and white tin cans or orange and blue, there were still too many of them discarded carelessly.

Despite the roaring fire at the hostel last night, my boots were still wet and squelchy, and as a result, the clean socks I'd put on that morning were now also wet and squelchy. It seemed like the further I got from Fort William, the clearer the skies became, and I wondered if it could be due to the rain shadow effect. As I recall it (quick school Geography lesson coming up now; please skip this paragraph if you wish), the dominant winds of the British Isles are south-westerly, meaning a lot of moist, warm air blows off the Atlantic and onto our Isles. When it encounters the higher grounds of the Lake District, the Pennines and the Western Highlands, this warm, moist air gets forced up and over these barriers, but as it rises it also cools. And as cooler air can't hold as much water as warm, it releases a lot of its moisture content and explains why more rain falls over higher ground. For those folks living on the east coast of the United Kingdom, by the time the air descends onto their side of the country, the worst of the moisture will already have fallen; hence the term, rain shadow. You would think this is reason enough to live on the east, but living on the west coast does have its own advantages. It has the benefit of receiving warm air straight from the Gulf Stream and so tends to be milder. Those in the east (and in the north-east especially) can spend their winters shivering as polar continental masses blow in from the Baltics... So, I think that probably makes it 1-1. However, as I doubted I'd gone far enough east to benefit from the rain shadow, I put the lack of rain down to sheer luck. But I did wonder, would it be noticeably drier between Inverness and John O'Groats than it had been between Glasgow and Fort William? It certainly couldn't get much wetter.

The inescapable noise of traffic was starting to irritate the hell out of me, and the A82 was arguably one of the busiest roads I'd ridden in the UK. Thoughts of leaving it behind once and for all cheered me up immensely... but *nothing* cheered me up as much as watching my milometer tick over onto the 1,000 miles mark; a momentous occasion. I was desperate to share this with someone. I wanted to yell *hey, look what I've done*, in the same way I had when I'd taught myself to swim in the English Channel as a child. But there were only the anonymous cars passing by, who saw me as an irritation and not as someone achieving something wonderful. But still, one *thousand* miles. I thought dreamily about where else that could take me. London to Rome, or New York to St Louis (one-third of the way across the USA), or even Melbourne to Brisbane. A whole world of possibilities was beginning to open up in my mind.

Only 3 miles from Fort Augustus and the pain in my posterior once again forced me off the bike. Another lay-by, another cigarette. (I had dumbly allowed these death sticks to slip back into my life on an almost daily basis.) I liked to admire my bicycle during these breaks. Steadfast, strong and reliable. I found myself looking at the frame in the same way a horse dealer might look at the lines and curves of an animal. My bicycle had transported me and all my luggage the length of the UK with barely a problem, save for one or two minor issues, and it sounds ridiculous but I was bursting with pride. Yes, I know; it's just an inanimate object, but I became very attached to that bicycle in a way I couldn't explain, until years later when a friend described it thus: '*It's as if all the thoughts, dreams and experiences you have whilst riding make up a part of the frame itself.*' And for me, this was so true. I was attached to my bicycle as though it were a second skin or a third leg.

The campsite at Fort Augustus was pleasant, clean and, most importantly, flat. (I've got to ask: campsites on sloping grounds, why even bother?) And there were the most incredible power showers, and all for a levy of just three pounds. After supper, I sat staring at the pay phone, biting my fingernails and trying to summon up courage... Despite all my best resolutions, I still couldn't wipe the thought of Steve from my mind. My opinions on the matter went around in circles, driving me crazy. One minute I convinced myself my feelings were strictly platonic, before admitting I did have a thing for him and wondering if he might like me too. Then I would try and scheme a way to return to Skipton so I could find out one way or another, before eventually resolving, yet again, to just let sleeping dogs lie and forget the whole impractical, uncertain, insane notion that we might end up in a relationship. But the resolve never lasted; It didn't stop me thinking about him and the whole cycle of potential outcomes would all start up again. In an effort to find answers to these conflicting thoughts, I decided I would be bold and just call him. I rehearsed thoroughly the exact level of casualness I would exude. The 'just ringing you because I was bored' routine, and the feigned indifference of 'maybe I'll swing by Skipton again sometime'. I dialled his number thinking, *keep it friendly, keep it casual, but behave in a demure and intelligent fashion.*

Steve answered on the third ring. 'Yo, pisshead, it's me.' Oh dear!

Actually, the conversation went pretty well, once I'd gotten over my initial nerves. It *was* chatty and causal and we *did* laugh a lot, and if I wasn't mistaken, Steve's delight at hearing from me smashed any illusions I had that our friendship was entirely platonic. Then came the awkward moment. I cleared my throat.

'So, I was thinking. Once I've finished up here, I have to go back to Sussex to see my family. But maybe I could stop by Skipton for a while, you know, so you can buy me that pint you owe me.

When I finally hung up the phone, my face was flushed by Steve's parting words: *he would be counting down the days to my next visit*. But back at my tent, my excitement quickly faded as reality set in. It would be another five weeks before that visit could happen; a time innumerable during the early days of romance. Unwittingly, I had just made my last 150 miles a damn sight harder.

DAY 35

(35 MILES)

*B*ecause I'd been to Inverness numerous times and explored the surrounding areas, I didn't need a map for this bit; I could visualise the route exactly. On leaving the campsite, I would cycle through Fort Augustus then turn right onto the B862; a very steep road which wound its way up and into the Monadhliath Mountains. Once up at the top, I would enjoy an easier ride along the high mountain road, and 5 miles before Inverness, the road would begin its descent into the town and down to the shores of the Beauly Firth. After Inverness, I would cycle north on the A9, swapping the more dramatic Highlands for the less mountainous counties of Sutherland and Caithness, and on this road, I'd stay, all the way to John O'Groats. It all sounded so simple and the end felt so close that I half expected to see John O' Groats around the next corner...

The B862 climbs 1,000 feet in just five and a half miles and despite being super fit, I still had to admit defeat and get off to push up the steepest sections. But I was comforted by the thought that this would be the last *really* steep hill on my ride (or so I believed at the time), and it acted as a carrot dangling in front of my nose. The B862 is one of General Wade's famous Military Roads, and in case you don't know, he was the man sent to tame (read: tear the wild heart out of) the Highlands and its people. After the Scottish Catholic King James VII lost his throne to his Protestant daughter Mary and son-in-law William of Orange in 1688, the Jacobites (the name for King James' supporters) were not at all impressed by these foreigners who had come to rule them, and so they began a campaign to restore what they saw as their true leader. Their battles became known as Jacobite Uprisings. Of course, the government in London didn't like the sound of this, so they sent a man to the Highlands to assess the seriousness of the situation. Step forward General Wade, a man who'd already proved himself top dog during several campaigns, including the Nine Years' War and War of Spanish Succession. Wade concluded that the Highlands and its people would be far easier to control if several strategic forts were built and linked by good roads. The government liked the idea and promoted Wade to Commander-in-Chief of North Britain. (Note: *of North Britain*, not Scotland, which I think says a lot about their attitudes.) Forts were built at Inverness, Fort Augustus and Fort William, and Wade saw to it that a coast-to-coast road connected them all. Did I say that Wade did? The actual donkey work was done by laymen (around one hundred in total), who no doubt worked their balls off through dubious Scottish weather and clouds of Highland midges. (And I bet a cheese and onion pie there are no plaques anywhere commemorating the real workers for their hard graft.) The southern section of this coast-to-coast road is more or less today's B862, and in fact, many military roads built around that time became the basis for the main roads throughout the Highlands today.

The B862 is very scenic but if you come this way, you'll miss out on Loch Ness, that most famous of Scottish lochs. Loch Ness is actually the flooded bottom of a valley so big that it is visible from space. Known as the Great Glen (what is it with Scotland and unimaginative names?), it is a geographical fault line carved out by glaciers some 10,000 years ago. It cuts across the entire width of the country from south-west to north-east, like a razor-sharp dart fired across the land. The loch itself covers 22 square miles, with a depth of up to 744 feet, and never freezes. Missing out on Loch Ness wasn't a problem for me, since I'd expended all my tourist tendencies on previous visits. (And I'd rather not mess with the lorries on the A82 any longer than I had to.) But should you desire it, opportunities abound between Fort Augustus and Inverness for visitors to indulge in the complete Loch Ness Monster experience; from boat spotting tours to photographs with a giant inflatable Nessie.

Despite the fact the road was relatively flat once I was up at the top, it still wasn't an easy ride; strong winds were battering me mercilessly from the back and sides. But I was happy as a lark, because this was my favourite all-time road and the Monadhliath Mountains had become almost as familiar to me as the places I'd spent my childhood. I'd explored them many times, both on foot and by bicycle, and on one memorable occasion had been lucky enough to cross them on horseback. I had escaped into their beauty, slept by their lochs, and even dreamed of their existence. And I always knew how I'd feel when I returned. The name *Monadh Liath* is Scottish Gaelic for "Grey Mountain Range" which I think does them a disservice. To my mind they are a black mountain range, crisp black, particularly when they have the sun behind them. There was no sun today, alas, but they looked crisp and enticing just the same. I had first clapped eyes on these mountains whilst on holiday with my parents. I was sixteen, I'd just finished school and to say I was a stroppy, headstrong broiling bag of hormones would be the understatement of the century. I *cringe* when I think back to what I put my parents through on that holiday. I believe I was subconsciously fighting the last threads of parental hold and I think it's fair to say, the only thing we agreed on by the end of it, was that it would be the last holiday we'd take together. (Or at least until I became a proper adult.) But despite my recalcitrant behaviour, none of us could miss the charm of the land. I think we all fell in love with it, as it lifted our spirits and brought us together in a way no family bonding exercise ever could.

After 10 miles struggling to stay upright in the gale, a welcome break appeared in in the form of a snack van in a lay-by. As I sipped piping hot tea, my eyes focused on a cyclist coming the other way. He too was being battered and blown across the road but with one major difference. The wind, which through most of Scotland had helped me along my way, was for him a full-on headwind. Fortunately, this was a part of the world where there's no need to pretend you haven't seen someone, and on noticing me with my bike, Michael joined me at the snack bar. I admit I had to fight an urge to blurt out, 'Screw riding into a headwind'. Or, 'Boy, am I glad to be going the other way', since that wouldn't have been very supportive, and I bit my tongue. I had been trying unsuccessfully to smoke a cigarette. (Have you ever tried smoking a roll-your-own in a gale?) Michael looked on disapprovingly at my bad habit for a moment before telling me he was an End-to-Ender himself. He had reached John O'Groats yesterday and decided he'd enjoyed it so much, that he'd turned straight around and was now cycling back to his home in Glasgow. I let that sink in for a minute. *Yesterday?* I thought. *Are you telling me this guy has cycled 140 miles since yesterday? Into this headwind? Was he shitting me?*

I long since came to the conclusion that some people are just born fit. Whilst some of us would have to train for months on end and suffer much sweat and pain to complete a 5k fun run, there are those who after months (even years) without exercise, do a couple of half-hearted training runs and then go to complete a 10k sprint without breaking a sweat. It's true, I've *met* them. They walk amongst us. I clearly belong to the former group, whilst Michael belonged to the latter. (Either that or he was shitting me.) I could bite my tongue no longer.

'Aren't you struggling with the headwind?' I should have guessed at his answer; the well-rehearsed tough guy demeanour. He shrugged his shoulders and described the

(30mph) headwind as *easy*. Hmm, now I was starting to smell a rat. I finished my tea and asked if he would like to make a donation into my collection tin. He asked if I would like to make one into his, and so we swapped fifty pence pieces and off he went; into his easy headwind. Just as I was leaving, I heard a whistle. The man running the snack van had been listening to our conversation with, I might add, considerable amusement. (Perhaps he smelt a rat too.) And he returned the fifty pence piece I'd paid for my tea with and insisted I have it for my collection tin. I thanked him profusely and shot off. Jet-propelled by my easy tailwind.

As beautiful as the Highlands are, it probably won't come as much of a surprise to learn they've been stripped of most of their original flora and fauna. The extensive forests were thought to be at their pinnacle some five or six thousand years ago, and by the time the Romans came to our shores, climate change had reduced forest cover by at least fifty percent. But as the footprint of Homo sapiens increased, so the machine of deforestation began. Over the centuries, people felled the forests for timber, charcoal and tanbark (although the need for timber helped protect forests to some extent). But slowly and surely, demand on the forests went beyond the natural world's ability to cope. Once interest in timber went into decline and sheep farming took over, the forests never regenerated. With the forests went many key wildlife species: wolf, bear, beaver and lynx, chased out by loss of habitat and then hunted to extinction. Today, only one percent of these native Caledonian forests remain, with a few ancient Scots pines scattered around which are thought to be around 500 years old; trees that would have borne witness to the Highland Clearances.

I could barely contain my excitement as I began my descent into Inverness; a place I'd already visited a dozen times, and a place which usually entailed an all-night train journey to reach. That I had cycled here this time seemed so incredible, I could barely register the fact. But there was something else: it was this road. *The road.* The one I'd dreamed I was riding two years ago and which had sparked my interest in cycle touring and led me to this adventure.

*

I sat in my favourite café with a pot of tea chatting to the waitress, Carmella. Carmella had worked here for a number of years now and I always made an effort to catch up with her whenever I came to town. Carmella may seem a strange name for a Scotswoman, but there is an intriguing story behind her name. She was born in the fifties after her nineteen-year-old mother, a lass from Edinburgh, had fallen pregnant after a whirlwind romance with an Italian tourist, and she'd named her baby girl Carmella as a nod to her Italian heritage. Carmella was an artist, a very good one actually, but as she earned a pittance from her paintings, she topped up her earnings by working at the café a few afternoons a week. I'd visited her "house" once; a one-room building she'd crudely converted from her friend's garage, where she lived happily, surrounded by her paint pots and easels.

As I drank my tea, Carmella expressed amazement as I told her about my journey, even asking me to repeat certain bits back to her to make sure she'd heard me correctly. (She always said she found my southern accent difficult to understand.) Right in the middle of our conversation, she excused herself and went out back to make a phone call. When she returned, she said there was someone she wanted me to meet and, full of intrigue, I finished my tea and walked with her through the streets of Inverness. As we walked, she said, 'I really think it's amazing what you've done, Dawn, and I think you should tell everyone because I'm sure people would want to donate to your appeal.' I didn't realise she literally meant *tell everyone*, until we reached our destination: the local radio broadcasting house. Carmella went inside to talk with an acquaintance, who turned out to be the local news reporter, whilst I stayed defiantly outside thinking there was no way I was going to set foot in the place. I'd come thus far without media attention and I couldn't see the point in starting now. But just as I was thinking this, Carmella reappeared.

'Dawn, they'd *love* to interview you.' With powers of persuasion that would have made a defence barrister proud, she somehow cajoled me into going inside. I'd never been into a radio broadcasting studio before, and it was actually rather fun. The presenter led me into a tiny sound-proof room and gave me a set of earphones to wear so the recording could begin. The woman asked me questions about my ride, whilst I tried to stifle nervous giggles and convey the facts about landmines. A thought suddenly struck me. *Gosh, I hope they won't ask me about Princess Diana.*

'So, Dawn, what are your feelings on the tragic death of Princess Diana?'

Next morning, I had the rather surreal experience of hearing my voice coming over the radio. But just at that moment, a works crew started up their pneumatic drill right outside my youth hostel, and so I never got to hear the whole interview. But what little of it I did hear, I sounded calm and knowledgeable. This came as a surprise, since the only time I'd heard my voice played back to me was after recording pretend radio shows on C60 cassettes as a child, and I'd always likened my voice to a rather nasally Minnie Mouse. What I didn't realise, though, was not only had the broadcasters afforded me an honorable slot on their local news, which was played every hour that day, but half the population of the Highlands had been listening as well.

DAY 36

(41 MILES)

I was back in the café with Carmella. We'd arranged to meet at ten o'clock and then head to the high street to hold a charity collection. I'd already explained my misgivings about this, especially after my toe-curling failure in Stratford-upon-Avon. But Carmella assured me she would come along for moral support. This support started with her buying breakfast, and I wasn't the only one who benefitted from her generosity that morning. Whilst I struggled to find a single vegetarian item on the menu, I watched as a local homeless man came into the café and asked the staff if they could donate some food to him. The request was clearly aimed at Carmella, leading me to suspect she frequently gave food away to the homeless when the manager wasn't around. I watched, secretly amused, as she hurriedly explained to the sixteen-year-old Saturday server that *she* would buy this man's breakfast, before too many questions were asked. Dear Carmella, why is it those who have the least that are often the most generous?

So, for the second time, I psyched myself up for what I expected would be another collection failure. Carmella found a couple of old buckets at the back of the café and we decorated them with *Landmines Clearance International* stickers, and as Inverness High Street began to fill up with Saturday morning shoppers, we began shaking them hopefully. Within *minutes*, the money came pouring in thick and fast. Everyone, it seemed, had heard my broadcast on the radio that morning. Those wonderful people of Inverness arrived in a constant stream to drop money into our buckets, often several pounds at a time, but curiously, each and every one of them shared with me their sorrows over the death of Princess Diana. I realise I was collecting for one of Diana's causes only days after her death, but it wasn't like the two events were connected. I guess that because the interviewer had asked me Diana-themed questions, I think people linked the two events in their minds; as if by donating to a landmine clearing charity, they were somehow paying their respects to her.

Whilst I understand it's normal to feel moved by the death of a celebrity, especially if we've long admired them, I've never fully understood people who get utterly grief-stricken; as if the deceased was a personal friend or relative. To me that seems a little mixed up. In Princess Diana's case, I believe the media drove the "national wave of grief" as they called it, and certainly in the weeks that followed, the news was wall-to-wall Diana and everyone was encouraged to take part. I myself was out of touch with mainstream media at the time and thus removed from the hysteria. I personally didn't feel the need to mourn excessively; for a person who'd had no real impact on my life. I was able to appreciate the sadness of a life taken far too young, pay my respects and then move on, and leave the serious grieving to the family and friends who actually knew her.

In under two hours, we'd collected over seventy pounds. (Take that, Stratford-upon-Avon.) Thrilled and humbled by this wonderful town, Carmella and I went for a celebratory pot of tea, and then it was time for me to leave... and a lump formed in my throat. I had put so much emphasis on reaching Inverness and associated it with being *so nearly there,* that I'd quite forgotten I still had rather a long way to go. (One hundred and thirty miles to be exact.) I was nowhere near psychologically prepared and I began to complain to myself.

It's too soon to leave... I only just got here. I had to force myself into action. I hugged Carmella goodbye, thanked her for all her help, engaged my autopilot and got on my way.

I left town along the hazardously busy A9 by way of the Kessock Bridge, an impressive 1,000-metre- long structure that crosses the Beauly Firth. As I went, I kept an eye out for those ever-elusive dolphins that frequent the bay but, as usual, I saw no sign of them. There were no cycle paths in those days, so I danced and diced with the deadly traffic, and although the dual carriageway ended in the village of Tore, the traffic was as heavy as ever. It was soon after Tore when I first noticed horns were being sounded at me, and my first instinct was to take this as a negative. *Here we go again. Just like Loch Lomond. Why do they hate bicycles so much in Scotland? Maybe if they bothered to build even one bloody cycle lane, I wouldn't have to ride on their precious roads.* And on and on I grumbled until I'd worked myself up into such a temper, I began shaking my fist and growling obscenities in retaliation. How comical I must have looked… it was only later that I noticed the cars going the other way (and on the *other* side of the road) were also sounding their horns at me, and it finally dawned on me: these drivers weren't showing aggression, they were honking to show their *support* (having presumably heard me on the radio). The emotional seismic graph flickered wildly once again. I was suddenly merry. Waving back at them with a grin stretching from ear to ear.

But things got stranger still when a battered Renault pulled up. For a second I wondered if it were Carmella. Perhaps I'd left something behind at the café. But instead, a younger woman got out of the car and produced a ten-pound note for my collection tin. I listened, gobsmacked, as she explained she'd heard me on the radio that morning and had driven from Ullapool (some 60 miles away) to come and find me. I was so bowled over that I barely knew what to say, aside from thanking her profusely. We stood there for a moment in awkward silence, her looking at me expectantly. What should I say? Had she come expecting to meet an incredible person or to hear an inspiring speech?

'So, how's it going?' she persisted. Somehow, I strung together a few sentences, talking about the hills and the weather, and about how generous everyone had been in Inverness that morning. But on the whole, I think my speech came out rather wooden, uninteresting, and not terribly inspiring. Crash went the sound of my pedestal hitting the floor.

'Well, thank you so much,' I repeated for the eighth time. 'I'd better get going, what with the late start this morning and all.' A 120-mile round trip just to meet me? She must have been disappointed.

Unlike the Highland regions I'd already traversed, it was a long time since I'd strayed north of Inverness and I was looking forward to seeing it again. As I rounded each corner and a new vista opened up, I remembered how the rugged mountains flatten out into gentler peaks and how an eerie quiet fell over the land. At the slow speed of a bicycle, I could almost hear the silence creeping up to meet me, and by the end of the afternoon, I was utterly enveloped in it. This desolation was lodged firmly in my psyche and would no doubt remain there until the end. In this state of mind, I started looking favourably at the cars passing; at least they were signs of life which made me feel less alone, although, of course, I was very alone in my endurance. Far from being the easy last leg I'd imagined, I realised this would probably be the toughest bit of all. Throughout Scotland, I'd kept up a tremendous pace, keen to visit the next familiar place, and the next. But after Inverness, that motivation had gone. My only desire now was to reach the end, and it was like replacing a carrot with a stick. As if to confirm my anxieties, the bright sunshine that had smiled on me since leaving Inverness disappeared behind an angry black cloud, and before I had time to even wonder which pannier bag my coat was in, a torrent of unforgiving water began hammering to earth. It beat down on the ground, it beat down on my head, and the world around me disappeared.

Then quite suddenly I began acting in a most peculiar fashion. Each time a car roared past and splashed me, I was hit by a powerful wave of emotion, each one different from the last. One minute I was waving and grinning at the driver, beckoning them to stop as if they were an old friend. Then a few minutes later another would pass and I would erupt in an outburst of anger; cursing and gesticulating rudely. For the first time in my life, I felt genuinely out of control; unhinged. I got off my bike and hurled it to the ground in a gesture that said: *That's it, I'm done* (shaking my fist at a random car). *It's your fault it's raining and I'm wet. The whole damn world can just piss off.* But just as quickly, the emotional turmoil subsided. I squatted on the ground where my bicycle lay, panting heavily, and closed my eyes against the rain. There were no tears now; no anger or self-pity left, just resignation at my situation. One moment I'd been a well-recognised and highly praised VIP, and the next, I was but a lonely, bedraggled stranger, shivering uncontrollably.

I picked Loopy Loo up off the ground and swung my leg over the saddle. I saw that I must now lower my expectations for the next few days, down to the level of just gritting my teeth and getting through it. ("It" being the cold, the wet and the isolation.) My legs went on to autopilot: round and around. My mind went blank and my eyes stared into the far-off distance. As I rode through the rain, my mouth began to move and twitch until the words of a song formed: *Bright Eyes* by Art Garfunkel. I sung it first in my own voice, then with a Scottish accent, followed by German, and then Australian. And when I became tired of that, I made up lame songs about the impending campsite, now only 6 miles away.

Please, please let it be a super campsite,
With room for me to lay my bed,
A hot shower for me to warm my toes,
A tumble dryer to dry my clothes,
A place to lock up Loopy Loo,
Not forgetting a cheap rate too,
Cause I'm so cold and tired, hell, yeah...

Perhaps the universe liked my silly song, because when I finally reached the campsite at Tarlogie, every wish I had came true.

The campsite owner took one look at my blue lips and uncontrollable shivers and ordered me to go and dry out and come back to pay later. Putting up the tent was nigh on impossible with numb hands, and I started to seriously worry that I might just die of hypothermia, right here, right now. I forced myself to take a few deep breaths, remain calm and try again. And somehow, I got the damn tent pitched up. From there, things got easier as routine took over:

1. Place sleeping bag and mat at the back of the tent where they'd stay dry and could be rolled out later.
2. Put my rear panniers inside the tent porch and leave front ones (my larders) on the bike.
3. Stuff a cheese and onion pie into my mouth to keep me going.
4. Grab my wash things: towel, clean clothes, toiletries, and make a dash for the shower block.

On this particular day, however, that walk from tent to shower block felt like the longest walk I'd ever done. But finally, I was there. Standing under the shower, stripping off sodden clothes. And the water that cascaded over my body was hot. Fabulously hot.

Half an hour later, I was finally warm enough to contemplate returning to the outside world. I blasted my hair under the hand dryer, pulled on dry clothes, leaving the wet ones rumbling in the clothes dryer, and off I went to pay the proprietor. Harold's office was toasty and warm, so I was totally unbothered when he pulled out a hefty pile of forms and began filling them in. I was also unfazed by the fact he talked slowly and incessantly. It occurred to me that this was the way things are done up here in the isolated north. There is a very real need to talk. The content wasn't really important, but general chat was vital for mental wellbeing, and after the afternoon I'd just had, I could now fully appreciate this. Harold spent some time telling me about unexploded Second World War bombs that were sometimes found in the area, and then because I asked, he also described in great detail the wildlife I should look out for whilst I was up here. And I hung on to his every word, grateful for the company of another human.

Much later, after I'd gathered my clothes from the dryer and returned to my tent, I snuggled up in my sleeping bag and worked out my times and distances for the day. I was amazed. Despite not having left Inverness until the afternoon, and despite my precarious emotions and my brush with hyperthermia, I had made my fastest average speed of the whole trip.

DAY 37

(53 MILES)

*A*ll I remembered from my last visit to Sutherland was that I'd found the place rather dreary, but as I'd travelled at the speed of a car and raced between the two varying landscapes, it was an easy mistake to make. One minute I had been in amongst the majestic Highlands and the next, reeling with shock at the starkness of Scotland's most northern counties. But this time it was different. By bicycle, my speed was slow enough for one landscape to merge slowly into the other, allowing me to appreciate every minute change in the colours and contours. From my position leaning over the handlebars, I felt I had a front-row seat to what was arguably some of the best scenery of my trip. The colours were dazzling in the sunshine, which reflected off the sea on my right, making me squint. Every happy, contented thought I had was answered by the sound of ancient wisdom; of waves crashing onto pebbled beaches, dragging the stones backwards and forwards in a constant rhythm to which I could dream to. And above me in the skies, buzzards hovered on the lift of the breeze, surveying the landscape below them as if they were the mighty rulers and we the mere mortals. This serendipitous scene mirrored Cornwall to some extent, except everything here felt on a larger scale. I realised now how much I'd missed the sea, which had been hidden from my sight for most of this journey. Up here, on the far northeast coast of the British Isles, I finally felt for the first time like I was actually living on an island.

I felt like I'd stumbled across a secret new world; a beautiful world that only I knew about. Like a child who dares to go exploring further than they would normally, and then discovers a fantastic new place in which to play; a place they keep secret from adults and other children (save for a few that they trust). I felt because I'd ventured off the well-beaten tourist trail, I'd discovered a new and secret land, where the beauty of it was known only to me and enjoyed only by me. And well I may have thought this, for I saw no others out doing the same.

*

At Helmsdale, I had a decision to make. I had been advised by the cycle tourist Simon (in Langsett) to leave the A9 here and cycle directly north on the A897: a single-track road which cut across a mountainous region. Simon had tantalisingly described this route as virtually traffic-free. Where once these words would have been music to my ears, now I was here, the blank spaces on the map left me recoiling in horror, and all I could think was: *isolation, desolation, depression.* As someone who has stared into the abyss a few times, I would like to make rule number twenty-five of cycle touring: taking care of your mental health must be a top priority. Whilst I have not said so in as many words, I think it's glaringly obvious from some of my descriptions that, if one is prone to depression, there are certain aspects of cycle touring that could potentially perpetuate a bad mental health episode: being alone for long periods of time, unfamiliar surroundings, too much time to think and always being the stranger. Even boredom could trigger an episode. Having said that (and not wanting to put people off), I can also vouch for there being many aspects of cycle touring highly recommended as ways to *beat* depression: exercise, fresh air, being in nature and a boost to self-confidence each and every day as you smash yet another personal goal. When I embarked on this tour, I was fortunate to be in a great frame of mind (unlike the year before), and I was all ready for my big adventure. But even this didn't stop me experiencing a few darker days. All I will say is, I think it's wise to pick one's time carefully: embarking on a lengthy lone tour in the middle of a mental health crisis may not be the best course of action. (There again, it may be just what some people need.) And during a tour, if things become too much, don't be afraid to alter your plans or even cut the trip short if necessary… there will always be time for another tour.

And so, the lonesome A897 got the kibosh and I made a beeline for John O'Groats. Besides, this far north, I wouldn't exactly describe the A9 as a busy road. But, more than anything, I just wanted to get back to being sociable again. The sound of my own thoughts running around and around my head was driving me crazy. I longed to sit in a group and laugh like mad about a common experience, and I craved familiar voices.

Around two o'clock, I reached Helmsdale, an attractive fishing village which seemed the perfect spot for a break: Bench? Check. Toilets? Check. Pay phone? Check. Shop selling cheese and onion pies? Check. I rang my mother at work and as always, I relayed the number of the phone box and she called me straight back. (She had an understanding boss.) But at that very moment in our conversation, when I was telling her how well everything was going, I was hit by a wave of exhaustion. Worse still, by the time our conversation ended, I was beginning to feel feverish as well. Up until now, I hadn't considered how hard I'd been pushing myself. Since Glasgow, I'd cycled over 300 miles in six days, come rain or shine and regardless of whether I had been tired or not, hurting or not. And to top it all off, yesterday I'd received a thorough drenching. Of course, as everybody knows, you don't catch a chill from *being* chilly, but it was hard to not want to believe that there might be a connection. As I sat shivering and aching, I felt angry. Why now? Why did this damn ague have to arrive when I was so close to the finish line? In another day, it wouldn't matter how ill I became. I could find a campsite to rest up for a while, or catch a train back to Inverness and check into a youth hostel. (I pictured myself curled up in bed sleeping all day whilst fellow backpackers fetched me paracetamol and fresh orange juice.)

But today, I was 55 miles of unknown topography away from John O'Groats and I needed all the strength I could muster. It was *not* a good day to be getting sick.

It reminded me of the unproven theory of Leisure Sickness: when people push themselves really hard (say at work or at school) in an effort to get everything completed before a vacation, and then fall ill the moment they go on holiday. This has in fact happened to me, and the theory that the mind can temporarily override physical infirmity for a greater emergency at hand (whether that be running away from a saber-toothed tiger or finishing a project for an angry boss) gets the thumbs-up from me. One explanation is that stress hormones may temporarily boost our immune systems, which helps keep infections at bay. Then, when the stress ends and adrenaline and cortisol levels drop, it leaves the door wide open for germs to multiply. This theory was easy for me to believe right now. Yesterday, I'd arrived in Inverness feeling like my ride was as good as over… but then I'd been forced to realise it was anything but, and reluctantly carried on. I'd mentally paid a high price for my premature jubilations. Now it looked as though I would pay the price physically as well.

After Helmsdale the road left the coastline and meandered its way inland, and up and over the mountains. Remember on that steep hill outside Fort Augustus, when I'd confidently described it as the last really steep ascent of the trip? Well, if anyone wants to print me out a t-shirt saying, *poor misguided fool,* then now would be a good time. I had to negotiate my way up and over several steep inclines and then scale the hairpin bends on the infamous Berridale

Braes: a 530ft rise over three-quarters of a mile. The bends are so sharp and steep that cars can only negotiate them in first gear, and it is not uncommon for large lorries to get stuck halfway around them. Back in Cornwall and Devon, I had struggled up hills just like this, lesser hills actually, and every night I'd lain too exhausted and disheartened to move. But fast forward 1,000 miles to the other end of our island, and I scaled that hill barely breaking a sweat; even with a dose of the flu.

Today was the first time I'd got a sense of my ride as one continuous expedition, rather than remembering it in dribs and drabs; as if the different bits had occurred at different times of my life. And I felt a sense of pride I'd not experienced before. Then something else put everything into perspective: I began to see other cyclists heading in the opposite direction. After the fourth passed me that afternoon, it dawned on me… they were End-to-Enders too. The realisation was electrifying. They were *me*. Setting out with the same excitement, courage and perhaps the same pinch of naivety that I had (although none of their bikes were as loaded down as mine). We grinned and waved as we passed one another. They were fresh-faced and eager as their adventure began but I didn't envy them one little bit, I was just relieved mine was nearly over. I noticed how most car drivers were waving and smiling at me as I was nearing the end, and all these thoughtful gestures persuaded me to push on through my fever. And I sang just for the joy of it.

The A9 swung east and I approached the sea once more, greeting it warmly like an old friend. When I stopped in a small village to get some water, a man with a strong local accent and slurred speech came over to talk with me. My initial reaction was to deem this man as drunk and I tried leaving as quickly as possible, but then I remembered what part of the world I was in. Once I'd dropped my preconceptions, I saw the man clearly for the first time. He was old, maybe a little eccentric, but only slurring because he was missing most of his teeth. And what was more, he mercifully chose to ignore my rude attempts to shun him and placed a pound coin into my collection tin. I stayed a little longer after this. Even though I couldn't make out what he was saying, I knew by now it wasn't really important. It was that old comfort factor of the north again: human contact and talking.

Now into Caithness and my final county, I headed for Dunbeath for the night. Just a stone's throw from the campsite was a garage and a shop where I bought my cheese and onion pies. The mother and grown-up daughter who ran the show asked me to sign their visitors' book, a sure sign not too many people pass this way. Whilst I scribbled, they bemoaned their customers. Tourists, the mother announced, were on the whole rude and did nothing but complain because their humble store didn't offer the choices of a larger supermarket. I was all too happy to sympathise with their gripe, when she stopped to enquire about where I was headed. *At last*, I thought, and proudly announced that I had cycled here all the way here from Land's End. Then the daughter spoke up and her voice was almost a sneer. 'That must have been easy. I know a man who ran it.' Her words were a sucker punch to the midriff and as I hurried outside, they rang around my head. *That must have been easy… I know a man who ran it… that must have been easy.* Those callous words threatened to take the most challenging, most exciting feat of my life thus far and turn it into something so ordinary, it shouldn't even be *called* an achievement. I slumped against the wall, blinking back the tears I knew were coming and stared vacantly for a long, long time. Had I been deluding myself; believing I was doing something worthwhile with my life whilst other people disparaged me?

The Dunbeath campsite was run by a welcoming English guy who didn't seem to mind living up here alone; in fact, he told me it had been his dream to move as far away from other people as possible. When I told him of my quest, he smiled and advised I pitch up my tent then head straight for the wee pub down the road for a celebratory drink. I guess on the outside I looked fit and confident I would finish my journey tomorrow, but on the inside lay a different story. I was weak in body from flu and weak in morale from unkindness. Would I finish off my ride tomorrow or would it finish me off? I decided I would give that celebratory drink a miss for now.

DAY 38

(45 MILES)

"But one thing was crystal clear; I was going to explore the Highlands by bicycle".

Come the morning, the wind which had kept me awake most of the night still raged and as no one was about to object, I took my stove into the shower block so I could make tea and breakfast out of the wind. As I watched tiny bubbles rising to the surface of the pan, butterflies began dancing in the pit of my stomach. In years to come, I would frequently feel nervous on the last day of each cycle tour; jitters I would come to know simply as "Last-day Nerves". I can't say precisely what I mean by Last-day Nerves, only that I suspect they are the general background anxiety that accompanies most people at some point in their lives. They are the voices that ask: *what if it all goes wrong?* The irrational fears a person has when they've been working towards a goal for a long time. *What if my bottom bracket breaks 10 miles from John O'Groats? What if I get hit by a lorry on my last day? What if I don't get the grades I need to get into university? What if my fiancé does a runner on the way to the church?* Ad infinitum. But trying to anticipate as yet non-existent mechanical problems was largely immaterial, considering the real problem at hand: 45 miles riding with a dose of influenza. I popped a couple of paracetamols and went to pay the proprietor, but like so many before him, he waved away my money. He would be the last one to do so. I relished his optimism when he said he didn't think it would rain today, and with fingers crossed, I swung myself into the saddle. That brief glimpse I'd had yesterday of my ride as one continuous journey had gone. It'd slunk away in the night and left me with the far more familiar notion: that my journey had begun only yesterday, 20 miles down the road.

The beautiful coastal vistas of yesterday were gone too, and today the A9 felt dreary, grey and thoroughly unappealing. Somehow, despite the fever, my legs continued to work, round and around on autopilot, and before I knew it, 23 miles had passed and the town of Wick appeared in the road ahead. As well as the requisite cheese and onion pie, I'd decided to shop for something a little more special for tonight and I slipped a packet of fresh four cheese ravioli pasta into my basket as well.

If you'd asked me what I remembered from the last time I'd visited Wick, my answer would be a strange one, for all I could recall was the minutiae of the public toilets.

With the awful stench and their walls covered in graffiti, I remember thinking how boring it must be to live here if the only entertainment for local youths was to vandalise the public toilets. But please forgive me, dear Wick, for now with more mature eyes, I could see better. With time to stop and observe properly, I saw the gatherings of locals appearing for a convivial lunchtime natter in the main square, seemingly oblivious to the autumnal wind now biting. And I sensed that this was a close-knit community. I also noted the casual glances my way as I shopped and ate, and suddenly I lost all nerve to go and ask people for donations. For surely this town must have been witness to almost every single End-to-End expedition that there ever was, and I was just one more in a big long chain, stretching back to 1863, when an American by the name of Elihu Burritt walked from London to John O'Groats, and then from London to Land's End.

Onwards and north. I looked ahead at the spartan road, then up at heavy grey skies, and again I was reminded of why I'd found this place so bleak first time around. In another time and place, I could have been quite taken with it: the grassy hillocks, the clouds stretching away to hidden horizons and the land reflecting a dark and moody sky. Now and again, I passed intriguing houses, either alone or in small clusters. I longed to peek inside and find out about the lives of those who dwelt in the far north. I also passed dozens of ruins; long-ago abandoned farmhouses crumbling to dust, and soon to be no more. It was these disintegrating buildings which really tugged at my heartstrings. It left me with the impression of a community driven away, not by the weather, for surely these were hardy folk, but a community driven out by financial hardship. Maybe they were the abandoned homes of crofters who found they could no longer survive on their cottage industries or through self-sufficiency, not when multi-national companies are gobbling up all traditional ways of life right across the globe.

"That's it, I encouraged myself, cycle at least as far as the Bodmin campsite... and then give up."

Like something out of a dream, I passed a signpost that told me I was only 2 miles from John O'Groats. By now, my fever was at its crescendo and as I rode, I shivered uncontrollably whilst my body began shouting at me, *Are you crazy? You should be tucked up in bed right now with paracetamol and a hot lemon infused drink.* I guess what I was really hoping for was to top a rise and unexpectedly come across John O'Groats, lying in wait at the bottom of the hill, bathed in golden sunshine. But 2 miles from the end and things had never been so tough. A cold northerly wind blew straight off the Pentland Firth and into my face, doing its damnedest to blow me off balance, and I zigzagged across the empty road in an attempt to lessen its force against me. Only 2 miles from the end and the heavens cruelly opened their floodgates, as they had enjoyed doing on so many occasions before. The sting of cold rain on my hands and face made me gasp. With only 2 miles to go, couldn't the elements have spared me this final punishment? Only 2 miles... just 2 more damned miles.

If I had been thinking clearly, I would have barred all thoughts of John O'Groats from my mind and let my autopilot take over, but after five weeks alone I had no mental stamina left, and my mind was devoid of anything other than what was written on that last signpost... *2 miles*. It felt as though every last trace of summer, which had been holding on by its fingertips, was being squeezed out by the snarling and salivating dark winter months that came galloping in to consume the land. Straining my eyes for sight of the end, the sea suddenly came into view and with it a small group of buildings appeared in the distance. But, feeling masochistic enough, I decided I wanted to do this properly and I delayed the end. I took a right-hand turning down a single-track road and headed for Duncansby Head; *another 2* miles away. The last 2 miles, which had taken an eternity to cover, didn't have a patch on these 2 miles. These 2 miles could only be measured in light years, they were so long. And as the steep road ran sharply up and down, the weather joined in with the road to laugh at me, by sending hailstones smashing into my face and eyes...

...Then very suddenly it ended. For the first time in 1,205 miles, there was no more road. I got off my bike and walked over to the cliff edge. And there I was, alone on Duncansby Head at last, staring out to sea at the nothingness. There was no more land, just sea. I was now the most north-easterly person (and bicycle) on the British mainland. There were no cheering crowds or flashing cameras, just me with some sixty million people behind me. Satisfied but shattered, I pushed my bicycle most of the way back to John O'Groats.

John O'Groats (or Jan de Groots, as it was originally called, after the Dutch settler who had first resided here) was chilly, grey and filled with none of the magic I had promised myself for a thousand miles. And what was worse, there appeared to be half a dozen other cyclists hanging around, giving the impression a conveyor belt was churning out End-to-Enders, who, I imagined, had all completed their ride faster, easier and more expertly than I. I decided I would mark the end officially and I paid to have my photograph taken in front of the John O'Groats signpost, which pointed back to where I'd stood five weeks earlier (874 miles as the crow flies). I had the photographer post up my own version of events, so it now read: *DAWN'S CYCLE. 1,205 MILES.* I took off my coat and posed with a fake smile and my knuckles clenched coldly together, and then that, as they say, was that.

*

I wasn't so glum that I didn't treat myself to a celebratory pint. The bar of the hotel was empty except for me, and I wondered how such a large place managed to stay in business. I supped slowly, briefly contemplating staying there the rest of the day, but I still needed to sort out somewhere to stay. Through the window I could see a small campsite by the edge of the sea with one lonely campervan in residence. I envisaged the night I'd have: trying to stop my tent blowing away with one arm and fighting off the flu with the other arm. No thank you. For the first time on my trip, I splurged my cash and treated myself to a bed and breakfast for two nights, and in hindsight, it was a very wise decision. For twenty-five pounds, I had a double room all to myself, and I recreated my camping routine within the sanctuary of those four walls. I tidied my panniers and hung out the wet clothes. I showered and then set up my camping stove on the bedside table and boiled up ravioli for my celebratory dinner. Then I ate it in bed whilst watching television. I thought of my parents just then. More than likely, they were sat at home watching the same television show as I, but they felt so far away. A tear escaped the corner of my eye. Were they thinking of me? I felt sure they would have liked to be here for this moment.

The howling wind continued unabated for two days whilst I stayed in my room and sweated out the fever, surviving on complimentary tea and packets of biscuits. By the second evening, I was feeling decidedly better and so I ventured out to the red telephone box. First, I rang home, longing to hear a familiar voice say 'well done you' but no one answered. I sighed. Then I rang the backpackers' hostel in Inverness and booked beds for myself and my friend Sarah, who would be arriving from London tomorrow evening. I chatted to the Australian voice on the other end of the line and before we had time to go into formalities, he asked, 'Is your name Dawn?'

'Erm... yes.'

'Did you stay at the Isle of Skye Backpackers' Hostel last winter?'

'Yes, I did,' I replied, perplexed. How could this stranger possibly have known that?

'I thought so,' he said, 'I was working there at the time. I'd recognise your voice anywhere.'

I eventually remembered Colin too. I was surprised he remembered me, since we'd only met the once, almost a year ago for about ten minutes, and I was rather flattered (especially when I recalled Colin's big brown eyes). On that lonely night, it felt good to hear a familiar voice, and we talked about what we'd both been up to since. When I explained my trip to Colin, he was full of awe and congratulated me for completing my ride. It was the recognition I'd been craving and my journey felt suddenly complete.

*

Next morning, everything had changed. For one thing, the sky was predominately blue, and I wasn't accustomed to the sun glaring directly into my face. Something else that was directly in my face was the wind, hitting me smack on, and I got a measure of just how different things might have been had I chosen to cycle the End-to-End the other way around. But the main change was that I was no longer going northwards. Thurso lay distinctly to the west, and that was where I was heading. And from there I would be taking a train south. I said the word aloud. SOUTH. South to where there were people who knew me and would welcome me, and where there was fun to be had.

The streets of Thurso were deserted when I arrived, and surprisingly for a Saturday morning, all the shops were shut too. I couldn't help feeling an "end-of-the-world" type of doom, but just as I was about to start feeling depressed and isolated again, I spied some children playing in the street. They came bounding over like puppy dogs when they saw me. They agreed to guide me through the deserted streets to the railway station and asked me why I wasn't in London for Princess Diana's funeral. Of course, that explained why everything was shut; everyone was indoors watching the televised events. As the rest of the nation thought about Diana, I thought about them. The people I had met, the kindness I'd received, the words of encouragement, the stares and looks of disapproval, the donations made and the very many miles between Cornwall and Scotland. As I sat in the empty railway station waiting for my train, from behind the closed shutters of the ticket office, Elton John's *Candle in the Wind* floated across the concourse as I reflected upon my journey.

EPILOGUE

I could write a book on the events following my ride…
and maybe someday I will, but for now, suffice it to
say that reaching John O'Groats was not an end but a
beginning. Despite all the times I'd sulkily declared *I'll never
ride my bicycle again,* it turns out I was ready for a little more
and with a renewed sense of excitement, I embarked on a
tour of the Orkney Isles with my friend Sarah. We pitched
our tent next to the ferry terminal in Thurso and patiently
waited five days whilst gale-force winds cancelled one ferry
crossing after another. On the second day, we gratefully
accepted an invitation from fellow travellers to move into
their caravan across the way, where we could wait it out in
the warm. Each day was spent idling contentedly: eating,
listening to music and catching up on the gossip, and only
occasionally did I glance at my tent through the window, still
flapping wildly where we'd left it. It was a relief to no longer
be out there too. I was done with roughing it.

For four weeks, Sarah and I made our way around the Highlands and Islands of Scotland by ferry and train, and used bicycles to reach the bits in between. I settled happily into this gentler pace of life whilst youth hostels along the way provided me with all the socialising I had dreamed of. It was a contented time for me… except now and again, I found myself feeling a little deflated. It turns out that dropping my daily mileage from 50 miles to 10 was enough to send my body into a sulk; imagine a workaholic losing their job and having nothing to do once the school run is over. Rule number twenty-six of cycle touring: it takes time to adjust back to normal life. Sometimes, I wondered if all I'd been through would simply become extraneous to my life, but I'm happy to report that I did pick up my thread of happiness again. I first noticed it when I travelled by train. I'd sit and stare out of the window for hours on end and then it would dawn on me that I'd cycled all this way, and further. Then, for a long time afterwards, I would settle down each night, turn off the lights and enjoy running through each and every day of my journey, remembering the roads where I'd cycled and the places I'd camped.

*

So, to tie up a few loose ends: my total distance ridden was 1,205 miles and I skipped 50 miles for logistical reasons. I spent £319 of my own money and raised £978 for *Landmines Clearance International*. And just in case anyone is dying to know… no, nothing ever became of myself and Slalom Steve. I did visit him again (twice in fact), but by the time we were reunited, I'm sorry to say that any inclination to take the friendship further had faded in the interim. I was so glad I hadn't made any rash declarations at the time.

And so, I returned to Sussex, keen to see what the future held. In terms of cycling, it would be rather eventful. In between jobs, marriage, health problems and divorce, there would be many more tours. Once the process of selective memory had wiped the negatives from my mind, I decided to complete my dream to ride as far north on the British Isles as the road would allow, and the very next spring, I visited the Shetland Isles. I should have taken heed of a comment I found in a visitors' book: *To cycle in the Shetland Isles, one needs the thighs of a rugby player and a head shaped like an axe.* But using the determination I'd learnt on my End-to-End, I persevered. Despite seasonal flooding and strong gales, I finally reached the end of the road, just north of Haroldswick. As I stood in the gloom blinking rain out of my eyes, something caught my attention. The bus shelter across the road had been decked out like a cosy living room, with a sofa, television set, cups of tea and cream buns (all plastic of course), and I laughed. Someone had prepared a warm welcome for travellers who'd reached their journey's end, and I took shelter there gratefully.

But, of course, it wasn't the end for me. After the Shetland Isles, my eyes were forever drawn to my world maps, and in the years that followed I toured other parts of the UK, Ireland and Europe. In my thirties, I cycled around parts of Asia and then rode across the United States. (I am in the process of writing a book about this.) And all on the same faithful red bicycle, Loopy Loo. My latest dream is to ride across Australia, but we'll see how things pan out, because rule number twenty-seven of cycle touring is of course: there are no rules.

If anyone reading this wishes to give cycle touring a try, whether it be a day trip or an entire round-the-world extravaganza, then I can wholeheartedly say, go for it. Because if inexperienced, unfit li'l ol' me can do it, then you sure can too. The bonus these days is the mass of information available on the internet to help you plan a trip, and it will provide far better advice than I can. The only downside is that volumes of traffic increase each year, but on the plus side, there are more cycle lanes now than ever before, so take advantage of them wherever you can.

I've loved cycle touring and seeing the world. Not every second of it, mind you… and it's probably best that you don't expect to either. But if there's one thing I've noticed riding around the globe, it's that attitudes towards cycling are pretty similar, and it can be summed up nicely by the following account. One day, as I cycled toured through the Chinese province of Zhejiang, I arrived at a guesthouse where the entire family came outside to greet me. As the matriarch took my money, she chatted away in Mandarin. Without understanding a single word of each other's language, just from a few simple hand gestures, I can tell you exactly how that conversation went.

'Where have you come from?'

'Shanghai.'

'Shanghai? All that way on a bicycle?'

'Yes'

'But that's crazy… why didn't you just come in a car?'

And how do I know this was what she said? Because it's the same conversation I've had the world over; from Shanghai to St Louis, and from Milan to Margate. Even at home, when I've ridden 5 miles to get my groceries, the question is invariably the same: *Why ride a bicycle when you can drive a car?*

It appears that a large proportion of the world's population loathes the idea of physical exertion, and they fill their lives with all manner of gadgets and inventions to help them avoid it. Of course, we have some fantastic inventions: we can now bring heat, light, clean water and medicine to millions of people, and we can save many more from back-breaking toil or dangerous work. But equally, and especially in developed countries, we have an ever-increasing number of gadgets that don't address any real needs. They are invented simply to keep consumer markets moving, and many cost way more than their actual worth to people's lives. But we are encouraged to buy them all the same, so manufacturers can continue to rake in their profits and then, presumably, fill *their* lives with even more elaborate and unnecessary gadgets. And on it goes.

Why does all this bother me? Because most of us are already living with the consequences of unnecessary production. Sedentary lives go hand in hand with poor health (heart disease is the world's number one killer). Mining the earth's resources to build stuff has wiped out great swathes of the natural world and left the oceans a seething mass of plastic. And what about the consequences to our mental health? Does a life filled with drive-thrus, ready meals, ever more powerful cars, and voice-recognition technology actually make us happy? Statistically speaking, it doesn't seem to. At the time of writing this (2020), one in six people in the UK have ongoing mental health problems. Suicide is the biggest killer of young men, and I'll wager there are an awful lot more people out there who are just plain bored or dissatisfied with their lives. Could there be a correlation between our misery and our extreme sedentary lives? These days, our food, heat, light, clothes, music, entertainment, children's entertainment, transportation and communication are readily supplied by faceless international chains. We have no personal involvement in their inception or production; we simply pay for them to be delivered into our lives. Putting aside the rather obvious problem, that most of us couldn't survive long if supply chains are disrupted, I'd also like to know what it means for us *spiritually* that we play no real part in our own survival anymore.

Just a few generations back, our ancestors could grow their own food, make clothes, chop firewood and manage livestock. They supplemented their diet with wild plants, or by using their hunting and fishing skills. And I bet they could walk wherever they needed to get to. And further back, the skills that our hunter gatherer ancestors acquired, just to even get us to this point, were even more incredible. What I find disturbing is that it's only in the last couple of hundred years (since the Industrial Revolution) that entire populations have lost their essential survival skills and handed over control of their very existence to external agencies. So that in less than one per cent of Homo sapiens' 300,000 years of existence, we've gone from multi-skilled, industrious energetic humans to cossetted, helpless and lazy children. Ouch.

So, what has all this got to do with cycling? I mention it here because I became aware of my own reliance on the corporate world at the same time I got into cycling. As I happily rode my bicycle around town – fit, healthy, not to mention financially much better off for not having purchased a car – I felt empowered by my independence and it started a chain reaction. I began to wonder what other self-sufficiency skills I could learn. I began to grow my own vegetables, forage for wild food, make clothes, bake bread and play the guitar. None in themselves were life-changing... but together they were life-affirming, and I became intoxicated by the thrill of each new skill learnt. And whilst I was never going to achieve total self-sufficiency, it was nice to be able to at least partially take care of myself and my family.

So here (finally), I get to the point about what cycling taught me. It began to dawn on me that we humans are born with a lot of energy... vast amounts actually. It is totally free to use and completely renewable, and yet up until I'd gone to Land's End, I'd barely been aware of it. As I learnt to do more and more things for myself, I gained a new perspective on life and discovered a contentment I never even knew I was missing. Whilst I'm not advocating that we return to a pre-industrial era, the more I thought about it, the more ludicrous it seemed that we sacrifice so much time working in soul-destroying jobs, just so we can buy things that *save our effort and time*. It doesn't make any sense. I'm not a Luddite or anything. I believe we can embrace the technology that saves and improves lives whilst shunning inventions that have little worth: those that are cost heavy to the environment, increase our waistlines, reduce our bank accounts and rob us of our ability to do basic things for ourselves. Every time I say no to a purchase because I can make, grow or mend something myself, I feel a surge of joy. And I firmly believe that the very essence of being human is to be energetic and creative, as our ancestors were for hundreds of thousands of years. But when we're removed from what we truly are, then we run the risk of despondency and ill health. I don't believe we humans were ever meant to be as cossetted and sedentary as we are now; why else is physical activity hailed as the great antidote to depression? It may not be everyone's cup of tea, but this new way of living has certainly helped me to feel more in control of my life again, as I try to find my way in an increasingly crazy and out-of-control world.

The dreaded A30

From the top of the Kirkstone Pass, about to head down
the other side

ABOUT THE AUTHOR

*B*orn in 1976, Dawn Rhodes grew up with a strong love for wildlife and nature. Since discovering the joys of cycle touring aged 21, she continued to tour the world, crossing Europe, The United States and parts of Asia and Australia. She now lives in the northeast of England with her husband and the two of them continue to explore the world by bicycle whenever they can.

For more information please visit my website

https://dawnrhodes-cycling.com/

This book is printed on paper from sustainable sources managed under the Forest Stewardship Council (FSC) scheme.

It has been printed in the UK to reduce transportation miles and their impact upon the environment.

For every new title that Matador publishes, we plant a tree to offset CO_2, partnering with the More Trees scheme.

For more about how Matador offsets its environmental impact, see www.troubador.co.uk/about/